Raising Poultry and Livestock Guardians

An Essential Guide to Happy Birds and a Protected Herd

Table of Contents

Part 1: Raising Poultry

The Ultimate Backyard Companion, Covering Chickens, Turkeys, Geese, Ducks, Guineas, Game Birds, and a Variety of Fowl

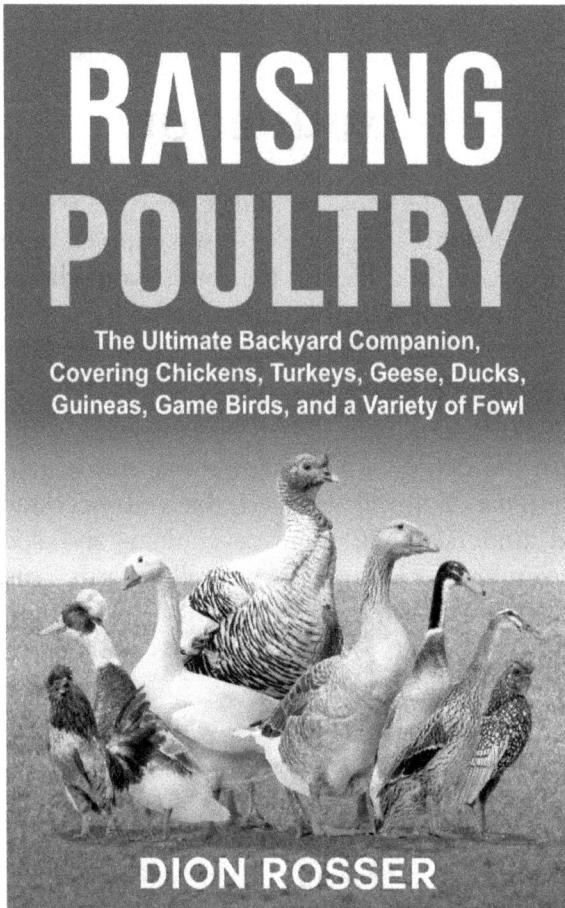

Introduction

Raising poultry is one of the most fulfilling endeavors you can embark on. This first step – reading this book – will unlock a new world of understanding the complex life of the birds you choose to farm. It provides a wide range of valuable tips, methods, and techniques for poultry farming that are hands-on, practical, easy to read, and suitable for beginners. These are delivered with an entertaining flavor that keeps you engaged until the end.

You will learn the details of housing poultry and keeping their health and wellness up to par. You will also learn the tools necessary for breeding your birds and understanding their psychology and social dynamics. Furthermore, you will learn to ethically farm sustainably and environmentally friendly. From top to bottom, everything you need to know about raising the birds of your choice is outlined with nutritional details and habitat requirements.

Since raising animals, especially birds, without the proper knowledge could have disastrous outcomes, you have made the right choice by picking up this book. It unpacks poultry farming in detail; carefully reading each section places you in a position to excel. As you work through the chapters, your eyes will be opened to the most commonly overlooked factors and considerations. By shining a light on the complexities of raising poultry, you will be put in an amazing position to succeed as a beginner. Many people desire to farm but never start because they have no idea how to get the ball rolling. The start-to-finish outline of the intricacies of poultry farming provided in these pages will make building your coop easier than you ever thought possible.

As you get into it, you will gain the skills that can only be learned through experience. Poultry farming provides meat, eggs, or companions if you want some feathered friends. A little bit of elbow grease and commitment can help you set up an operation that runs smoothly for years to come. Don't be scared. Take that risk and jump right into the deep end. You will not regret becoming a poultry farmer!

Chapter 1: Backyard Poultry 101

Do you know that birds are the descendants of dinosaurs? Yes, those cute and small creatures evolved from huge and scary reptiles. How is it possible that all dinosaurs have been extinct for millions of years? This can't be another case of Jurassic Park, right? Well, not exactly. One lineage survived that catastrophic comet. That was the birds. Although all birds come from the dinosaur family tree, chickens are more primitive than all others. They also resemble dinosaurs the most. Basically, when you are raising chickens, you have tiny dinosaurs running around in your backyard.

Raising poultry has many benefits; it isn't just having a constant supply of fresh products. This chapter covers these benefits, the common misconceptions about poultry, and some of the birds you can raise.

Why Backyard Poultry?

If you are hesitant about having backyard birds, this section will change your mind. There is a reason these funny and feathery creatures are very popular among both farmers and non-farmers. Wouldn't you love to have access to fresh eggs all the time? Besides the obvious benefits, raising poultry is also an extremely rewarding experience.

There is a reason these funny and feathery creatures are very popular among both farmers and non-farmers.[1]

Whether you want to start a small business, keep these birds as pets, or simply live a self-sufficient and greener lifestyle, there are so many benefits to reap from backyard poultry.

Fresh Products

The most apparent advantage of raising poultry is getting fresh eggs. These are much healthier and environmentally friendly than the ones you buy at the grocery store. They don't go through shipping or processing, which can put them at risk. You will also be involved in every step, from choosing the birds to collecting and storing the eggs. You are in control of what to feed your birds and which environmental conditions are best to guarantee safe produce that will give you peace of mind. You won't have to worry about pesticides, steroids, chemicals, hormones, or unethical farming practices.

Fresh eggs also taste better and are richer in color. Unlike store-bought ones, they don't contain as much bad cholesterol or saturated fats.

Have you noticed the prices of organic eggs in the supermarket lately? Raising farm birds will save you a lot of money in the long run. If you plan to sell them, you will also make a good profit.

You can raise birds for their meat instead of buying it from unethical farms. You will have access to a natural meat resource free of hormones.

This creates a synergy between you and your birds as they depend on you for survival, and you depend on them for sustenance.

Environmentally Friendly

As you won't rely on commercial egg production, you can positively impact the environment by raising your own poultry. Big farms usually rely on water, lighting, and electricity, which harm the planet. Raising farm birds, on the other hand, requires fewer resources. It reduces your carbon footprint and allows you to do your part to protect the environment.

Backyard poultry also provides you with a more sustainable option, making you directly involved in your food supply chain. You will become self-reliant and less dependent on commercial goods. This lifestyle will make you more appreciative of all the natural resources contributing to your meals.

Low Maintenance

When people decide to become self-sufficient and raise farm animals, they usually prefer to raise birds over cows or sheep. Unlike most animals, birds easily adapt and are self-sufficient. They are extremely low maintenance and don't require much responsibility. All you need to do is set up a living space for them. Things get much easier afterward since they can take care of themselves.

Raising chickens, ducks, etc., will be a great first step if you plan on expanding and venturing into livestock or farming.

Great Company

Birds can bring joy to your life. These cute and funny little creatures can liven up your backyard for hours on end. They are very interesting birds. They love exploring the world around them and play just like children. You can have breakfast every morning in your backyard and watch them peck around for seeds or establish their pecking order. This can be very therapeutic and help you connect with nature and unwind. Kids will also enjoy playing and running around with them.

Birds are amusing creatures with gentle sounds that can reduce anxiety and calm you. After a long day at work, spending time with your birds will give you peace of mind and make you forget about all the stress you experienced during the day.

Producing Fertilizers

Chickens and other birds produce manure rich in nutrients, which acts as a natural fertilizer. It contains potassium, phosphorus, and nitrogen that encourage plant growth. Manure can improve the soil's fertility and nutrient content so plants can thrive. This results in an eco-friendly garden. Using manure to fertilize your soil is a sustainable way to feed your plants and reduce your dependence on unnatural alternatives.

Gardening

Having backyard poultry in your garden can boost its health, output, and even its fertility. Chickens reduce pests since they feed on various organisms like snails and grasshoppers, which can damage your garden. They also eat ticks and mosquitoes, so you and your family can spend time outdoors during the spring and summer without worrying about insect bites.

Chicken can also reduce weed growth by scratching and pecking to dig up seeds. They can loosen the soil, which encourages plant growth.

Making a Small Business

If you want to earn extra cash, you can sell the meat or eggs to friends, family, local restaurants, or farmer's markets.

Kids Will Love Them

You can raise poultry for their eggs and meat, but your child may want to keep one as a pet. This will teach them responsibility and to love and care for something other than themselves. They will also want to spend more time outdoors to play with their bird pet and get some fresh air instead of staying at home and playing video games.

Eating Kitchen Scraps

Backyard chickens eat kitchen scraps, which reduces the trash output. They can eat anything, even meat. Yes, that's right. Chickens are carnivores, and many people feed them on meat or even other bird bones. Collect all the scraps daily in a big bowl with your leftover food and leave it in your chicken coop. They will enjoy it.

More Humane

Have you ever seen how industrial farms treat birds and animals? They are kept in small spaces just for breeding. They can't leave their quarters to walk around, play, stretch their wings, or socialize with other birds. By raising your own poultry, you won't be supporting these farms.

According to a 2010 Cambridge University study, birds that can move around freely and peck for food produce more nutritious eggs with higher omega-3 fatty acids and vitamin E levels than eggs from industrial farms.

Therapy Animals

You often see people adopting a cat or a dog to help them cope with their anxiety, ADHD, or other mental health problems. Did you know that birds can be therapeutic as well? Many countries use them as therapy animals in nursing homes where residents care for them and sell their eggs.

Improve Your Mental Health

Keeping birds as pets can reduce stress, increase resilience, fulfill your social needs, boost self-esteem, and teach responsibility, especially to kids. It can also improve social relationships, reduce loneliness and depression, and improve overall well-being.

Improves Physical Health

You will notice an improvement in your physical health since you eat organic meat and food with higher nutrients. Organic eggs contain less cholesterol, more beta carotene, and fatty acids than store-bought eggs.

Pest Control

Did you know that one chicken can clear bugs from 120 square feet of land every week? Chickens aren't picky eaters and can feed on grubs, beetles, and all types of insects. Basically, they will eat any insect that crosses their path.

Bird Watching

Bird-watching is extremely therapeutic. Getting out in the fresh air will make you feel rejuvenated. It also allows you to spend time alone in nature without any distractions so you can unwind and calm your nerves. It also keeps the mind active and improves memory, especially in dementia patients.

Sense of Accomplishment

Raising your own poultry will give you a sense of accomplishment and drive you to chase your dreams and goals. You believe, "If I can take care of these beautiful creatures, I can do anything."

Common Myths Debunked

You have probably heard a few things about poultry keeping that have discouraged you from raising chickens or other birds at home. There is a lot of misinformation about the subject that will be cleared up in this section.

Myth #1: Raising Poultry for Meat Is Expensive

This isn't true. Although feeding costs are on the rise, it is still cheaper to raise poultry at home. In fact, one pound of organic backyard poultry costs less than one pound of store-bought meat.

Myth #2: Bird Meat Is Harmful

If you choose the right birds, feed them properly, and care for their well-being, you won't face any problems, and your birds' meat will be healthy and delicious.

Myth #3: Raising Birds for Meat Is Time-Consuming

Whether you are raising poultry for meat or eggs, birds are low-maintenance and self-sufficient. Caring for them is easy and will only take 10 to 20 minutes daily.

Myth #4: Birds Raised for Meat Are Violent

Birds raised for meat, like any other bird, love to play, sit in the shade, and won't fight back if your child picks them up or plays with them.

Myth #5: Chickens Are Noisy

Do you remember that Friends episode when Chandler and Joey's chicken woke Rachel and Monica up? Although it turned out to be a rooster, most people think all chickens are loud and will disturb them, their families, and their neighbors. Roosters may be loud, but hens are generally quiet except when startled or laying eggs.

Myth #6: Birds Have a Bad Odor

This is another common misconception that couldn't be further from the truth. In fact, birds are very clean and usually preen their feathers or dust bathing. So, if you notice a bad odor, it is probably because the coop needs cleaning.

Myth #7: Hens Lay Eggs Every Day

Do you think chickens would survive if they laid eggs every day? This myth came from children's story books and illustrations that show chickens doing nothing but sitting on their nests. Most breeds produce three eggs a week.

Myth #8: Backyard Poultry Attract Wild Animals

Some believe backyard poultry attracts rats, coyotes, raccoons, and other wild animals. However, those animals are drawn to pet bowls, wild bird feeders, garbage, barbecue grills, or backyard compost, but never to your birds.

Myth #9: You Will Need Roosters

It is understandable why many people have this misconception. They believe that you will need a male (rooster) and a female (hen) to create babies or eggs. Although this is true, it doesn't apply to shell eggs. This is a natural process all hens go through without the help of a rooster.

Myth #10: Blue and Brown Eggs Are Bad

Many people believe that eggs are dirty or rotten if they aren't white. That is false. The color of the eggshell changes depending on the bird's breed. There are different colors of eggshells, like pink, blue, and brown, and they are all safe to consume.

Myth #11: Raising Poultry Lowers Property Value

Your neighbor might tell you to eliminate your birds because they are lowering the neighborhood's value. There is no evidence that raising poultry in your backyard impacts the property value.

Myth #12: Birds' Eggs Are Difficult to Harvest

This can only be true if you use the wrong nest boxes. If you provide one box for every five hens, they will easily lay their eggs, and you won't have any difficulty harvesting them.

Myth #13: Chicken Carry Diseases

This is an old myth that many people still believe today. Chickens are clean animals and are extremely safe to consume and handle. In fact, they can protect you from diseases by removing pests from your garden. It never hurts to wash your hands after handling your birds, though.

Myth #14: You Can't Raise Poultry in the City

As long as you have a small yard, you can raise poultry whether you live in the country or the city.

Myth #15: Roosters Only Crow in the Morning

Although roosters crow every day at dawn to greet the morning, they also crow during the day.

Myth #16: Chickens Are Dumb

Chickens have always been associated with cowardice and lack of intelligence. However, they are brave and intelligent animals you can teach to recognize colors, do tricks, and count.

Myth #17: You Can't Have Birds If You Live Near Predators

Predators are everywhere, and this shouldn't stop you from raising poultry. You can do things to protect your birds, like adding netting or installing a predator apron.

Myth #18: You Should Only Raise the Same Type of Birds Together

You can raise different types of birds and chickens together.

Myth #19: Bird Coops Must Be Heated

Some types of birds, like chickens, thrive in cold weather, and heaters should be avoided since they are a fire hazard.

Myth #20: Bird Coops Are Ugly

Birds' coops come in different colors and styles, and many can be nice decor for your backyard.

Different Types of Poultry Birds

This section focuses on different types of poultry birds so you can decide which one is right for you to raise.

There are different types of poultry birds, so you must decide which one is right for you to raise.[2]

Chickens

Chickens are the most popular backyard birds in the world. You can raise them for meat, eggs, or as pets. They usually start laying eggs between 16 and 18 weeks old.

Most Common Breeds:

- Sussex
- Orpington
- Leghorn
- New Hampshire
- Rhode Island

Distinctive Characteristics:

- Average size
- Small heads
- Short wings
- Short beaks
- Featherless legs
- Round body
- Four claws on each foot

Needs:

- A nest to lay eggs
- Other chickens
- Exercises
- Coops
- Coop cleaning
- Collecting eggs
- Protection from predators and the weather

Fun Fact: *Chickens have great memories. They can recognize about 100 distinct humans and fowls. If you are ever separated from your chicken, it will most likely remember you when it sees you.*

Ducks

Ducks live in water and on land and can fly as well. They are commonly raised in the U.S., U.K., and the Netherlands. Like chicken, people raise them for their meat and eggs. They also sell their feathers. A female duck is called "duck," and a male duck is called "drake." They lay about 300 eggs a year.

Most Common Breeds:

- Domestic duck
- Whistling duck
- Teal
- Sea duck
- Perching duck

Distinctive Characteristics:

- Long, flat bill
- Webbed feet
- Short necks
- Small size

Needs:

- A healthy diet
- Protection from the weather
- Sunlight
- Water for swimming
- Protection from predators

Fun Fact: Ducks have waterproof feathers, so they can move and fly easily when out of the water.

Pigeons

People raise pigeons for sport, as messengers, or for their meat. They start nesting when they are about 30 days old and lay eggs daily.

Most Common Breeds:

- Utility breed
- Fancy breed
- Fliers

Distinctive Characteristics:

- Small
- Gentle
- Plump
- Bobbing head
- Long wings

Needs:

- Pigeon aviary
- Other pigeons
- Protection against harsh weather and predators
- Exercises
- Wood shavings
- Clean water

Fun Fact: If a pigeon sees a picture of itself and other birds, it can recognize itself. They can also differentiate between pictures of different people.

Turkey

Turkey is one of the biggest types of poultry in the world. They are mainly raised for meat production. Although they lay eggs, consuming them isn't that common. In Africa, people raise them as pets or for security. They produce 45 eggs yearly, each taking 28 days to hatch. In America, people usually eat their meat on Thanksgiving and Christmas.

Life Stages:

- **Roasters**: Turkeys under four months
- **Hens**: Female turkeys around five months
- **Tom:** Male turkeys at 12 months
- **Mature**: Turkeys over 15 months

Most Common Breeds:

- Bourbon reds
- Blue state
- Black turkey
- Beltsville small white

Distinctive Characteristics:

- Long red ornament
- A fleshy wattle on the throat
- Black feathers
- Dark with a bronze-green iridescence

Needs:

- Food
- Water
- Bedding
- Heat
- Nests
- A safe place to run

Fun Fact: Turkeys' heads change color to reflect their mood and emotions. For instance, if they are terrified, their heads can turn red.

Geese

Similar to ducks, geese live in water and on land. They were raised by the ancient Egyptians thousands of years ago and were the first type of poultry to be domesticated. People raise them for meat and egg production; some sell their feathers. They produce about 65 eggs per year.

Most Common Breeds:

- Toulouse
- Lands
- Kuban
- Huoyan goose
- Czechoslovakian White
- Embden

Distinctive Characteristics:
- Short necks
- Humped bill at the base
- Legs further forward than ducks

Needs:
- Clean water
- Protection from predators
- Grass
- Kiddie pool for swimming

Fun Fact: Geese mate for life, are extremely loyal to their partners, and are protective of their offspring.

Quail

People raise quails for egg and meat production. Their eggs are used for medicinal purposes and to treat multiple conditions like allergies. They eat berries, leaves, seeds, and insects. They lay 200 eggs annually, each taking 23 days to hatch.

Most Common Breeds:
- Gambel's quail
- British Range quail
- English White quail
- Italian quail
- Japanese quail

Distinctive Characteristics:
- Small body
- Long pointed wings
- Curved, short beaks
- Long, brown legs

Needs:
- Food
- Water
- Clean shelter
- Protection against harsh weather

Fun Fact: *Quail can camouflage and blend in with their surroundings to hide from predators.*

Raising poultry is a fun and relaxing hobby. You will feel a sense of accomplishment as you care for these birds and watch them grow. In addition to consuming safe and clean products, your mental health and well-being will thrive.

Chapter 2: Choosing the Right Birds

The key to raising poultry is making informed decisions right from the start. You need to consider selecting the right birds, the unique characteristics of your backyard, personal objectives, and the level of care you can provide. This chapter aims to give insights into the considerations shaping your choices.

Considerations for Poultry Selection

Space Constraints

The available space in your backyard plays a role in the type and number of birds you can keep. Consider the size of the coop and the outdoor area for free-ranging. Certain breeds are well-suited for smaller spaces, while others thrive in bigger environments. Understanding your space constraints is crucial for the health and well-being of your birds. The Brahma chicken, for example, thrives well in smaller spaces, whereas the Delaware chicken prefers living in large coops.

Climate Compatibility

Different poultry breeds exhibit varying levels of adaptability to climate conditions. Some breeds are built to withstand cold temperatures, while others can only survive in fairly warmer climates. Knowing the region's climate and the temperature shifts during seasonal changes provides insights to make the selection easier and ensure your poultry remains comfortable and productive throughout the seasons.

Purpose

Ask yourself why you want to raise poultry. Are you looking for a fresh supply of eggs? Do you need to raise poultry for meat? Will this be a hobby? Or do you want to experiment before expanding? Whatever it is, having the reason in mind narrows down your options. For example, some bird species are renowned for their meat quality, while others have a striking appearance. Having a clear idea of why you want to raise birds will save you time and allow you to pick a breed that aligns with your goals.

Amount of Care Required

Be honest about how much time and effort you can dedicate to care. Some breeds are more independent and require minimal maintenance, making them suitable for beginners or individuals with busy schedules. Other breeds may demand more attention, especially regarding grooming, health monitoring, and specialized care.

Common Poultry Types and Considerations

Egg-Laying Breeds

If your primary goal is a consistent supply of fresh eggs, consider breeds renowned for their laying capabilities.[3]

If your primary goal is a consistent supply of fresh eggs, consider breeds renowned for their laying capabilities. Popular choices include the Rhode Island Red, Leghorn, and Sussex. These breeds are known for their reliability in egg production and are well-suited for backyard enthusiasts looking for a daily output.

Meat-Producing Breeds

For those interested in homegrown meat, breeds like the Cornish Cross or the Broiler are common choices. These are bred for efficient and rapid growth, providing a source of high-quality meat for your table. They may require more care and attention to ensure optimal growth and well-being.

Dual-Purpose Breeds

Dual-purpose breeds, like the Plymouth Rock or the Australorp, are versatile choices that balance egg production and meat quality. These breeds are well-suited for backyard settings where eggs and meat are desired, providing a comprehensive sustainable poultry-keeping solution.

Ornamental Breeds

For those seeking the aesthetic charm of poultry, ornamental breeds like the Silkie or the Polish chicken are popular choices. They often feature unique plumage, distinctive color patterns, or captivating personalities, adding a delightful touch to your backyard environment. Keep in mind that ornamental breeds may have specific care requirements.

Considerations for Poultry Selection

Here are some considerations when selecting poultry breeds and real-life scenarios that reveal how each factor influences the selection.

Space Constraints

- Evaluate the square footage of your backyard and assess the space available for the coop and outdoor roaming. Consider breeds suitable for confined spaces if your backyard is limited.

- Provide ample space to prevent stress and territorial disputes among your flock.

- Understand that larger, more active breeds may require more room.

- Consider the layout of your backyard, including trees, bushes, and other structures, to ensure a well-organized and safe environment.

The Johnsons, nestled in the suburbs with a petite backyard, chose Bantam chickens. Their small size and gentle nature suited the limited space and brought a delightful charm to the family, turning the backyard into a miniature haven for their feathered friends.

Climate Compatibility

- Research your region's climate, considering temperature extremes, humidity, and other weather factors.

- Choose breeds known for their adaptability to your specific climate, ensuring they remain comfortable and healthy throughout the seasons.

- Implement appropriate shelter and ventilation measures based on your climate to safeguard your poultry.

- Plan for seasonal changes and extreme weather events, providing additional protections when needed.

Up in the northern reaches, the Thompsons faced biting winters. Opting for resilient breeds like the Plymouth Rock and Wyandotte was not just a choice but a necessity. These cold-hardy birds weathered the chill and added a sense of resilience to the Thompsons' homestead.

Purpose

- Research breeds that align with your goals – some excel in egg production, others in meat quality, and certain breeds are prized for their ornamental characteristics.

- Align your purpose with the inherent traits of the chosen breeds to maximize productivity.

- Consider the market demand for specific poultry products in your area if your purpose includes potential sales.

Fueled by a passion for sustainability, Maria found her purpose in heritage breeds. The Sussex and Dorking, with their historical significance, became not just layers of eggs or sources of meat but ambassadors of conservation, preserving genetic diversity and connecting Maria to a broader community of like-minded enthusiasts.

Amount of Care Required

- Assess your daily schedule and be realistic about the time and effort you can dedicate to poultry care.

- Different breeds have varying care requirements; some are more independent and low-maintenance, while others may need meticulous grooming, health monitoring, and specialized care.

- Consider your experience and choose breeds that match your comfort level and resources.

- Research specific health considerations for each breed, including susceptibility to common diseases and required vaccinations.

The Millers, juggling the chaos of family life, gravitated toward low-maintenance breeds. The Rhode Island Red and Australorp supplied fresh eggs with minimal fuss and became resilient companions, perfectly fitting into their busy daily lives.

The goal can extend beyond eggs, meat, and ornamental purposes. Here's a scenario for inspiration. The Petersons, grappling with a persistent slug invasion, took in Khaki Campbell ducks. Beyond their role as pest controllers, these quacking allies added a playful element to the Petersons' backyard, turning an everyday task into a spectacle of nature's quirky pest management.

Behavioral Characteristics

- Understand the temperament and behavior of different poultry breeds. Some breeds are docile and easily handled, while others may be more skittish or territorial.

- Consider the social dynamics of each breed, especially if you plan to keep multiple types of poultry. Some breeds thrive in flocks, while others exhibit aggressive behavior.

- Evaluate noise levels, especially if you have close neighbors. Some breeds are known for being quieter than others.

Choosing suitable poultry breeds demands meticulous attention to detail and considerations like space, climate, purpose, care requirements, behavioral traits, egg and meat characteristics, and the unique qualities of each breed. After thinking about these factors, optimize the conditions for your poultry and set the stage for a fulfilling and sustainable poultry-keeping experience.

Purpose-Driven Selection

Selecting suitable poultry breeds is often purpose-driven, with specific goals shaping enthusiasts' and farmers' choices. Whether the aim is abundant egg production, high-quality meat, an ornamental display, or contributing to conservation efforts, each purpose influences bird selection in distinctive ways.

Egg Production

For those prioritizing a consistent supply of fresh eggs, breeds renowned for their prolific laying capabilities become the top choice. Considerations include the number of eggs per week, egg size, and the ability to sustain egg production throughout the year.

- Assess the balance between egg quantity and size based on your preferences and requirements.
- Consider factors beyond egg quantity, like color and taste.
- Explore breeds known for producing specific types of eggs, like those with brown, white, or colored shells.
- Research the nutritional content of eggs produced by different breeds.
- Assess whether you prefer breeds that lay consistently or exhibit seasonal variations in egg production.
- Research egg-laying capabilities, considering the number of eggs laid weekly, egg size, and persistence throughout the year.
- Explore the potential for broodiness, as some breeds may be more inclined to hatch eggs.

Top Choices: Leghorns, Rhode Island Reds, and Sussex are favored for their impressive egg-laying prowess, making them ideal selections for egg-centric goals.

Meat Production

When the primary objective is raising poultry for high-quality meat, breeds with efficient growth rates, good feed conversion, and tender meat are the go-to. The focus is on breeds that deliver optimal meat yield without compromising taste and texture.

- Understand the growth rate and feed efficiency of meat-producing breeds.
- Acknowledge the need for attentive care and controlled growth to ensure optimal health and meat quality.
- Research the processing requirements for different meat-producing breeds, including their suitability for home processing.
- Research the taste, texture, and tenderness of meat produced by different breeds.

- Consider the growth rate of meat-producing breeds and how it aligns with your timeline.
- Explore heritage breeds known for superior meat quality and flavor.
- Understand the processing requirements for meat production, including potential challenges associated with specific breeds.
- Explore breeds that offer a balance between egg production and meat quality, providing a comprehensive solution for sustainable poultry keeping.
- Consider dual-purpose breeds like the Plymouth Rock or Australorp for both egg and meat production.
- Acknowledge that these breeds may excel less than specialized breeds in either category but offer a well-rounded option.
- Research the average lifespan of dual-purpose breeds to plan for long-term sustainability.

Top Choices: Broilers, Cornish Cross, and heritage breeds like Dorking are popular for those aiming for superior meat production.

Ornamental Display

Individuals looking to enhance the aesthetic appeal of their flock often prioritize breeds known for striking plumage, unique color patterns, or captivating personalities. The emphasis is on breeds that serve as living artworks, adding visual charm to the surroundings.

- Recognize the unique characteristics of ornamental breeds, such as distinctive plumage, color patterns, or captivating personalities.
- Understand that ornamental breeds, like the Silkie or Polish chicken, may have specific care requirements, including grooming and protection from predators.
- Consider the aesthetic appeal and temperament of ornamental breeds to enhance the visual charm of your backyard.
- Explore breeds with unique behavioral traits, such as breeds known for being particularly friendly or those with entertaining behaviors.

Top Choices: Silkie chickens, Polish chickens, and ornamental bantams are sought after for their distinctive and visually appealing features, contributing to an ornamental display.

Heritage Breeds

People involved in conservation are primarily concerned with *breed conservation*. However, before starting conservation efforts, it's necessary to consider the following factors and understand the specific requirements of the breed to ensure they thrive in the provided conditions.

- Explore heritage breeds known for their historical significance, resilience, and adaptability.
- Consider the conservation aspects of raising heritage breeds to contribute to preserving genetic diversity.
- Acknowledge that heritage breeds may have slower growth rates and different egg-laying patterns than modern commercial breeds.
- Research the unique characteristics and cultural importance of specific heritage breeds.

Conservation

Conservation-minded individuals contribute to preserving genetic diversity and rare poultry breeds facing endangerment. They focus on raising breeds at risk, helping maintain a living gene pool, and preventing the loss of valuable genetic traits.

Top Choices: Breeds like the Delaware, Dominique, or Cream Legbar, classified as threatened or critical, become ambassadors for genetic conservation, fostering a sense of responsibility toward poultry biodiversity.

Understanding the purpose behind poultry selection dictates the traits and characteristics prioritized in the chosen breeds. Whether aiming for prolific egg layers, superior meat quality, an ornamental ensemble, or active participation in conservation, aligning bird choices with specific goals ensures a purpose-driven and fulfilling poultry-keeping experience.

Bird Temperament

When it comes to poultry keeping, understanding the intricacies of bird temperaments is a fundamental aspect that can significantly impact the overall well-being of the flock. This involves knowing the breed's behavioral aspects, their compatibility with other birds, and the suitability of specific breeds for families with children or other pets.

Behavioral Aspects

Each poultry breed has unique behavioral traits that influence how they interact with their environment and caretakers. For instance, breeds like the Rhode Island Red, known for their docile temperament, are often more amenable to handling and human interaction. Conversely, with their energetic disposition, breeds like the Leghorn may thrive in more active and free-ranging setups. Recognizing and understanding these behavioral nuances allows poultry keepers to create an environment that aligns with their preferred level of interaction and the overall experience they seek in poultry keeping.

Compatibility with Other Birds

Poultry, by nature, is social. Some breeds exhibit communal and tolerant behaviors, creating a cooperative and harmonious environment when housed together. Other breeds may display territorial tendencies or aggression, influencing the social dynamics of the flock. Breeds celebrated for their friendly and sociable nature, like Sussex or Australorp, are excellent choices for mixed flocks. This understanding keeps the social structure within the flock cohesive and stress-free.

Suitability for Families

Introducing poultry into a family setting requires consideration of how well a particular breed adapts to interactions with children or other pets. Some breeds inherently possess gentle and patient temperaments, making them ideal companions in family environments. Silkie chickens, for example, are renowned for their gentle disposition and are often well-suited for families with children. Being mindful of a breed's tolerance levels ensures a positive and enriching experience for all household members, promoting safe and enjoyable interactions.

Some breeds inherently possess gentle and patient temperaments, making them ideal companions in family environments.'

Likewise, getting family members on board is crucial when raising poultry in the backyard. It's beneficial for the breeds you want to raise as it increases the level of care the birds will receive, ensuring they thrive without an issue. If you have small children, educate them on these birds and demonstrate over time about adequate poultry care, how they can approach these feathered cuties, and build a bond of trust. Teaching these skills enhances the child's understanding of nature and increases their positive personality attributes like empathy, providing care, and decision-making.

Issues like overcrowding, raising different breeds in a confined space, poor nutrition, lack of attention, and numerous other factors can further deteriorate bird temperament. In the coming chapters, you will learn more about housing, care, nutrition, incubation, and much more; several of these components of poultry raising affect bird temperament. The practical tips listed below can make a difference and guarantee that your birds thrive without a problem.

- Frequently visit your feathered friends, making your presence a non-threatening part of their environment.
- You can use treats or small amounts of their favorite feed to create a positive association with human interaction.
- Take your reinforcement training to the next level by using a clicker. The breed you raise will slowly associate the clicking sound with treats or positive interactions with their caretaker.
- Avoid putting too many birds in a limited space, as it only leads to aggression and stress and increases the risk of developing diseases.
- When preparing the housing area, select a quiet and noise-free place.
- Be consistent in the feeding times and ensure the feed is nutritious and balanced.
- Whether you alone – or with the whole family – have a consistent team of caretakers so the birds can become familiar with faces that come daily to provide care.
- During inspections or maintenance, avoid catching and handling the birds aggressively.

- When clipping wings, perform it gently to avoid distressing the birds.
- Whenever you notice a bird exhibiting aggressive behavior, separate the bird immediately and keep it under monitoring to address the cause of this aggressive behavior.
- Instead of feeding them in one specific area, implement foraging opportunities by scattering grains or seeds on a larger area if possible.
- Nearby predators can also cause distress in the flock, which must be mitigated as soon as possible.
- Introduce hanging objects and interactive toys to improve their overall mood.
- Always keep the coop clean and maintain feasible temperature and humidity. Birds can develop stress in unhealthy environments and even become prone to several diseases.

A comprehensive understanding of bird temperaments involves recognizing the unique behavioral aspects of each breed and considering their compatibility within a flock and their suitability for specific family dynamics. Ensuring the flock stays healthy, thriving, and calm involves paying attention to nutrition, housing, disease prevention, brooding, and much more. Understanding the overall picture and taking informed steps is the right way forward. Maintaining this thoughtful approach guarantees that the chosen poultry breeds contribute to a harmonious, enjoyable, and enriching experience for poultry keepers and their feathery friends.

Chapter 3: Housing, Nesting, and Rooting

Creating an optimal living space for your feathered friends is paramount to their well-being, productivity, and health. This chapter delves into the importance of a well-designed habitat, exploring its impact on various aspects of avian life. You'll find several examples to guide you in crafting suitable housing setups tailored to different backyard sizes and budgets.

The Necessity of a Well-Designed Space

A well-designed living space for birds is not just a physical structure; it is a pivotal factor that profoundly influences your avian companions' overall well-being, productivity, and health. In this section, you'll explore in detail why a carefully planned habitat is essential for creating a haven that contributes to the holistic welfare of poultry birds.

When designing the coop, nesting and perching areas must be properly assigned.[5]

Promoting Well-Being

A thoughtfully designed habitat allows birds to improve their mental and physical well-being. This includes perching, foraging, and nesting, creating a sense of security and contentment. When designing the coop, nesting and perching areas must be properly assigned. Likewise, keeping the area free from predators and allowing the birds to roam and gather food all promote natural behavior and calm your furry friends.

Reducing Stress

Providing ample space and enriching features reduces stress among birds. Stress leads to various health issues and negatively impacts the flock's overall quality of life. A well-designed space keeps your birds relaxed, makes them keen to explore the surroundings, and allows them to keep stress at bay.

Behavioral Expression

No matter how many breeds you want to raise together, the design should always cater to the diverse behavioral needs of different bird species. Whether it's providing platforms for courtship, suitable nesting areas, or spaces for communal activities, fulfilling these design considerations allows birds to express their natural behaviors freely.

Egg Quality

A comfortable and stress-free environment is crucial to consistent and quality egg production. Adequate spacing minimizes stress levels among birds, encouraging consistent egg laying. Thoughtful design includes strategically placed nesting boxes, ensuring easy access for hens, and reducing the likelihood of eggs being laid in undesirable locations. This contributes to improved egg quality, strong and durable shells, reduced contamination, and better hygiene.

Reproductive Success

Properly designed nesting areas contribute to reproductive success. Nesting boxes or platforms should mimic the birds' instincts, encouraging successful egg-laying and raising their young.

Encouraging Social Interaction

Well-designed habitats facilitate social interactions among birds. Socializing is crucial, especially for species that thrive in flocks. Communal spaces, perches, and designated areas for group activities contribute to a harmonious and socially engaged flock.

Meat Quality

Regarding meat quality, a well-managed space is vital in ensuring healthy and robust poultry. Optimal spacing reduces aggressive behaviors, minimizing injuries and pecking incidents. Uninjured birds contribute to superior meat quality. Additionally, proper spacing ensures fair access to food, reducing competition among birds and promoting nutrient absorption. A stress-free environment positively influences the reproductive system, producing better meat quality. Overall, a well-designed space for poultry is integral to achieving optimal egg and meat quality, essential for the success and sustainability of poultry farming operations.

Ventilation and Cleanliness

Proper ventilation is vital for maintaining a healthy environment. Well-designed habitats ensure good airflow, reducing the risk of respiratory issues. Furthermore, keeping cleaning and waste management in mind contributes to a hygienic space, minimizing the spread of diseases.

Temperature Regulation

Adequate spacing and strategically placed elements in the habitat help regulate temperature. Birds are sensitive to extreme temperatures, and a well-designed habitat ensures they can find shelter, shade, or warmth as needed. Several factors, like using insulation material and controlling moisture, must be considered to achieve optimum temperature regulation. If several breeds are being raised in the same area, consider temperature zoning, where you designate zones in the coop according to age, and create microclimates feasible for each age group or breed.

Preventing Diseases

Thoughtful design incorporates measures to prevent the spread of diseases. This includes spacing structures appropriately, isolating sick birds when necessary, and minimizing potential breeding grounds for parasites or pathogens. These spaces support healthy growth, reducing mortality and optimizing feed conversion rates.

The importance of a thoughtfully designed avian habitat cannot be overstated. This habitat goes beyond meeting basic shelter needs. It becomes a dynamic environment supporting a bird's life's physical, mental, and social aspects.

Creating spaces that align with their natural behaviors, encourage social interaction, and prioritize health considerations fosters an environment where birds can thrive, express themselves, and lead fulfilling lives. A well-designed avian haven is a testament to your commitment to the well-being of your feathered friends, ensuring a life of comfort, productivity, and health within their carefully crafted homes.

Insulation for Temperature Regulation

Maintaining Optimal Conditions

Adequate insulation is crucial to regulate temperatures within the poultry housing. Insulation helps maintain a stable environment, protecting birds from extreme heat or cold. This ensures optimal growth, egg production, and overall health.

Preventing Heat Stress

In warmer climates, proper insulation prevents heat stress by minimizing the impact of external temperature fluctuations. It creates a more comfortable living space, reducing the poultry's risk of heat-related health issues.

Addressing Cold Environments

During colder seasons, insulation retains heat within the structure, preventing drafts and ensuring that birds remain warm. This is vital for preventing frostbite and respiratory problems associated with exposure to low temperatures.

The Use of Ventilation Systems

Promoting Airflow

Adequate ventilation is essential for promoting airflow and maintaining fresh air within the poultry housing. Stagnant air can lead to the buildup of harmful gases, moisture, and airborne pathogens, negatively impacting the respiratory health of birds.

Minimizing Respiratory Issues

Proper ventilation reduces the concentration of ammonia and other airborne pollutants. This minimizes the risk of respiratory issues, enhancing the overall respiratory health of the flock.

Regulating Humidity Levels

Ventilation systems also play a role in regulating humidity levels. Controlling humidity is essential for preventing mold and bacteria growth, contributing to a healthier living environment for poultry.

Predator-Proofing Measures

Securing Outdoor Spaces

Designing outdoor areas with secure fencing and netting protects poultry from predators. Thoughtful design that incorporates secure fencing, buried hardware cloth, and reinforced structures is essential. Installing predator-resistant fencing, like hardware cloth with small mesh sizes, prevents access to small predators like raccoons and snakes. Burying the fencing material beneath the soil surface creates an additional barrier, deterring burrowing predators like foxes. Reinforcing structures, such as coops and roosts, with sturdy materials and locks further enhances protection.

Regular outdoor area maintenance and inspections are crucial to identify and promptly address potential vulnerabilities. Likewise, adequate lighting around the perimeter can also discourage nocturnal predators.

Sturdy Construction

Ensure the poultry housing is constructed with sturdy materials and features secure locks. To begin, selecting durable materials resistant to weathering and wear is crucial. Thick and strong wood or metal provides a solid foundation, minimizing vulnerabilities that predators could exploit. Reinforcing vulnerable points, such as entry doors and windows, with additional locks or latches enhances security.

Moreover, paying attention to structural details is vital. Ensuring there are no gaps, cracks, or weak points in the construction eliminates potential predator entry points. Seal any openings with predator-resistant materials like hardware cloth with small mesh sizes.

Elevated Roosts and Nesting Boxes

Elevating roosts and nesting boxes can deter ground-based predators. This reduces the risk of predation during vulnerable times, such as when birds are resting or laying eggs.

Creating an environment that caters to the specific needs of laying hens is fundamental for ensuring optimal egg-laying conditions. This next section delves into the intricacies of choosing suitable nesting materials, offering layout suggestions for nesting boxes, and implementing privacy measures to enhance the comfort of your hens during the egg-laying process.

Choosing Suitable Nesting Materials

Straw and Hay

Using straw or hay as nesting materials presents a multi-faceted advantage. These materials provide a soft and insulating bed for the hens to lay eggs. Straw and hay also absorb moisture effectively, ensuring a dry and comfortable environment conducive to egg-laying.

Wood Shavings

Wood shavings are an excellent option for nesting material due to their absorbent nature. They create a clean and dry surface, minimizing the risk of eggs becoming soiled. It is crucial, however, to ensure that the wood shavings are free from sharp edges or splinters to prevent any harm to the hens.

Nesting Pads or Mats

Pre-made nesting pads or mats, crafted from materials such as felt or rubber, offer a consistent and comfortable surface. These materials are easy to clean and maintain, contributing to a hygienic nesting space that promotes the overall well-being of the laying hens.

Layout Suggestions for Nesting Boxes

Consider Box Size

Thoughtful consideration of nesting box dimensions is pivotal. Boxes should be appropriately sized to ensure comfort for the hens. Boxes that are too large may inadvertently encourage multiple hens to share, potentially leading to broken eggs.

Elevate Nesting Boxes

Elevating nesting boxes off the ground serves multiple purposes. Not only does it provide a sense of security for the hens, but it also minimizes the risk of them scratching and soiling the nesting materials. Elevated boxes reduce the chances of predation, creating a calm and secure environment for egg-laying.

Adequate Number of Boxes

Providing an adequate number of nesting boxes is essential. Overcrowding can lead to competition for nesting spaces, causing stress among the hens and negatively impacting egg production. Having a sufficient number of boxes promotes a harmonious and stress-free environment.

Ensuring Privacy for Optimum Egg-Laying Conditions

Screening or Curtains

Implementing screening or curtains within the nesting area creates a private and secluded space. This privacy measure contributes to a sense of security for the hens, encouraging them to lay eggs undisturbed.

Dim Lighting

Providing dim lighting in the nesting area caters to the hens' natural preferences. Hens favor dimly lit spaces for laying eggs, and this thoughtful design element contributes to a more relaxed egg-laying environment and reduces stress.

Separate Laying Area

Designating a specific area for nesting separates it from other daily pursuits. This separation reduces disruptions and provides the hens with a quiet and dedicated space, further enhancing the overall comfort during the egg-laying process.

The nuances of nesting are crucial for creating an environment that prioritizes the comfort and well-being of laying hens. The meticulous choice of nesting materials, thoughtful layout suggestions, and the implementation of privacy measures collectively contribute to an atmosphere that maximizes productivity and fosters a stress-free and contented egg-laying process. By paying attention to these details with precision and care, you elevate the conditions for your poultry flock, ensuring that their nesting experience is characterized by comfort, security, and optimal well-being.

Creating a Restful Environment

Creating a conducive roosting environment is crucial for your poultry's well-being and restful nights. You'll now be introduced to the necessity of appropriate roosting bars, height considerations, and spacing between roosts to provide optimal conditions for your birds' nightly repose.

Appropriate Roosting Bars

Material and Diameter

The choice of roosting bar material and diameter significantly influences your birds' comfort. Opt for materials that are comfortable for the hens to grip, such as smooth wood or PVC. The diameter of the roosting bars should be conducive to a secure grip, preventing foot problems like bumblefoot.

Spacing and Placement

Proper spacing between roosting bars is essential. Aim for a distance that allows each bird enough space to perch comfortably without encroaching on the neighboring one's territory. Adequate spacing prevents overcrowding and minimizes the risk of aggressive behaviors.

Adjustable vs. Fixed Bars

Consider the benefits of adjustable roosting bars, allowing you to modify the height as your birds grow or as you introduce new poultry to the flock. Fixed bars may limit flexibility, especially if you have a mixed-age flock.

Height Considerations

Natural Instincts

Chickens have a natural instinct to roost at higher elevations, mimicking their wild behavior of seeking elevated spots for safety during the night. Providing roosts at an appropriate height aligns with this instinct and promotes an overall sense of security for the birds.

Avoiding Height Disparities

Maintain a consistent height for roosting bars within the coop. Avoid sharp disparities in height, as this can lead to hierarchy issues within the flock. A level roosting surface contributes to a harmonious and stress-free roosting experience.

Accessibility for All Birds

Consider the accessibility of roosting bars for all birds, including those with physical limitations. If you have older or injured chickens, providing lower roosts ensures that every member of the flock can comfortably access their designated roosting spot.

Preventing Overcrowding

Adequate spacing between roosts is vital for preventing overcrowding. Birds need personal space for comfort and to exhibit natural behaviors like preening and stretching. Sufficient space also minimizes the risk of injury caused by territorial disputes.

Accommodating Different Breeds

Different chicken breeds have varying sizes and preferences when it comes to roosting. By offering varied spacing between roosts, you accommodate the diverse needs of your flock, ensuring that each bird can find a spot that suits them.

Facilitating Easy Movement

The arrangement of roosts allows for easy movement within the coop. Birds should be able to navigate to and from their roosting spots without hindrance. This facilitates a stress-free bedtime routine for your poultry.

Understanding and implementing the realities of roosting contribute significantly to the overall well-being and restful nights of your flock. Appropriate roosting bars, careful height considerations, and thoughtfully spaced roosts ensure that each bird can enjoy a secure, comfortable, and stress-free roosting experience. By prioritizing these roosting realities, you create an environment that promotes the natural behaviors and instincts of your poultry, fostering a contented and harmonious coop atmosphere.

Safeguarding Flocks from Disease

Biosecurity is a critical component of poultry management with the aim of preventing the introduction and spread of diseases within the flock and housing environment. By implementing stringent biosecurity measures, poultry farmers can enhance the overall health and productivity of their flocks. Here's an in-depth exploration of biosecurity practices:

Perimeter Fencing

Establish a secure perimeter around the poultry housing facility using appropriate fencing. This prevents unauthorized access and reduces the risk of disease introduction by external sources, such as wild birds or animals.

Controlled Access Points

Designate controlled access points for personnel, equipment, and visitors. Implement biosecurity protocols at these entry points, including foot baths, hand sanitization, and protective clothing, to minimize the risk of introducing contaminants.

Quarantine Practices

Introduce a comprehensive quarantine system for new birds entering the flock. This involves isolating new additions for a specified period, allowing for observation and health checks to identify potential diseases before integration.

Regular Health Monitoring

Implement regular health monitoring programs for the entire flock. This involves routine checks for signs of illness, monitoring feed and water consumption, and promptly addressing any abnormalities.

Cleaning and Disinfection

Establish strict cleaning and disinfection protocols for equipment and vehicles entering the poultry facility. This prevents the transmission of pathogens on surfaces, reducing the risk of disease spread.

Equipment Use

Designate specific equipment for use within the poultry facility whenever possible to avoid cross-contamination from other farming activities.

Biosecurity Training

Provide comprehensive biosecurity training to everyone involved. This includes proper handling procedures, hygiene practices, and the importance of adhering to biosecurity protocols.

Biosecurity Education

Educate staff, if you have any, on the potential risks associated with poultry diseases, emphasizing the role each individual plays in maintaining a bio-secure environment. Regular training sessions and updates are essential to reinforce these practices.

Bird Netting and Deterrents

Install bird netting or deterrents to minimize contact between poultry and wild birds. Wild birds can carry diseases that pose a threat to domestic poultry, making it crucial to prevent direct or indirect interactions.

Wildlife Management Plans

Develop and implement wildlife management plans to address potential threats from mammals that can transmit diseases. This may involve securing feed storage areas and implementing measures to discourage wildlife from entering the premises.

Sustainable Practices in Poultry

Sustainability in poultry housing involves adopting practices that minimize environmental impact, promote resource efficiency, and contribute to the overall well-being of the flock. Here's an in-depth exploration of sustainable practices in poultry housing:

Natural Lighting Solutions

Incorporate natural lighting solutions in poultry housing to reduce dependence on artificial lighting. This saves energy and promotes the well-being of birds as they respond positively to natural light cycles.

Energy-Efficient Equipment

Invest in energy-efficient heating, ventilation, and cooling systems. This reduces energy consumption and operational costs while maintaining optimal environmental conditions within the poultry facility.

Manure Management

Implement efficient manure management systems, such as composting or utilization as fertilizer. Proper disposal and recycling of manure contribute to soil health and minimize environmental impact.

Recycling and Reusing Materials

Embrace recycling practices by reusing materials within the poultry housing structure. This includes repurposing materials like wood or metal for construction, reducing the need for new resources.

Landscaping for Environmental Harmony

Incorporate landscaping around the poultry facility to enhance environmental harmony. This includes planting native vegetation, creating green spaces, and designing surroundings that support biodiversity.

Water Conservation Practices

Implement water conservation practices, such as rainwater harvesting or the use of efficient watering systems. This minimizes water wastage and promotes responsible water usage within the poultry housing facility.

Solar or Wind Power

Explore the feasibility of incorporating alternative energy sources, such as solar panels or wind turbines. Renewable energy contributes to sustainability by reducing reliance on traditional power grids.

Energy-Efficient Heating Systems

Opt for energy-efficient heating systems that utilize renewable energy sources or advanced technologies to minimize energy consumption.

Preserving Natural Habitats

Design poultry housing facilities with consideration for preserving natural habitats and biodiversity. Avoid encroaching on ecologically sensitive areas, and adopt designs that coexist harmoniously with the natural environment.

Planting Hedgerows or Windbreaks

Planting hedgerows or windbreaks serves multiple purposes, including biodiversity preservation, wind protection, and creating microenvironments that benefit both poultry and wildlife.

Feed and Bedding Procurement

Source poultry feed and bedding materials locally when possible, promoting sustainability in the supply chain. This reduces transportation-related carbon emissions and supports local economies.

Sustainable Construction Materials

Use sustainable construction materials for building and maintaining poultry housing structures. This may include recycled or locally sourced materials with lower environmental impact.

Incorporating biosecurity measures and sustainable practices in poultry housing is essential to achieve a balance between ecology and productivity. Robust biosecurity safeguards flocks from diseases, ensuring a healthy and productive environment. Simultaneously, sustainable practices contribute to environmental stewardship, resource efficiency, and the long-term viability of poultry farming. By integrating these principles, farmers can create facilities that prioritize the well-being of the flock, minimize environmental impact, and promote overall sustainability in poultry management.

Chapter 4: Feeding and Nutrition

Feeding and nutrition are at the heart of keeping poultry healthy and productive. If you want to protect your birds and guarantee safe and healthy products, you should pay attention to what you are feeding them. A balanced diet improves your birds' immunity and protects them from fungal, bacterial, and viral infections. It also makes their feathers look even nicer, improves their temperament, and enhances their well-being.

This chapter covers basic poultry nutrition, commercial feed components, and the benefits and potential hazards of treats and supplements.

The Connection between a Balanced Diet and Optimal Bird Health

FRUITS

Mango's
Kiwi
Papaya
Melons (no rind)
Berries
Pomegranates
Grapes
Cranberries
Banana's
Apples

VEGGIES

Carrots (Tops Included)
Sweet Potatoes
Leafy Greens
Peppers, Assorted Colors
Green Beans
Sweet Peas
Sugar Snap Peas
Squash
Pumpkin
Corn

50-60% Of Diet Should Comprise
of Well-Balanced Pellets

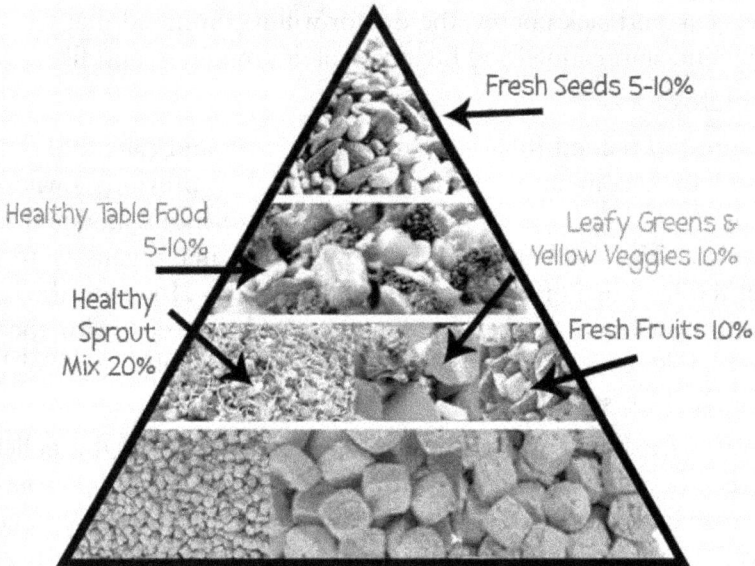

Fresh Seeds 5-10%

Healthy Table Food
5-10%

Leafy Greens &
Yellow Veggies 10%

Healthy
Sprout
Mix 20%

Fresh Fruits 10%

AVIAN FOOD PYRAMID

Avocado's, Uncooked Beans, Chocolate, Alcohol, Caffiene,
Shellfish & Undercooked Meat. Remove Fresh Foods After 2-3hrs.

When people decide to raise poultry, they often plan in advance the type of bird they want to have and where they will raise their flock. However, many don't pay attention to poultry feed and just buy any high-quality brand without looking at the ingredients to check for chemicals or harmful additives. When you feed your birds with nutrient-rich food, they will be strong and energetic and produce high-quality eggs with disease-free chicks.

To get the most out of your birds, feed them a balanced diet from the start. A well-balanced diet greatly impacts their laying capacity, immune system, growth rate, and yolk sac utilization.

If you raise the birds for eggs and meat, you should feed them high amounts of fiber and protein to keep them full and increase the amount of good bacteria in their stomachs. Feed them food rich in vitamins to guarantee constant egg production, hatchability, healthy chicks, and good fertility. A poor diet reduces egg production, weakens the shells, and impacts the birds' overall health.

Feed plays a huge role in your birds' well-being and behavior. In fact, the right diet can revive a malnourished bird. Similar to human beings, if you are weak and lack energy, the doctor will recommend that you change your diet and start eating food high in protein, minerals, and fiber.

Real Life Story

A young girl named Julia rescued a cute parrot and called it Lily. Sadly, Lily used to live in an abusive home, and her previous owners were negligent and didn't properly feed her. She was malnourished and severely underweight. Her feathers were falling off, and her organs were failing. Julia started feeding her seeds and fresh vegetables. However, the bird was still losing weight. So, she added pellets to Lily's diet with the seeds. Although Lily was eating the food, she remained underweight and malnourished for six months.

Julia was frustrated and wanted Lily to focus more on the pellets than the seeds. She removed the seeds from the diet and mainly put out pellets and vegetables. Lily started gaining weight and was feeling more energetic. However, her weight gain was slow. So, Julia decided to take her to the vet.

The vet recommended a type of high-quality organic food. Julia listened and only fed Lily the organic diet. After a couple of months, Lily gained weight and was full of energy. Her feathers looked better than ever, and she was finally happy.

It isn't an exaggeration to say that a well-balanced diet saved Lily's life. It turned her from a malnourished and sick bird who was on the verge of death to a full-of-life and joyful one.

The Basics of Poultry Nutrition

Now that you understand the significance of feeding your birds a well-balanced diet, you are ready to discover the essential nutrients that will keep them healthy and protect them from diseases.

Water

Water is necessary for transporting nutrients in birds' bodies, regulating their temperature, and keeping them hydrated. Make sure that your birds always have access to clean and fresh water. They should drink twice as much water as the amount of their feed.

Protein

Proteins build body tissues like the beak, feathers, skin, cartilage, nerves, and muscles. They are also responsible for the birds' maintenance, development, and growth. Proteins are made of essential and non-essential amino acids. Birds' bodies can produce non-essential amino acids, but you should provide them with food rich in essential ones.

If you raise birds for eggs, give them food rich in protein like corn gluten, meat, fish, legumes, canola, or soybean.

Inadequate protein levels can cause many health issues and reduce egg and meat yield.

Minerals

Minerals help bone and blood cell formulation, boost metabolism, activate enzymes, and prevent blood clotting. You should give your bird food high in zinc, selenium, manganese, iron, iodine, sodium, potassium, magnesium, chlorine, phosphorus, and calcium. Calcium improves bones and eggshell quality. Phosphorus boosts bone health, and chlorine increases the levels of hydrochloric acid, which aids in digestion. Potassium and sodium protect the nerves and muscles.

Birds require calcium during eggshell formation. They will use the calcium reserves in their skeletons if they don't receive enough. This can cause serious issues, and the hen will stop laying eggs.

Vitamins

Make sure your birds get vitamin A to support their growth and development, vitamin D for eggshell formation, and vitamin B to increase energy levels and boost metabolism. Many of these vitamins can be given in the form of supplements. Others require external factors like vitamin D that can be produced by constant exposure to the sun.

Energy

Ensure your birds consume enough calories daily to increase their energy levels and fuel all chemical reactions in their bodies.

Birds need energy for reproduction, digestion, maintenance, and growth. Luckily, almost all ingredients contain energy. If you want your birds to be more energetic, feed them corn, wheat, barley, meat, and fat.

Fats

Fats are necessary for meat and poultry. They increase the birds' energy and boost their productivity.

Carbohydrates

Carbohydrates boost the energy that fuels maintenance, growth, and daily activities. You should aim to strike a balance between carbs and fats in your birds' diet.

Decoding Feed Labels

Like most bird or animal owners, you will mainly rely on commercial feed for your flock's meals. Commercial feed is store-bought food made specifically for poultry. There are many types to choose from; some are expensive brands that are made from high-quality ingredients, while others are lower quality and can contain harmful substances. Sometimes, high-quality brands are your best option since manufacturers usually test all ingredients in advance to guarantee their safety.

Before you choose a type of feed, check the components first to make sure it is made from healthy ingredients and doesn't contain harmful additives or chemicals.

Commercial Feed Components

This section sheds light on all the common components you will find on commercial feed packages and what they mean.

Cereal Grains

Cereal grains are dry grains and cereal by-products that sustain your poultry and boost their energy. There are usually different types of grains used in feed. In Asian countries, Brazil and the US use corn as the main ingredient and energy source. Canada, Europe, Russia, New Zealand, and Australia use wheat as the main source of poultry dietary energy. However, many manufacturers don't really focus on the nutritional benefits of the grain but make their choice based on its price. For instance, China and the US use wheat if it is cheaper. In Australia, they sometimes use sorghum instead of wheat. Sweden, Denmark, and Norway use rye and barley when grain prices are high.

Any changes manufacturers make to their products depend mainly on cost. That doesn't mean they should keep adding or removing ingredients whenever they feel like it. Any change, whether big or small, should be handled with caution. In fact, many manufacturers avoid making big changes to the feed components since they can cause digestive issues to the birds and reduce their productivity.

Different factors can impact the grains' quality, such as storage and seasonal conditions. If the grains aren't stored properly or grown in poor conditions, their energy content will reduce drastically. These conditions can also expose the grains to toxins or harmful organisms like fungi.

Environmental and genetic factors can also impact the quality of the grains and their nutritive value. These can make them hard to digest and cause serious issues for the birds.

Cereal by-products like rice bran and wheat bran are also used in the feed components.

Protein Meals

Animal and vegetable proteins like fish, legumes, and oilseeds are used in poultry feed. Vegetable protein sources are usually the by-products of oilseed crops like sesame seed, linseed, peanut, copra, palm kernel, sunflower, canola, and soybean. They are made from the residue of the extracted oil. Similar to grain, countries also use different vegetable protein sources. Some use soybeans or sunflowers, and others use lupins, peas, or cottonseed. Manufacturers may use more than one vegetable resource if their prices are reasonable.

Animal protein sources used in poultry feed are feather meal, blood meal, poultry by-product meal, fish meal, meat meal, and meat and bone meal.

The animal industry has evolved in the last few years, and they have put more focus on increasing nutrient levels and improving the flavor.

Using animal resources in poultry feed can be challenging because a few people raise their concerns about it. Food safety has been put into question, with people worrying about recycling animal products and using them as feed ingredients. However, there haven't been any reports of birds getting sick. Some people were also worried that animal protein meals could cause Salmonella. It has been stated that harmful bacteria are usually destroyed through rendering, and recontamination is impossible. In most cases, birds get Salmonella through environmental factors instead of feed.

Animal protein meals contain high levels of amino acids and minerals and are also considered a source of energy.

Although there are some concerns surrounding animal protein meals, they have been incorporated into poultry feed for years. Using this ingredient is significant since it increases the economic and nutrient value of the feed and plays a role in producing high-quality meat and eggs.

Fats and Oils

Fats and oils are often used in bird feed because they increase their energy and contain more nutrients than proteins and carbohydrates. They also contain fatty acids like linoleic acid. Various types of fats and oils, like cottonseed oil, palm oil, linseed oil, sunflower oil, canola oil, and soy oil, are used in poultry feed.

Vitamins and Minerals

Minerals encourage development and normal growth in fowls. Feeds usually contain high levels of phosphorus and calcium, which increase egg production. You will also find other minerals like molybdenum, iodine, cobalt, selenium, zinc, manganese, iron, and copper. Lacking these minerals will cause health issues – and even death – for the birds.

The feeds also contain vitamins A, D, E, K, and B12, pantothenic acid, pyridoxine, thiamine, riboflavin, niacin, folic acid, choline, and biotin, which promote the bird's well-being and improve their health.

Additives

Additives enhance feed qualities, improve the bird's digestion, productivity, growth, and health, and prevent disease.

Antioxidants

Fat is usually added to bird feeds, especially in fish meals. However, products high in fats are at risk of going bad. To protect the feed and give it a long shelf life, manufacturers add antioxidants.

Antibiotics

There are microbes and bad bacteria in the digestive tract of all animals and birds. This bacteria can cause serious health issues, like damaging the intestines. Adding antibiotics to the feed will eliminate the bad bacteria and keep the bird protected from infections.

Antibiotic Alternatives

Some people are against the use of antibiotics because they eliminate the good bacteria as well. This is why manufacturers have developed and used alternatives that kill bad bacteria and increase the number of good ones.

Free-Flowing Agents

The feed should flow easily in the feeders so it doesn't get stuck and leave the birds hungry. Manufacturers add free-flowing agents to prevent the feeds from packing down. These agents don't react with any of the ingredients.

Coccidiostats

Coccidiosis is a parasitic disease that infects birds' intestine tracts. It isn't serious if the coccidia is at low levels. At high levels, this condition can kill your poultry. Adding coccidiostats to the feed will prevent the parasite from spreading and boost their immune system.

Coccidiostats isn't a treatment. It only provides protection.

Pelleting Additives

Pelleting additives are added to the feed to enhance its efficiency and ensure the ingredients are packed together in small pellets so the bird can eat them with ease.

Mold Inhibitors

Cereals can be infected with mold during harvesting, processing, or storing. Even though the mold can be removed, it will still release mycotoxins, which can be fatal to the poultry. Mold inhibitors prevent contamination and mold growth.

Feeding Enzymes

Some of the ingredients used in poultry feed have anti-nutritional properties, rendering them useless. Feeding enzymes can break down these properties to increase the potential of alternative grains.

Quality Indicators

Naturally, you want to get the best quality feed for your poultry. You may think that the most expensive or popular brands are the safest option. However, this isn't always the case. There are simple things you can do to guarantee you are getting the best feed for your birds.

- Look at the ingredients and make sure they contain proteins, carbohydrates, vitamins, minerals, fats, and grains.
- Check to see the additives they are using and make sure they haven't added any toxic or harmful chemicals.
- Read the feed preview online and see what other people are saying.
- Smell it before using it. If it has a strange odor, it probably isn't high-quality.

Supplements and Treats

If your birds are suffering from vitamin deficiency, you may want to give them supplements to boost their energy and improve their strength. You still shouldn't give them something that can affect their eggs, meat, or health.

Advantages of Using Supplements for Poultry

- Improve digestion
- Aid in absorbing nutrients from feed
- Boost the immune system
- Reduce infection
- Protect against diseases
- Increase egg production and quality
- Improve growth rate
- Strengthen bones
- Keep poultry active
- Enhance laying duration
- Improve overall health

Potential Hazards of Using Supplements for Poultry

- They aren't substitutes for nutrients
- They increase antimicrobial resistance
- Expose the poultry to harmful amounts of endotoxins, which can impact your health as well.

You love your poultry, and you probably want to spoil them every now and then. Giving them treats will make them happy and improve their mood, especially if they have been stressed. Just like supplements, there are advantages and disadvantages to treats.

Benefits of Using Treats

- Boost birds' immune system
- Add minerals and vitamins to their diet
- Boost their mood
- Improve their behavior

Potential Hazards of Giving Poultry Treats

- It can inadvertently replace nutritious food
- Obesity
- Reduce egg production
- Feather picking

Heart issues Give your poultry healthy snacks to avoid these potential hazards:

- Oatmeal
- Cottage cheese
- Pasta and noodles
- Mealworms
- Corn
- Ginger
- Watermelon
- Pumpkin
- Meat

Natural Foraging for Backyard Poultry

Natural foraging is letting your birds fetch their food by themselves. Many farmers prefer to let their animals wander around and search for food. Before you make a decision about backyard foraging, consider its advantages and disadvantages.

Natural foraging is letting your birds fetch their food by themselves.[6]

Advantages of Natural Foraging

- Environmentally friendly
- You give back to the environment
- You give your birds the chance to be out in nature, get fresh air, and be exposed to the sun, which is a natural source of Vitamin D
- The chickens become more sustainable
- Reduces the number of insects
- They will get animal proteins and Vitamin B from eating those insects
- Foraging is better and healthier than commercial feed as the birds will consume more saturated fats and vitamins
- It is more cost-effective since you won't have to buy commercial food

- Your poultry will have the chance to socialize with other birds
- It is great exercise for them and prevents them from gaining weight
- Keeps your birds active
- Eggs will be more nutritious

Potential Hazards of Natural Foraging

- Your poultry will be easy prey for predators
- They will make big holes while searching for food, which prevents the grass from regrowing
- Poultry that forage will make a mess by discharging wherever
- The birds are at risk of inhaling or ingesting harmful substances
- They will eat anything from your garden, including potting plants and flowers
- You will struggle to find the eggs since they can lay them anywhere they can reach

If you want to raise healthy poultry and consume their eggs and meat, you should pay close attention to what you are feeding them. One small mistake can make your birds sick and affect their products. Remember, you also love these funny, feathery creatures, so protect them and help them stay healthy by making sure their feed is highly nutritious.

Before buying commercial food, read the ingredient list on the package thoroughly. Make sure there are no harmful chemicals or additives that can harm your poultry. Check the expiration date as well; expired products are dangerous and often lack proper nutrients.

Whether you want to let your poultry forage or not is your choice. You just need to consider the advantages and disadvantages very well before making a decision.

Chapter 5: Poultry Health and Wellness

The health and wellness of poultry are intricately connected to proactive care and the early detection of ailments. This relationship is pivotal in enhancing your birds' longevity and productivity. By adopting a vigilant and preemptive approach to poultry health, caretakers can address potential issues before they escalate, safeguarding the flock's well-being and optimizing their performance.

The health and wellness of poultry are intricately connected to proactive care and the early detection of ailments.[7]

Proactive care involves a comprehensive regimen that encompasses preventive measures, regular health assessments, and a keen awareness of the environmental factors impacting the birds. This proactive approach sets the foundation for early detection, where subtle signs of illness or distress can be identified before they manifest into severe health issues.

Early detection, in turn, becomes a linchpin for maintaining the longevity and productivity of poultry. Detecting illnesses in their nascent stages allows for timely intervention, reducing the severity and duration of the ailment. This guarantees the individual well-being of each bird and prevents the spread of diseases within the flock. Moreover, addressing health concerns early on minimizes the impact on the overall productivity of poultry, allowing them to continue contributing to egg production, meat quality, or other desired outcomes.

Implementing a proactive healthcare strategy means arranging regular health check-ups and vaccination programs, maintaining optimal living conditions, and always giving a prompt response to any behavioral changes or symptoms observed. Caretakers who adopt these practices establish a robust foundation for sustained poultry health and, consequently, prolonged periods of productivity.

In essence, the intrinsic link between proactive care, early detection of ailments, and the longevity and productivity of birds underscores the importance of a holistic and vigilant approach to poultry health and wellness. Prioritizing these aspects contributes to the entire flock's collective resilience and efficiency, ultimately fostering a thriving and sustainable poultry environment.

Common Poultry Diseases

Poultry diseases can pose significant challenges to the health and productivity of your flock. Understanding the characteristics of common diseases is essential for early detection and effective management.

Coccidiosis

Causative Agent: Protozoan parasites (Eimeria spp.).

Symptoms: Bloody diarrhea, lethargy, decreased feed intake, and reduced weight gain.

Prevention: Maintain clean and dry bedding to reduce oocyst survival, provide medicated feed containing coccidiostats, and practice strict biosecurity.

Treatment: Administer anticoccidial medications as prescribed by a veterinarian. Supportive care includes maintaining hydration and proper nutrition.

Real-Life Recovery Story

Emma's farm included vibrant and spirited broiler chickens. One morning, Emma noticed that a few chickens from her flock had their feathers ruffled, and their eyes looked dull and weary. Recognizing the urgency of the situation, Emma decided to investigate further. She noticed a concerning sign – the droppings were tinged with blood, confirming the symptom of bloody diarrhea. Fear gripped Emma's heart as she remembered stories of farm owners sharing their stories of chickens succumbing to the notorious coccidiosis.

Without wasting a moment, Emma isolated the suspected chickens and reached out to a trusted veterinarian,

The vet confirmed the presence of an infective parasite causing coccidiosis and tailored a treatment plan for the isolated chicken. In a week, the feathers started regaining their luster and became completely healthy at the end of the treatment. This story highlights the importance of keen observation, prompt intervention, and seeking professional help to ensure the well-being of your feathered friends.

Holistic Solutions

Beyond medication, holistic approaches include maintaining a clean and dry environment, providing balanced nutrition, and regular check-ups. Daisy's recovery highlights how a holistic strategy can contribute to overall well-being.

Infectious Bronchitis

Causative Agent: Avian coronavirus.

Symptoms: Respiratory distress, coughing, sneezing, and decreased egg production.

Prevention: Implement vaccination programs, practice strict biosecurity measures to limit exposure, and isolate new birds. Adequate ventilation in coops is essential.

Treatment: Supportive care to manage respiratory symptoms. Antibiotics may be prescribed in severe cases under veterinary guidance.

Real-Life Recovery Story

In a coop nestled on a countryside farm, the coop owner (Ben) found himself hearing raspy coughs from a hen. He ignored the sound and went to work on his daily farm duties. However, in a few days, the entire flock started producing the same cough sound. Recognizing the urgency, Ben immediately contacted one of his friends who was raising livestock poultry himself. His friend, Alex, advised Ben to isolate the birds that were actively coughing and seemed in distress.

The vet was called in to run diagnostic tests, which confirmed the development of infective bronchitis in the flock. The second thing Alex noticed was the high levels of humidity, which is an aggravating factor in the spread of bronchitis within the flock. Targeted vaccination was advised by the vet, whereas the design of the coop was changed to convert it into a ventilation coop to reduce humidity and limit the exposure to other birds in the flock.

In a matter of weeks, the once somber coop transformed into a bustling haven again, and the hens went back to their egg-laying routine. As advised by the vet, Ben continued to uphold a robust health management plan, ensuring the well-being of the flock for years to come.

Holistic Solutions

Aside from vaccination, holistic care involves clean habitats, optimal nutrition, and mental stimulation. Charlie's recovery highlights the need for a holistic approach to combat respiratory diseases.

Newcastle Disease

Causative Agent: Avian paramyxovirus type 1.

Symptoms: Respiratory distress, nervous system disorders, and a drop in egg production.

Prevention: Vaccinate against Newcastle disease, implement strict biosecurity measures, and properly dispose of infected carcasses.

Treatment: There is no specific cure. Focus on supportive care. Euthanasia may be considered in severe cases.

Holistic Solution

A holistic approach includes clean environments, balanced nutrition, and regular mental stimulation. This showcases the resilience achieved through a comprehensive health strategy.

Avian Influenza

Causative Agent: Influenza A virus.

Symptoms: Respiratory distress, swollen heads, and a sudden drop in egg production.

Prevention: Strict biosecurity practices, surveillance for early detection, and vaccination in high-risk areas.

Treatment: Supportive care. Culling may be necessary to prevent the disease from spreading in severe cases.

Real-Life Recovery Story

In a cozy backyard lived a cheerful rooster with a few hens and their caring owner, Charlie. One day, the rooster started acting strange – breathing heavily, having a swollen head, and looking a bit tired. Charlie knew something was wrong and remembered reading about avian influenza.

Worried about the rooster, Charlie quickly reached out to the local vet. The veterinarian advised moving the rooster to an isolated space, separate from the rest of the birds, and suggested an antiviral treatment. In a matter of days, the antiviral treatment and the care Charlie provided enabled the rooster to recover in no time to crow and greet the day again. Immediate isolation, administering the right treatment, and providing the required care enable most poultry birds to recover unless it's a terminal illness or a life-threatening disease.

Holistic Solutions

Beyond medication, holistic strategies include maintaining strict biosecurity to prevent viral spread. Proper ventilation and hygiene in the coop, alongside a balanced diet, supports overall flock health. Oliver's recovery underscores the role of vaccination and regular health checks in preventing future outbreaks.

Fowl Pox

Causative Agent: Avian poxvirus.

Symptoms: Skin and mucous membrane lesions, reduced feed intake, and a drop in egg production.

Prevention: Vaccination and mosquito control are necessary to prevent transmission and isolation of infected birds.

Treatment: Supportive care. Recovery is generally spontaneous, but isolation is crucial to preventing its spread.

Real-Life Recovery Story

Meet Rosie, a friendly hen who faced fowl pox and survived. The hen was raised by a family but was abandoned due to unfortunate circumstances. Sam brought Rosie home from an animal shelter, adding the hen to his backyard coop. Within a week, the hen started developing lesions on the wattles and comb. Sam immediately recognized the lesions as some birds in his flock had already been affected by fowl pox and recovered after adequate management.

After isolating the hen, Sam gently cleaned the lesions and applied the topical ointment recommended by the vet. He also ensured Rosie ate nutritious treats to keep her strength up. Over time, the pox started to fade away, and the hen recovered within a few days. Sam's quick actions and caring efforts made all the difference. It's a reminder that with a little understanding and some tender care, anyone can help their feathered friends bounce back from challenges like fowl pox and keep the whole flock healthy.

Holistic Solutions

Holistic measures involve mosquito control, as mosquitoes transmit the flupox virus. This underscores the significance of a well-balanced, vitamin-rich diet to boost the immune system. Regular coop cleaning and avoiding overcrowding contribute to preventing fowlpox in the flock.

Marek's Disease

Causative Agent: Marek's disease virus (herpesvirus).

Symptoms: Paralysis, weight loss, and the development of tumors.

Prevention: Vaccination of day-old chicks, strict biosecurity measures, and maintaining a virus-free environment.

Treatment: There is no cure for this. Focus on supportive care. Euthanasia may be considered for affected birds.

Holistic Solutions

Holistic strategies include genetic selection for resistance to Marek's disease and maintaining stress-free environments. Max's recovery underscores the role of nutrition in supporting the immune system. Regular flock health assessments and vaccination protocols are essential for preventing Marek's disease.

Respiratory Diseases

Causative Agents: Mycoplasma, infectious Coryza.

Symptoms: Sneezing, nasal discharge, coughing, and swollen sinuses.

Prevention: Practice strict biosecurity, vaccination against respiratory diseases, and maintain optimal living conditions with proper ventilation.

Treatment: Antibiotics prescribed by a veterinarian based on diagnostic tests.

Real-Life Recovery Story

In a suburban backyard, Ruby, a spirited backyard hen, caught a menacing respiratory infection. It started with subtle signs – a hint of lethargy and a change in the melodic clucks. Ruby's owner, Sara, noticed nasal discharge and swollen sinuses near the beak, and the tone of clucks had changed – plus, Ruby showed clear signs of feeling tired throughout the day. Swiftly, Sara sought the expertise of Dr. Anderson, the local avian veterinarian. Early diagnosis revealed a respiratory infection that threatened Ruby's well-being and could potentially affect the entire backyard flock. Dr. Anderson recommended immediate isolation to curb the spread and initiated a targeted antibiotic treatment to combat the infection.

With each passing day, the antibiotic treatment worked its magic, and the sparkle returned to Ruby's eyes. The once-muted clucks transformed into joyful sounds echoing through the backyard. This tale of Ruby underlines the critical role of quick intervention, expert guidance, and a vigilant owner in overcoming respiratory challenges in backyard poultry.

Holistic Solutions

Holistic approaches involve proper ventilation, minimizing dust and ammonia levels, and reducing stress. Ruby's recovery underscores the importance of nutrition in supporting respiratory health. Regular cleaning and disinfection of the coop contribute to preventing respiratory diseases.

External Parasites

Causative Agents: Mites, lice.

Symptoms: Feather loss, irritation, decreased egg production.

Prevention: Regularly clean the coop and nesting areas, provide dust baths, and treat affected birds promptly.

Treatment: Use insecticides and acaricides as recommended by a veterinarian. Implement preventive measures to avoid reinfestation.

Real-Life Recovery Story

Max, an animal activist living in Mexico, rescued a rooster from a cockfighting match. Unfortunately, the rooster had already fought in cockfighting matches and was carrying several cuts and bruises. Max brought the rooster to his home to attend to the injuries. Within a few days, the rooster started recovering and regaining strength.

Max already had a pair of playful labradors he rescued recently. Although the friendly pet dogs welcomed the new feathered friend, they were suffering from a mite infestation, which ultimately made its way to the rooster's feathers.

Recognizing the urgency, Max started cleaning the rooster cage, removing any potential hiding spots for the pesky intruders. Armed with an appropriate parasite treatment recommended by the local veterinarian, Max nursed the rooster back to health.

As the days passed, the feathers regained their luster, and his crowing echoed triumphantly through the coop once more. This tale highlights the necessity of regular inspections, quick intervention, and a vigilant owner in maintaining the well-being of poultry birds.

Holistic Solutions

Holistic measures include maintaining a clean coop, dust baths, and using natural remedies to repel parasites. Percy's recovery underscores the importance of providing a stress-free environment. Regular parasite prevention protocols contribute to overall flock well-being.

Intestinal Worms

Causative Agents: Roundworms, tapeworms.

Symptoms: Weight loss, decreased egg production, diarrhea.

Prevention: Regular deworming programs, maintaining clean living conditions, and preventing access to contaminated areas.

Treatment: Administer anthelmintic medications as prescribed by a veterinarian based on fecal examinations.

Real-Life Recovery Story

Sammy is a livestock farmer who loves raising free-range chickens. Although the flock was well-fed and taken care of, a few hens from the flock seemed lethargic. In the next few days, the egg production decreased, persuading Sammy to isolate the hens and take them to the vet for a health check. The vet suggested monitoring the birds and running a diagnostic test for parasite infestation on fecal samples Sammy brought for testing.

The diagnosis confirmed the wormy woes, and a deworming treatment was prescribed to send those intruders packing. But that wasn't all; Sammy cleaned the coop, inspected the free-range area for worm infestations, and added a special menu to boost the immune system. As the days went by, Sammy's free-range chicken became more spirited than ever - thanks to the vet's expert advice and adequate care!

Holistic Solutions

Holistic measures include rotational grazing and maintaining a clean environment to reduce worm exposure. Sammy's recovery underscores the role of a well-balanced diet in supporting the immune system. Regular deworming protocols and monitoring contribute to overall intestinal health.

Egg Drop Syndrome (EDS)

Causative Agent: Avian adenovirus.

Symptoms: Drop in egg production, soft-shelled or misshapen eggs, and reproductive tract disorders.

Prevention: Biosecurity measures, vaccination, and proper management of breeding flocks.

Treatment: There is no specific treatment. Focus on preventing the spread through vaccination.

Real-Life Recovery Story

Ella, a layer hen, was the first in the flock to produce eggs but suddenly developed the mysterious egg drop syndrome. While every layer hen was taken care of, Ella got special attention as her egg production stopped, making the owner, Jenna, concerned. She took the hen for a vet health checkup, but no definitive diagnosis was made. A few days later, Ella laid a soft-shelled egg – a telltale sign pointing toward egg drop syndrome (something the vet had mentioned on the previous visit).

As there was no specific treatment for the syndrome, Jenna started researching it to create an effective management plan. She prepared a stress-free corner of the farm for Ella with a few special treats to make her comfortable and help her release any stress. Jenna religiously cared for Ella for several days, and at last, the hen started laying eggs again!

Holistic Solutions

Holistic approaches involve stress reduction through proper management practices. Ella's recovery underscores the significance of providing a well-balanced diet to support egg production. Regular health assessments and preventive measures contribute to sustained egg quality.

Botulism

Causative Agent: Clostridium botulinum toxin.

Symptoms: Weakness, paralysis, drooping wings, and difficulty in breathing.

Prevention: Ensure clean water sources, proper carcass disposal, and avoid stagnant water.

Treatment: Antitoxin administration and supportive care.

Holistic Solutions

Holistic approaches involve preventing access to contaminated water sources. Benny's recovery underscores the role of maintaining a clean environment and providing proper nutrition. Regular water source monitoring and preventive measures contribute to botulism prevention.

Erysipelas

Causative Agent: Erysipelothrix rhusiopathiae bacteria.

Symptoms: Swollen wattles, joints, and lameness.

Prevention: Sanitation, vaccination, and controlling exposure to infected environments.

Treatment: Antibiotics prescribed by a veterinarian.

Holistic Solutions

Holistic measures involve strict biosecurity to prevent the introduction of the bacterium-causing erysipelas. Emily's recovery underscores the significance of a well-balanced diet and stress reduction. Regular health checks and vaccinations contribute to erysipelas prevention.

Fatty Liver Hemorrhagic Syndrome (FLHS)

Causative Factor: Excessive fat accumulation in the liver.

Symptoms: Sudden death, pale comb, and hemorrhages in liver tissues.

Prevention: Balanced nutrition, especially for laying hens, and preventing obesity.

Treatment: Adjusting the diet and providing supportive care.

Holistic Solutions

Holistic approaches involve providing a well-balanced diet with appropriate energy levels. Freddie's recovery underscores the role of stress reduction in preventing fatty liver hemorrhagic syndrome. Regular monitoring and dietary adjustments contribute to overall liver health.

Ascites (Water Belly)

Causative Factors: Heart or lung issues leading to fluid accumulation in the abdomen.

Symptoms: Abdominal swelling, difficulty breathing, and decreased activity.

Prevention: Proper ventilation, balanced nutrition, and maintaining optimal environmental conditions.

Treatment: Addressing underlying causes, diuretics, and supportive care.

Holistic Solutions

Holistic measures involve managing growth rates and providing an appropriate diet. Alice's recovery underscores the significance of controlling environmental factors like temperature and ventilation. Regular monitoring and preventive measures contribute to ascites prevention.

Gout

Causative Factors: Kidney dysfunction leading to uric acid accumulation.

Symptoms: Swollen joints, lameness, and visceral gout affecting internal organs.

Prevention: Providing a balanced diet and maintaining proper hydration.

Treatment: Addressing underlying Gout.

Holistic Solutions

Holistic approaches involve providing a well-balanced diet with controlled protein levels. George's recovery underscores the role of stress reduction and maintaining proper hydration. Regular monitoring and dietary adjustments contribute to gout prevention.

Infectious Bursal Disease (Gumboro)

Causative Agent: Infectious bursal disease virus.

Symptoms: Immunosuppression, bursal atrophy, and increased susceptibility to other diseases.

Prevention: Vaccination, biosecurity measures, and proper management practices.

Treatment: No specific treatment; focus on prevention through vaccination.

Regular veterinary consultation and a comprehensive health management plan are essential components of maintaining a healthy flock.

Holistic Solutions

Holistic measures involve maintaining strict biosecurity and vaccination protocols. Isabella's recovery underscores the role of providing a stress-free environment and balanced nutrition. Regular health checks and preventive measures contribute to IBD prevention.

Maintaining a Healthy Flock

Biosecurity

Biosecurity measures play a key role in preventing the introduction and spread of diseases. This involves controlling access to the poultry area, disinfecting equipment, and isolating new birds before introducing them to the flock.

Vaccinations

Vaccination is a key preventive measure. Establish a vaccination program tailored to the prevalent diseases in your region. Regular consultation with a veterinarian is vital for developing an effective vaccination schedule.

Clean and Dry Environment

Maintaining a clean and dry environment is essential for reducing the risk of disease transmission. Regular cleaning and disinfection of the coop, along with proper waste management, can minimize the buildup of pathogens.

Nutritional Management

Proper nutrition is fundamental for a strong immune system. Provide a well-balanced and nutritionally rich diet for your poultry to support overall health and reduce susceptibility to diseases.

Quarantine New Birds

Isolating new birds for a period before introducing them to the existing flock is a critical biosecurity measure. This prevents the introduction of potential pathogens and allows for the early detection of any underlying health issues.

Monitoring and Early Intervention

Regular monitoring of the flock for signs of illness is essential. Early detection allows for prompt intervention, minimizing the impact of diseases on the overall health and productivity of the poultry. Establishing a close relationship with a poultry veterinarian enables timely and effective responses to emerging health challenges.

By diligently implementing these preventive measures and tailoring them to the specific needs of your flock, you can create a resilient and thriving poultry environment that contributes to the longevity and productivity of your birds. Regular veterinary consultations and ongoing education about local disease challenges are key components of successful poultry health management.

Proactive Care

Maintaining a healthy flock extends beyond medical interventions. Proactive care involves a multifaceted approach, emphasizing cleanliness, quarantine practices, and regular inspections as crucial components in preventing diseases and ensuring the overall well-being of poultry.

Cleanliness

Importance of Clean Coops

Clean living environments are paramount for preventing the spread of diseases. Regularly clean and disinfect coops, nesting areas, and feeding equipment to eliminate potential sources of contamination. This reduces the risk of bacterial and parasitic infections, fostering a healthier environment for your flock.

Effective Waste Management

Proper waste management is integral to maintaining cleanliness. Promptly remove droppings and spilled feed to decrease the risk of pathogens. A well-managed waste system mitigates the risk of diseases associated with bacterial and parasitic contamination.

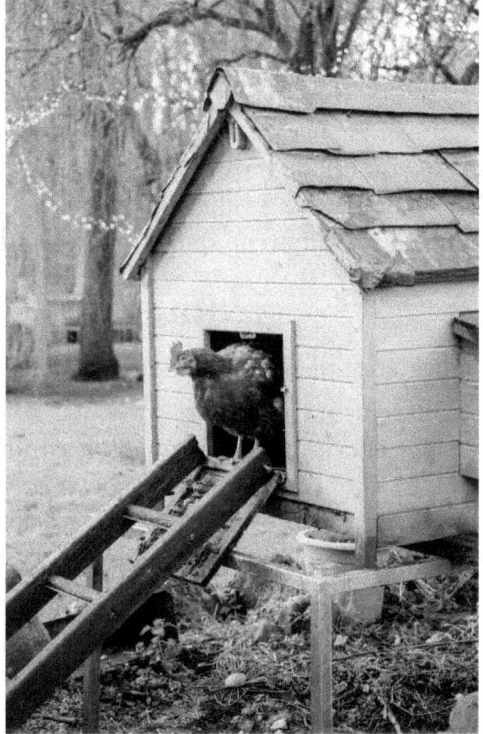

Clean living environments are paramount for preventing the spread of diseases.[8]

Hygiene Practices

Practicing personal hygiene when handling poultry is equally important. Wash your hands thoroughly after interacting with the flock to prevent the unintentional transmission of pathogens. Regularly clean equipment and tools to avoid cross-contamination.

Quarantine Practices

Purpose of Quarantine

Quarantine serves as protection against the introduction of diseases. When introducing new birds to the flock, isolate them for a specific period. This allows you to monitor for any signs of illness without jeopardizing the health of the flock. Quarantine is especially crucial when adding poultry from different sources.

Observation Period

During the quarantine period, observe new birds closely for any illness symptoms. Common signs may include lethargy, respiratory distress, or changes in droppings. This cautious approach prevents the potential introduction of diseases that might otherwise go unnoticed.

Biosecurity Measures

Integrate biosecurity measures into quarantine practices. Limit access to quarantined birds, use separate equipment, and change clothing between handling different groups. This minimizes the risk of disease transmission between quarantined and established flock members.

Regular Inspections

Importance of Regular Check-Ups

Regular inspections play a pivotal role in disease prevention. Schedule routine check-ups for your flock conducted by a veterinarian. These can lead to the early detection of potential health issues, enabling timely intervention and preventing the escalation of diseases.

Signs of Good Health

Familiarize yourself with the signs of good health in poultry. Active behavior, glossy plumage, bright eyes, and normal droppings are indicators of a healthy bird. Identifying deviations from these norms gives you the chance to act as soon as possible.

Environmental Assessments

Regularly assess environmental conditions such as ventilation, lighting, and temperature. Make sure these factors align with optimal poultry health. A well-maintained environment reduces stress and boosts the flock's immune system.

Incorporating these proactive care practices into your poultry management routine creates a robust foundation for disease prevention. Beyond relying solely on medications, a holistic approach that prioritizes cleanliness, quarantine measures, and regular inspections is key to sustaining a healthy and thriving flock. Regular consultation with a veterinarian further enhances your ability to tailor these practices to the specific needs of your poultry.

Mental Well-Being and Stimulation for Poultry

Maintaining the mental well-being of your poultry is crucial for a healthy and happy flock. Introducing toys, foraging activities, and environmental enrichment can keep them mentally engaged, reduce stress, and promote overall welfare.

Pecking Balls

Purpose: Provides entertainment and encourages natural pecking behavior.

Benefits: Reduces boredom, frustration, and aggressive pecking.

Types: Hanging pecking balls.

Mirror Toys

Purpose: Reflective surfaces stimulate curiosity and social interaction.

Benefits: Reduces loneliness and promotes socialization.

Types: Mirrors placed strategically in the coop or run.

Swinging Perches

Purpose: Mimic natural movements, offering physical and mental stimulation.

Benefits: Engages birds in balancing activities, promoting agility.

Types: Hanging perches or swings within the coop.

Scatter Feeding

Purpose: Encourage natural foraging behaviors.

Benefits: Reduces stress, stimulates mental activity, and prevents boredom.

Types: Scatter grains or seeds around the area for birds to peck.

Hanging Vegetables

Purpose: Provide a challenging foraging experience.

Benefits: Promotes physical activity and mental engagement.

Types: Hang vegetables, such as cabbage or lettuce, for birds to peck.

Dust Bath Areas

Purpose: Facilitate natural dust bathing behavior.

Benefits: Aids in feather maintenance and reduces stress.

Types: Create dedicated areas with dust or sand for birds to bathe.

Vegetation and Hideouts

Purpose: Create a dynamic environment with hiding spots.

Benefits: Mimics a natural setting, reducing stress and promoting exploration.

Types: Plant vegetation or add shelters like wooden boxes.

Perches and Platforms

Purpose: Offer elevated spaces for roosting and observation.

Benefits: Birds feel secure, and it provides opportunities for mental stimulation.

Types: Install wooden perches or raised platforms.

Colorful Objects

Purpose: Introduce visual stimulation.

Benefits: Adds variety to the environment, reducing monotony.

Types: Hang colorful objects, like cloth strips or shiny materials.

Considerations for Implementation:

Safety First

- Make sure that all enrichments are safe and free from sharp edges or toxic materials.

Rotation of Items

- Regularly rotate or introduce new toys and enrichments to maintain interest.

Observation

- Monitor how birds interact with enrichments to gauge preferences.

Adapt to Seasons

- Adjust enrichments based on weather conditions to guarantee year-round suitability.

Integrating these mental stimulation strategies into your poultry management practices leads to a more enriched and content flock. Happy and mentally engaged birds are more likely to exhibit natural behavior, experience reduced stress, and contribute to a healthier overall environment. Regular observation and adaptation to the preferences of your specific flock enhances the effectiveness of these initiatives.

Chapter 6: Breeding and Incubation

Breeding and incubation in poultry are complex processes, and each egg symbolizes the promise of a new beginning. Exploring the science of fertility provides an intricate understanding of the processes governing the journey from mating to hatchling. This chapter invites you to navigate a comprehensive journey where the art of caregiving converges with the science of life, creating life from egg to hatchling in meticulous detail.

From Egg to Hatchling

Breeding and incubation represent a profound journey where the caretaker becomes a witness to the unfolding miracle of life. Observing the metamorphosis of a seemingly ordinary egg into a lively hatchling establishes a connection that goes beyond the routine, adding an element of wonder to each step in the process.

The Enigmatic Nature of Incubation

This marks the initiation of a profound bond between caretakers and the potential hatchlings.[9]

Incubation is a process that combines anticipation with the miracle of development. It involves carefully managing the warmth required for eggs to hatch, accompanied by the rhythmic pulsation of life within. This marks the initiation of a profound bond between caretakers and the potential hatchlings. To become familiar with the enigmatic nature of incubation, here's a real-life example depicting its power.

In a rustic farm nestled in the hills, Joe meticulously managed his incubator, a treasure trove of potential life. One brisk morning, as he checked the eggs, he discovered a surprise—a tiny quail egg tucked among the chicken eggs. The quail, oblivious to the mix-up, hatched alongside its larger companions. The farmer, amused by this unexpected addition, marveled at the unpredictability of life and the surprises each incubation cycle could bring.

Factors Shaping Breeding Success

Breeding success is contingent on numerous interacting factors. The health and genetic makeup of the breeding pair, environmental conditions, and nutritional considerations collectively influence the outcome of the journey from egg to hatchling. A nuanced understanding of these factors empowers poultry keepers to optimize conditions, ensuring a fruitful breeding experience.

Incubation Process and Milestones

Pre-Incubation

Day 1-3

- Roosters court hens, leading to fertilization.
- Hens lay eggs, marking the beginning of the incubation process.

The Incubation Chamber

Day 1-7

The incubation process begins with carefully placing fertilized eggs in an incubator. The eggs must be positioned with the pointed end slightly lower to facilitate proper embryonic development.

- Gather eggs, ensuring cleanliness.
- Place eggs in the incubator with proper orientation.

Day 7-14

- Embryo development begins.
- Initial candling to observe embryonic growth.

Mid-Incubation

Day 14-18

- Continued embryo development.
- Regular candling to track progress.

Day 18-19

- Stop turning eggs.
- Increase humidity for hatching readiness.

Hatching

Day 19-21

- **Pipping:** This is the process where the chick starts to break through the eggshell using its egg tooth.
- **Hatching:** The final milestone is the actual hatching of the chicks. This process can take anywhere from a few hours to a day. Chicks use their egg tooth to make a small hole (pipping) and gradually work their way out of the shell.

Day 21-22

- Transfer chicks to the brooder.
- Initial feedings and health checks.

The Incubation Process

Whether you're a novice or a seasoned enthusiast, this step-by-step guide will lead you through setting up your incubator, regulating temperature and humidity, and closely monitoring the development of embryos for a successful hatching experience.

Step 1: Setting Up the Incubator

Choose the Right Incubator

Begin by selecting an incubator that aligns with your specific requirements. Consider factors such as egg capacity, automatic turning features, and temperature control capabilities.

Placement Matters

Make sure that the incubator is positioned in a stable environment, away from direct sunlight and drafts. Consistent temperature regulation is crucial for the success of the incubation process.

Sanitize and Prepare

Thoroughly clean the incubator, including trays and any accessories, to eliminate potential contaminants. Sterilize the incubator with a mild disinfectant to establish a hygienic environment.

Calibrate the Incubator

Calibrate the incubator to guarantee accurate temperature readings. Use a reliable thermometer to cross-verify the incubator's temperature settings, ensuring precision.

Step 2: Temperature and Humidity Regulation

Set the Initial Temperature

Eggs generally require an initial temperature of approximately 99.5°F (37.5°C). Adjust the incubator's thermostat to achieve and maintain this temperature. These conditions simulate the natural environment necessary for embryo development. Keep a close eye on the temperature by checking it regularly. Any fluctuations can significantly impact embryo development. Adjust promptly to maintain stability.

Humidity Control

Maintain humidity levels within the recommended range for your specific eggs. Typically, a 40-50% relative humidity is suitable for the first 18 days, increasing to 65-75% during the lockdown period.

Water Management

Use a hygrometer to accurately measure humidity. Adjust it by adding water to the incubator trays, considering a larger water surface area to increase humidity.

Step 3: Turning Eggs and Lockdown

Regularly turning eggs is critical to prevent the embryo from sticking to the shell. Birds instinctively do this in nature, but this process is replicated mechanically or manually in an incubator.

Automatic Turners

If your incubator has an automatic turner, make sure it is activated. Turning the eggs at regular intervals is essential for embryo development. For manual turning, do this at least three times a day.

Lockdown Preparation

On day 18, stop turning the eggs and prepare for lockdown. Increase humidity by adding more water to the trays. Lockdown simulates the natural nest environment, creating ideal conditions for hatching.

Step 4: Monitoring Embryo Development

Candling

Around day seven and day 14, start candling to assess signs of development. Look for veins, embryo movement, and healthy growth. Remove any clear or non-viable eggs to maintain optimal conditions.

Record Keeping

Maintain a comprehensive log of vital information, including incubator settings, candling observations, and any adjustments made. Meticulous record-keeping helps with troubleshooting and serves as a valuable reference for future incubations.

You establish an optimal environment for successful incubation by diligently following these detailed steps. Remember, each egg holds the promise of life, and your careful attention guarantees a seamless journey from incubation to the joyous moment of hatching.

Practicing Patience

It's the cornerstone of a breeder's journey. The incubation process unfolds gradually, requiring steadfast patience. This process demands waiting, and waiting demands patience. It's a delicate dance where time plays a crucial role in the development of life within the eggs. Patience allows nature to unfurl at its own pace.

Patience in observation aids in detecting early signs of potential issues. Recognizing irregularities allows for timely adjustments, fostering a proactive approach to incubation management.

Post-Hatching Care

Welcoming a new batch of chicks into the world is a joyous occasion, but it comes with the responsibility to provide impeccable care during the critical first days post-hatch. This section will delve into chick care, brooding, and early nutrition to ensure a healthy and thriving start for your newfound feathered friends.

Chick Care

Drying Off

Welcoming chicks into the world involves allowing them to undergo a natural process of drying off after hatching. This initial step is crucial in ensuring the health and well-being of the newly hatched chicks.

Natural Drying Process

Chicks emerge from their eggs wet. This moisture is a result of the hatching process and the remnants of the eggshell's contents. The chicks, however, possess a natural instinct to commence the drying process almost immediately after hatching.

Allowing chicks to dry off naturally is vital. The dampness on their bodies serves a purpose in the wild, where it helps insulate the chicks during the hatching process. This down, once dried, contributes to the chick's ability to regulate its body temperature.

During the initial moments post-hatch, resist the urge to intervene. Observing the chicks as they fluff their feathers and dry naturally provides valuable insights into their vitality. Active, healthy chicks exhibit vigorous movements to shed excess moisture.

Implementing Biosecurity Measures

Isolation and Quarantine

Establish a dedicated area for the brooder that is physically separate from other poultry or animals. This minimizes the risk of potential disease transmission between different groups of birds.

Restricted Access

Limit access to the brooder area strictly to essential personnel. Enforce stringent hygiene protocols, including the use of dedicated clothing and footwear when entering the space, to prevent the introduction of contaminants.

Hand Hygiene

Enforce thorough hand hygiene practices for anyone handling chicks. Provide easily accessible handwashing stations equipped with soap and water or hand sanitizer near the brooder area to reduce the risk of disease spread.

Footwear Sanitization

Set up footbaths (or foot mats containing disinfectant) solutions at the entrance of the brooder area. This measure ensures that footwear, a potential carrier of pathogens, is disinfected before entering the space.

Clean and Disinfect Equipment

Regularly clean and disinfect all equipment used in the brooder, including feeders, waterers, and any other tools. Use effective disinfectants recommended for poultry facilities to eliminate potential disease vectors.

Avoiding Interference

While assisting in the drying process might be tempting, interference is generally unnecessary. The warmth of the incubator or brooder gradually provides the ideal environment for the chicks to dry off without external assistance.

Separating Weak Chicks

As part of the immediate care routine, assessing each chick for signs of weakness or lethargy is essential. If identified, weak chicks should be gently separated for special attention to give them the care they need to thrive.

Prevent Overcrowding

Overcrowding can lead to stress, injuries, and competition for resources. Ensure that the brooder space allows each chick sufficient room to move, eat, and drink comfortably.

Biosecurity is crucial to prevent the spread of diseases. Practicing good hygiene, including regular cleaning of the brooder, disinfecting equipment, and washing hands before handling chicks, contributes to maintaining a healthy environment.

Gradual Introduction to Solid Food

Around the second or third day, chicks can be introduced to solid food in addition to the starter feed. This broader diet stimulates their natural foraging instincts.

Adjust Brooder Conditions Gradually

As the chicks grow, they gradually adjust the brooder conditions to mimic the natural environment. Lowering the temperature and providing opportunities for exploration and socialization contribute to their overall well-being.

Transferring to Brooder

Once the chicks are visibly dry and active, it's time to transfer them to the brooder. The brooder replicates the warmth and security of a natural nesting environment, creating a conducive space for the chicks' further development.

Brooding Essentials

Creating the right environment for newly hatched chicks is crucial for their health, growth, and overall well-being. The brooding essentials encompass a range of factors that contribute to a comfortable and secure space.

Appropriate Temperature

Maintaining the right temperature within the brooder is paramount for the chicks' survival. During the first week, aim for a temperature of around 95°F (35°C) and gradually decrease it by 5°F (2.8°C) each week until the chicks feather out. Use a reliable thermometer placed at the chick level for accurate readings.

Bedding Material

Choose a suitable bedding material for the brooder. Pine shavings are a popular choice, providing a non-slippery surface for chicks to move around. The bedding maintains cleanliness and provides insulation against temperature fluctuations.

Ample Space

Make sure that the brooder offers sufficient space for the chicks to move freely. Overcrowding can lead to stress and potential health issues. Adequate space also prevents competition for resources and encourages natural behaviors.

Access to Feed and Water

Place chick feed in shallow containers to facilitate easy access. Fresh, clean water should be available at all times. Dip each chick's beak in the water upon introduction to help them locate the water source. Adequate feeder and waterer space prevents crowding and ensures all chicks have access.

Lighting Conditions

Maintain appropriate lighting conditions in the brooder. Provide a balance between light and dark periods, allowing chicks to rest. Adequate lighting supports healthy circadian rhythms and helps chicks establish a regular feeding and resting routine.

Ventilation

Ensure proper ventilation in the brooder to prevent ammonia buildup and maintain air quality. Drafts, however, should be avoided, as they can lead to chilling. Strike a balance between fresh air circulation and maintaining a warm environment.

Brooder Placement

Choose a strategic location for the brooder. It should be situated away from drafts, direct sunlight, and areas with extreme temperature fluctuations. Placing the brooder in a quiet and low-traffic area helps reduce stress for the chicks.

Monitoring Equipment

Use monitoring equipment, like a thermometer and hygrometer, to regularly check the temperature and humidity levels. These tools assist in making necessary adjustments to create an optimal environment.

Supplemental Heat Sources

Depending on the brooding setup, supplemental heat sources like heat lamps or radiant heaters may be required. Position these sources to create a temperature gradient within the brooder, allowing chicks to choose their preferred comfort zone.

Creating a comfortable space within the brooder involves meticulously considering temperature, space, cleanliness, and environmental factors. Addressing these brooding essentials establishes the foundation for a healthy and thriving flock as the chicks grow and develop.

Early Nutrition

The early stages of a chick's life are critical for establishing a foundation of health and vitality. Early nutrition plays a pivotal role in supporting their growth and development. The following section covers the various aspects of providing optimal nutrition to ensure a strong start for your chicks.

Selecting the Right Feed

Choosing a high-quality chick starter feed is fundamental to meeting the nutritional needs of growing chicks. Look for a feed with around 18-20% protein content, designed specifically for the early stages of poultry development. The balanced formulation should include essential vitamins and minerals for bone, muscle, and organ development.

Supplementation

Consider supplementing the chicks' diet with a vitamin-electrolyte supplement in their water during the first few days. This supplementation supports their immune system, helps counteract any stress during the transition, and ensures they receive essential nutrients for optimal health.

Feeder Accessibility

The feed should be easily accessible in shallow containers within the brooder. Chicks should be able to reach the feed to encourage consistent and adequate consumption. Positioning the feeders at an appropriate height facilitates easy access for all chicks.

Water Accessibility

Provide fresh, clean water at all times. Chicks need to stay hydrated, particularly during their early days. Dip each chick's beak in the water upon introduction to familiarize them with its location. Hydration is crucial for digestion, nutrient absorption, and overall well-being.

Monitoring Feed Consumption

Regularly monitor the chicks' feed consumption. Healthy chicks will exhibit a consistent appetite. Adjust feeding amounts if needed, considering environmental conditions and individual chick requirements.

All chicks should have equal access to feed.

Brooder Temperature and Nutrition

The brooder's temperature influences the chicks' metabolic rate and, consequently, their nutritional requirements. Adjust the feed and water supply based on temperature changes, ensuring the chicks receive adequate nutrition to support their growth and maintain body temperature.

Health Monitoring

Nutrition is closely linked to overall health. Monitor the chicks for malnutrition or deficiencies, such as lethargy, stunted growth, or abnormal feather development. Address any nutritional concerns promptly. Furthermore, maintain a detailed record of the chicks' feeding patterns and any observed changes in behavior or health. This record is valuable for adjusting their diet as they progress through different developmental stages.

Transition to Grower Feed

As the chicks mature, transition them to a grower feed with a slightly lower protein content. This gradual shift aligns with their changing nutritional requirements and supports the development of feathers and skeletal structure.

Performing Health Checks

Maintaining the health of your chicks is a continuous process that involves thorough health checks and keen observation. Regular assessments ensure that any potential issues are identified and addressed promptly, contributing to the overall well-being of your flock.

Daily Health Assessments

Conduct daily health assessments of each chick. This allows you to identify any subtle changes in behavior, appearance, or activity levels. Healthy chicks exhibit alertness, curiosity, and responsive behavior.

Physical Appearance

Examine the chicks for any abnormalities in their physical appearance. Check for clear eyes, well-groomed feathers, and clean vents. Abnormalities like disheveled feathers, discharge from the eyes or nostrils, or changes in posture can indicate potential health issues.

Active Behavior

Monitor the chicks for active and engaged behavior. Lively chicks exploring their surroundings, pecking, and interacting with their environment are signs of good health. Lethargy, excessive sleepiness, or reluctance to move may indicate underlying problems.

Feeding Behavior

Observe the chicks during feeding times. A healthy appetite is a positive sign. Any changes in feeding behavior, such as a sudden decrease in consumption or increased aggression during feeding, should be noted.

Social Interaction

Chickens are social animals, and healthy chicks engage in social interactions.[10]

Chickens are social animals, and healthy chicks engage in social interactions. Observe their behavior with each other, ensuring that all chicks are integrated into the flock. Isolation or aggressive pecking may signal social issues or potential health concerns.

Respiratory Health

Monitor respiratory health by listening for normal breathing sounds. Respiratory distress, audible wheezing, or labored breathing can be indicators of respiratory infections. Inspect the nares (nostrils) for any signs of discharge.

Vent Check

Regularly check the vents of the chicks for cleanliness. This is where eggs are laid. A clean vent indicates proper digestive health. Any signs of diarrhea or abnormalities in fecal consistency should be addressed straight away.

Weight Monitoring

Implement periodic weight monitoring. Gradual weight gain is a positive sign of healthy development. Sudden weight loss or fluctuations may signal underlying issues and should be investigated.

Record Keeping

Maintain a detailed record of health observations, including any abnormalities, interventions, and outcomes. This record becomes a valuable resource for identifying patterns, tracking progress, and informing future care strategies.

Prompt Intervention

If any health concerns are identified during checks, intervene promptly. Isolate affected chicks, if necessary, consult with a veterinarian, and implement appropriate measures to address the issue.

Environmental Factors

Consider environmental factors that may impact health, such as changes in temperature, humidity, or ventilation. Ensure that the brooder environment remains conducive to optimal health.

You establish a proactive approach to their well-being by consistently conducting health checks and keenly observing your chicks. Early detection of potential issues allows for timely intervention, ensuring a healthier and more robust flock as your chicks progress through their developmental stages.

Chapter 7: The "Pecking Order": Social Dynamics

At first glance, it may seem like there is no social structure among farm birds. Anyone who has not observed chickens, ducks, or turkeys for an extended time can be forgiven for making this uninformed assumption. To successfully raise poultry, you need to be familiar with how the birds you choose interact socially so you can manage your flock according to their nature. Birds do not have the mental complexity that people do, so you must get onto their level of thinking to understand them. Moreover, seeing how their communication methods are vastly different from those of people, you must learn their language.

Poultry birds mostly arrange their groups in a hierarchical social structure known as a pecking order.[11]

Poultry birds mostly arrange their groups in a hierarchical social structure known as a pecking order. There may be slight delineations between species, but the idea remains relatively the same. When you understand the social dynamics of your flock, you can create an environment that minimizes injury and facilitates reproduction. Birds can be aggressive, but in the same vein, they have a collective and cooperative society.

The environment will affect how your birds behave. Competition for food and mates can become a problem if it is not managed. For example, in overcrowded conditions, some chickens starve to death because the fights are so brutal. Weaker birds avoid fighting, so they never get to eat. Many poultry species live in groups, so they can be tribal. Understanding their vocalizations and body language will allow you to respond to various behaviors.

You can become a poultry mind reader by noticing a few behavioral cues. Birds do not express their emotions and concerns like people do, nor do they resolve their conflicts in the same way. You need to be a mediating force to direct the outcome you desire in your flock. Your oversight and knowledge basically make you the president of your mini-bird nation. Great governance of your flock requires you to tap into the variety of social expressions it exhibits.

Origins of Order

Evolution by natural selection is the foundation of all the behavior of living organisms. Survival of the fittest is often misinterpreted to mean that might is right or that the strongest animals rise to the top. This is not necessarily the case. As much as huge elephants are evolutionarily successful, tiny butterflies were also chosen by nature. Therefore, survival of the fittest means that nature will keep traits most suited to environmental conditions. Evolutionarily, birds are some of the oldest species on the planet, and there's even evidence they're related to dinosaurs. However, you can see some traces of their ancestry when you look at ostriches or emus, which can be terrifying if you are not accustomed to their intimidating appearances.

All adaptations are based on the availability of resources and the drive to reproduce. The hierarchical structure of fowl society has been instilled over millions of years of evolution. Although some traits of many farmed species have been artificially bred into existence by humans, the ways poultry structure their social groups predate human intervention. If you look at wild ducks or turkeys, they have the same types of societal organization as their domesticated cousins. All behaviors evolve in an environmental context. The societies that various poultry birds have developed are what have allowed them to remain on the planet for so long. Making the connection between why behaviors develop in particular environments and why they are evolutionarily beneficial will grant you the keys to understanding their psychology. Some of the natural behaviors that these birds display could be in opposition to the type of raising operation you are establishing. To encourage the behaviors you want, you must manipulate their environment. Therefore, you need to guide them toward the behaviors you would like to see with the help of psychology and evolutionary biology by making conscious changes so that your birds adopt favorable expressions.

Domestic ducks most likely descend from two duck species, namely the wild mallard and the Chinese spot-billed duck. Selective breeding and differing environments also play a role in shifting the social behavior of fowl species. Certain behaviors are kept from their evolutionary past. For example, many duck species pair bond and have courting displays for mating. Typically, the male of the species will make elaborate movements to attract a female. The competition amongst males will be fierce, with many suitors fighting for the opportunity to show off their skills. Furthermore, the mating seasons for some bird species come along once a year for a short period of time, so they are keenly aware that they have little time to woo a partner.

It is believed that this tough competition is a result of the female population being lower than the males. This is because females, in addition to being physically weaker, also perform tasks that put them in increased danger, like nesting. Therefore, not every male will get a mate, and the female has to choose wisely whose genes she wants to pass on. The elaborate courtship rituals allow the female to make an informed choice by examining the physicality of her potential partners.

There is power in numbers. Many fowl species have evolved social cohesion because they can respond to threats better when sticking together. Groups are better able to ward off predators with warning systems, and they can forage better because there are more ways to look out for food. Chicken societies are remarkably close to humans. They have surprisingly complex relationships that have evolved over millions of years. Humans can process about 150 social relations, while chickens can process about 30. The stereotype of a "bird brain" being stupid is far from accurate. Chickens know exactly where they sit on their social ladder. Since chickens can only remember about 30 relationships, it becomes tougher to introduce new birds into a large group.

Fowl hierarchies may seem violent at first glance, but the social order that these birds develop is an evolutionary trait that emerged to reduce fights. If a duck knows where it stands in the social order, it will not typically fight members higher up in the ranks. This creates a solid society with reduced instability. Natural selection chose the social structure of fowl because it protects them from predators, allows them to get food, and reduces fights within a flock.

In a social order, there must be ways to communicate. If not, the structure will quickly fall apart. Fowls have developed vocalizations and body language to communicate their needs and disagreements. You need to be familiar with these sounds and movements to maintain the well-being of your flock. Observation is your main tool because it will inform any other actions that you take concerning your flock.

The environments that birds live in profoundly impact their behavior, showing evolutionary development in real time. For example, city ducks have a louder quack than those in rural areas because the noise levels are higher in densely populated and industrialized regions. Similar to humans, there are cultural differences between birds of the same species based on where they are from. This adaptation shows how powerful human interference can be. The environment you build for your animals will change how they interact, so you must be keenly aware of how your actions impact your flock. If you are not careful about how you engage with your birds, any small change you make could have a huge impact. To get into a bird's mind, use empathy instead of visual cues.

Many different kinds of fowl show deep family connections that have evolved for the purposes of safety and resource acquisition. In turkey populations, after about six months, the males will form sibling groups that typically last a lifetime. Amongst swans and ducks, pairs mate for life, with some widows and widowers refusing to mate with a new partner even after the death of their partner. Much like human families act as a support to help people thrive and survive, animals like ducks, turkeys, and swans employ the same strategy.

Sticking together, minimizing competition, collectively searching for food, and having access to mates are the underpinnings of most evolutionary fowl behavior. Understanding what your birds are doing through these lenses will help your flock produce the outcomes you desire. You are meant to hack the adaptations of your birds to direct them toward your goals. You must understand how they evolved to provide them with adequate care that satisfies all of their needs. When you begin poultry farming, you are adopted as an honorary member of the flock that has the most responsibilities.

Signs and Signals

Just like humans have various signs and signals they use to communicate their state of being, so do fowls. Someone might start talking louder and getting redder if they are angry, or they may laugh out loud when they are happy. A woman might give a man a look hinting she is interested, and he may reply with a winning smile to show his interest. All these social dynamics frame the way humans relate to one another. There are many overlaps in the fowl kingdom. Although the males do not have any teeth to flash a movie star smile, and some species don't turn red when angry, they have their unique body language and vocalizations to communicate their needs and displeasures. The environment they are kept in will influence their actions, and their behavior can vary depending on what you do as a farmer.

Sally had started a permaculture homestead where she grew a variety of produce and kept many different kinds of animals. She decided to breed ducks to sell them to contribute to the maintenance of her farm. She noticed that when she introduced new ducks into her flock, they were attacked and prevented from feeding. That almost always led her to separate them. After learning a bit more about the social dynamics of ducks, she devised a new method to introduce new members of the flock. Sally constructed a cage adjacent to where her other ducks were kept. She would let them interact through the mesh fence. By gradually introducing new ducks, she was able to manage the violent aggression that her birds showed.

Ducks hiss and spread their wings when they are angry. This is done to intimidate threats and make themselves look bigger. When there are too many males in a flock, this behavior becomes common, especially if there is not a lot of space. Duck fights increase during mating season because males are hardwired to compete for mates. Even on a farm where females outnumber males, they may still fight during the mating season.

There are many interesting ways different kinds of fowl species express themselves. Turkeys change color according to their emotional state. The featherless turkey head will be lighter shades when they are calm but will transform into a deep red if they are angry or stressed. The snood, which is that little bit of wrinkly, dangling flesh near the turkey's beak, works in combination with its head color changing. Red does not always equal aggression. The snood will contract if a turkey is scared and about to fly away. For an aggressive or relaxed turkey, the snood will hang loosely. An angry one might charge to warn or intimidate you. This behavior must be monitored because domestic turkeys have a greater chance of fatally injuring one another than their wild counterparts because they live in such proximity to one another.

Identifying the roles your birds play in their social order is a big part of being able to manage them. If you can identify those at the top of the hierarchy, you know the ones that you need your new members to impress. Sounds and body language can help you find the alpha out of the bunch. If you look at turkeys, for example, the classic gobble noise you hear coming from them is either to attract females or to assert dominance. If you hear a few members of your flock gobbling more than others, they are probably the leaders. They are the ones that need the most convincing when introducing new birds. Turkeys are especially hostile to outsiders because they rely on their group for survival. They will need some convincing for new members to enter.

Many other vocalizations will tell you the mood your turkeys are in. You need to know what every sound means because how your turkeys are doing will determine the peacefulness of your flock. When turkeys are content, they cluck and purr. When you hear these noises, know that your flock is in a great position socially. Mothers usually let out loud and continuous yelps to gather their young. Even though this sound pierces your ears, there is no problem that needs addressing at that moment.

With chickens, although roosters are persistently competing for the top position, there are also social classes among hens as well. The head hen is the one that eats first. She will get her choice of the best nesting position. The rooster hierarchy is linked but separated from the hens. If a rooster chooses to interfere with the hierarchy that the hens have built, they will sometimes gang up on him to attack the one in charge. The hens will rotate guard duty to look out for predators, but the alpha hen does most of the work. When there is danger approaching, the hen on the lookout will let out an eardrum-rattling screech to warn the others. The pecking order of hens may be on the verge of transition when you see challenges arise. The hens competing for the number one spot will stare one another down and puff out their neck feathers before fighting. These challenges could happen repeatedly until either one of the competitors gives up. If you cannot risk your birds getting injured, it may be advisable to separate them at times like this. Alpha hens will emerge even if there are no roosters in your flock.

Managing Disruptions

There are four major causes of conflict among fowl species. Fowls like having a lot of space. When you put them in cramped conditions, it increases their stress, which results in more fighting. Mating is another cause for conflict, so you need to maintain your male-to-female ratio at an acceptable level. Food resources could also be a cause for conflict. Fighting over food goes hand in hand with being in cramped spaces, which is why battery-caged chicken farmers remove the beaks of their flock to reduce damage. Lastly, since many fowl species form deep social bonds, they may also fight if new birds are introduced in a type of tribal gang violence. Much like pack or herd animals, poultry birds are territorial because of the competition for resources. You need to get your flock to understand that the newest member is part of the group.

When you put them in cramped conditions, it increases their stress, which results in more fighting.[13]

Poultry is similar to humans when it comes to how adverse conditions stoke the flames of antisocial behavior. To keep your flock well-behaved, make sure they are well-fed, have ample space to explore and perch, as well as a good mixture of males and females. That does not mean there will never be any hiccups. Fowls have their societal perception, so battles will emerge for hierarchical positioning. You cannot completely eradicate fighting, but you can minimize it. A calm, spacious area reduces the short-tempered birds' irritability.

Farm birds do not reserve their aggression for each other. When an alpha rooster emerges, you may find that they start attacking you. Chevanni started a backyard chicken coop for egg production and to add to the overall feel of his home. One of the roosters, named Frango, which means chicken in Portuguese, became overly aggressive. He was the only chicken with a name because he had the most personality. Frango would not let anybody walk past from a distance closer than about four feet. It'd flap its wings and lunge at you, pecking any bit of exposed skin. It terrified people, although it was not able to cause much harm. It became unpleasant because whenever children visited, they would have to watch out for Frango. Many people made sure they took the long way around the house just to avoid it.

In cases like this, there are some steps you can take to address the undesirable behavior. Ignoring the attacks will not make them go away. The longer you wait, the more the behavior will become ingrained. Remember that a rooster does not hate people. It sees you as a threat, so all it is doing is protecting the hens. Some people use water spray bottles to keep them at bay. Spraying a rooster with water is uncomfortable but does not hurt the animal. Your best option in this case, if you are brave enough, is flipping your rooster. When it starts acting in violent ways, grab it, flip it upside down, and hold it close to your body until it calms down. This would need to be repeated regularly until it begins adjusting its behavior.

Ducks can be notoriously territorial. Unlike roosters, their attacks are extremely painful and will leave you with giant bruises. There are several ways to get aggressive ducks under control. The first technique you could try is to eliminate hand feeding. Hand feeding can cause aggression amongst your animals because hierarchies are established when some animals get more feed than others. Instead of hand feeding, scatter the food and allow them to forage. The feed you choose could also impact your animal's temperament. For ducks, choose food that contains more greens and that is protein-rich. An abundance of energy could be the culprit for their unpredictable behavior. You can use toys or take them for a swim to use up some of their excess energy. Lastly, you can pin the duck down on their back. This takes away their primary defenses, their beaks, and wings. It also asserts your dominance as their leader, but you must be careful because there is still a chance of getting injured in the process.

Be mindful of how your actions are perceived by your animals. You may assume that you are behaving appropriately, but birds do not interpret actions the same way as humans do. You may think you are spoiling your ducks by giving them treats, but this teaches them to expect food from humans, and, in some cases, this could turn ugly. You need to be hyper-aware of the psychology of your birds and frame all your actions according to what they understand and how you would like your coop to be run.

Chapter 8: Fowl Play: Dealing with Predators

Imagine putting in all the effort to understand what goes into choosing the right birds, taking all the necessary health precautions, fully grasping the dynamics of breeding, and understanding their social interactions just for a sneaky devil to munch on your entire flock. Waking up to dead birds is both traumatizing and heartbreaking. Dealing with predators can become a constant mission, but with hard work and the right information, you can manage to keep them away.

Combatting predators is all about how you house your birds. However, this task can become complicated due to the lack of a one-size-fits-all solution. Preparing your coop for fox attacks and leaving it vulnerable to snakes will not work. You need to be able to identify predators in your area and equip your enclosures to respond to all possible challenges. From fencing and housing to the identification of predators and adjusting to the local environment, the following chapter will assist you in responding to all predator threats.

As much as it can be devastating for your birds to be harmed, it does not justify acting violently against predators, especially if they are federally protected like owls and hawks. Harming protected animals carries harsh legal repercussions. Protecting your birds should be humane and be carried out with respect for the well-being of the predators. In some cases, you can contact government bodies to remove the predators.

Exploring your options may come with a lot of mistakes along the way. There is no exact science to predator prevention. What you have at your exposal is not the same as what the next person has. Conducting a detailed analysis and researching all the variables about your birds and their predators is the foundation on which you should start building. Once your coop and fencing are up, predators may find some weak spots. You will use this to conduct reconnaissance about the predator's behavior and make changes according to the gaps. As the seasons change, this battle will be a constant one. When your structures deteriorate, be ready to continuously observe and respond. The cat-and-mouse game you play with predators may be unending, but once your main structure is in place, you will only need to make small repairs and changes.

Predator Profiles

Whether you are keeping your birds in a major city or out in the most isolated woods, predators are always a major threat. Domesticated dogs and cats can be just as dangerous as foxes or coyotes. Other unexpected visitors might show up – like raccoons or rats looking to nibble on chicks or have an egg as a midnight snack. Different regions have varying predators, so it helps to know which animals are common in your area so that you can adjust your preparations accordingly. If your flock has already been attacked, there are some steps you can take to determine what the threat is. How your animals are killed (and which tracks or droppings are left behind) are all clues to point you in the direction of the right culprit.

Coyotes are common re-offenders when it comes to taking out poultry.[13]

Coyotes are common re-offenders when it comes to taking out poultry. They easily sneak past defenses and are often cunning enough not to get caught. They are creative and find unusual ways to get into your enclosures. If you hear regular howling in your area, you may have a problem with coyotes. Although the mere presence of scat is not an indicator that it came from a predator, it can help to identify the droppings. Coyotes, for example, use droppings to communicate, so those will be easy to spot. It often contains hair and bones. They have similar tracks to dogs, except their prints are slimmer, streamlined, and more oval. Their tendency to find unexpected points of entry means that following their tracks could help you determine where they broke in. You will probably not find many parts of your bird because coyotes kill and carry away the animal, so blood and feathers will be all that's left.

Foxes are a lot like coyotes in their slyness and appearance.[14]

Foxes are a lot like coyotes in their slyness and appearance. Coyotes have brown coats, while foxes have red and gray coats. Foxes are found in many states around the US and even in Canada. They live in holes they dig into the ground near trees or walls. If you find these dens on or near your property, you are most definitely dealing with foxes. Wildlife organizations are often willing to relocate them if you find any on your property. This is done to stop farmers from killing these animals so they can thrive in the wild.

Rats are not picky eaters, so they enjoy both chicks and eggs.[15]

One unexpected predator is rats. They cannot attack fully grown birds, but you may find some bites on their legs. Rats are not picky eaters, so they enjoy both chicks and eggs. Keeping them out can be extremely tough, so many farmers resort to poisoning. You will find the small droppings along the corners of your coop, and you may also discover parts of chicks stuck in holes that the rats burrowed in or squeezed through.

Weasels, minks, and skunks are all small predators that, like rats, are difficult to keep out of your coop. To keep them out, you must be thorough with your construction because there cannot be gaps bigger than about half an inch. Weasels can be particularly brutal because they not only kill for prey but also take enjoyment in hunting. If you find a decapitated chicken, there is likely a weasel in the picture. Weasels can take out large parts of your flock at once because of their capacity to kill for fun. If you do not discover them in the act, you'll enter your coop to discover massive destruction with bites on your birds' necks and backs. Skunks and weasels also leave behind a musky smell, so a potent fragrance is a giveaway of their presence.

Raccoons have hand-like paws, so they can open simple locks, and they find crafty ways to break into your coop.[16]

Opossums and raccoons are in trouble in cities and rural areas alike. You do not have to worry that much about opossums because they are lazy hunters and will only kill sick birds. As long as you make it difficult for them to enter, you should be okay. The main problem with opossums is not their killing capabilities but the diseases they carry. Raccoons, on the other hand, are a nuisance. They have hand-like paws so they can open simple locks, and they find crafty ways to break into your coop. If there are raccoons around, your birds need to be well-secured. They are destructive and will leave a trail of half-eaten bodies lying around. The clean-up after a raccoon attack can be extremely nasty. Leaving animals headless and limbless is their calling card.

Domestic pets like cats and dogs can be massive problems, too. Make sure that your animals are trained and accustomed to the birds you have on your land. Pets are usually fed by their owners, so these animals do not kill birds for food but rather a predatory instinct. A good sign that cats or dogs are the culprits is that the birds will be dead but not eaten. Pets usually kill for sport instead of food. Your pets can be trained, but sometimes your neighbor's animals get into your yard, so you need a good relationship with the people who live around you so you can work together to protect your flock.

Bobcats are small but deadly.[17]

Bobcats terrorize many parts of rural and urban North America. These cats are small but deadly. They are stealthy hunters, so it is unlikely that you will spot one on your property unless you have cameras. They almost always aim for the head. If you find your bird headless, a bobcat might be the one to blame. Their droppings contain fragments of vegetation and look similar to those of a domesticated house cat. Their prints resemble house cats as well, but are bigger. If you smell cat urine, there is a chance that it belongs to a bobcat.

Depending on where you live, you will most probably not be defending your animals against one type of predator. A holistic approach that caters to several variables is the best route to take. The predators on your land may change according to season, so stay prepared for all possibilities. Whether the predators are punching, scurrying, flying, or slithering, you must have an answer to the attack techniques. Using paws, fecal matter, killing methods, and smells, you can see exactly what you are dealing with so that you can act aligned with what you have discovered. Going in equipped with a bunch of signs to look for puts you ahead of the game so that you can react quickly.

Fortifying the Flock

In commercial farms, predators are not much of an issue because birds are typically kept inside buildings until they are mature enough for slaughter. However, with smaller homesteads, organic farms, and backyard operations, predator attacks are likely. When you construct an enclosure for your animals, there are several factors you need to consider, like the number of birds you have, the predators and risks you have in your area, and the costs and supplies you have available. Building a coop is a constant process of trial and error to find what works best for your unique needs. Constant adjustments must be made until you find what is functional.

Many organic farmers are set in their old ways of dealing with predators. Killing or poisoning animals are not ideal options for protecting your birds. The local ecosystem is sensitive, so you should always strive to make ethical and humane decisions. Some animals are protected by law, but this does not stop farmers from shooting and burying animals on their property. This is by no means an ethical approach, especially if you are embracing organic farming to protect the environment and ethically raise livestock. A prime example of an organic farmer who embodies ethical agriculture is Will Harris, who runs the family farm White Oak Pastures in Georgia.

Harris had a problem with bald eagles making easy pickings of his flock. The farmer admired the birds and lived alongside them. However, he began reconsidering his pacifist attitude when the birds began attacking his turkeys in addition to his chickens. He looks at the losses as a sacrifice or tithe to nature. He believes in permaculture organic farming. Instead of killing the birds like many farmers do, Harris contacted the Georgia Department of Natural Resources or DNR. There is not much that the department could do for the overgrown eagle population, so Harris still lives with the birds taking on the losses. He believes that if all the farmers in the area used organic farming methods, the eagles would naturally spread and scatter, but he admits that this small-scale farming revolution is unlikely to happen. At the last count, 75 eagles were living on and around the property. These huge numbers of eagles killed thousands of his birds.

Predator-friendly farming, like Will Harris adopted, is an option, but not everyone has a large enough farm or the resources to take such losses. One of the first options you can explore to protect your animals is constructing floorless grazing coops. These will stand about two to three feet high, depending on the species you are farming. The width and length of the coop will depend on how many birds you have. These coops protect your animals from aerial attacks during the day. Therefore, they are handy for birds of prey that hunt during sunlight hours, like eagles or hawks. Some birds, like owls, hunt at night. To prevent these attacks, you should build a safe, roofed structure to put your livestock into at night after they are done feeding. Make use of orange netting because it distracts the vision of birds like hawks and owls.

Motion-sensing lights are a great deterrent for nocturnal animals. These hunters usually have brilliant eyesight in the dark, but this could make them sensitive to extreme changes in light. The bright and instant flash that comes from motion sensors can scare these predators, keeping them away from your precious livestock. Moreover, the increased visibility on your land can help you spot predators better in the dark so you can know exactly which animals you are dealing with and craft your prevention methods specifically for them.

An age-old method of pest control is the use of guard animals. Domestic cats are great for keeping rats and even snakes away from your birds, while dogs can deal with bigger predators like coyotes or foxes. If you use guard animals, they need to be well-trained and used to living with poultry because sometimes they can be problems themselves. Cats can be dangerous for local bird populations, so they aren't always a great choice for sustainability, but they are effective for small predators. The downside of using guard animals is that they kill the predators, which is not the most humane way to get rid of them.

Sometimes, you need to think outside of the box. The box, in this case, creates a solid, unbreakable coop. You may find yourself continuously having to restructure your pens because different predators keep finding their way in, but you must expand your gaze outwards. For example, birds of prey could be hanging around your property because it is comfortable and attractive to them. Removing perches taller than 100 yards will encourage the squatters to leave. You may need to cut down some trees on your property to get rid of pesky flying predators.

With mesh fencing, wood, metals, and some basic building expertise, you can construct coops that will keep the majority of predators out. Unlike commercial farms that have protected concrete buildings with fowl cramped in battery cages, your free-range setup is not as secure. Your vigilance and ingenuity are your biggest weapons against predator encroachment. Use what you have wisely, and cater your protection plans to the psychology of the species threatening your population.

When Breaches Happen

You may think that you have a solid, foolproof plan to protect your birds, but small damages to your enclosures or simple oversights can result in predators gaining entry to your coop. You need to respond quickly when this happens because you know that predators have an open pathway to an all-you-can-eat buffet. Keep some repair materials around at all times, like metals, mesh fencing, wood, zinc, nails, glue, and construction tools like hammers, saws, and drills. You can quickly put together a makeshift patch until you come up with a better solution. These repair patches could be the difference between losing your entire flock or losing just a few birds and eggs.

Joyce Bupp struggled with predators killing her chickens. At this point, her birds produced very few eggs, and they were more like pets. Losing them affected her deeply. She struggled to know exactly which animals were eating her pets because there were several different predators on her farm. Eventually, she discovered a small hole through which a raccoon was entering under the cover of night. They trapped the omnivorous culprit using sweet corn as bait, and two more were also captured on the days that followed. You can use a humane cage trap to catch raccoons and avoid harming them. Take the trapped animals to a wildlife specialist or governmental body in your area. If you want to release them yourself, be extra careful because they may carry rabies. If you get bitten, go to the hospital immediately.

Reinforcing your cages and surrounding your perimeter with electric fences to ward off wolves, coyotes, and foxes is a brilliant investment; however, there are other less obvious methods you can use to protect your flock. For example, you can seal food and keep your trash cans locked up so that you do not attract curious and hungry visitors. A lot of times, predators do not go directly for your fowl but are enticed nearer with food attractions. Therefore, identifying food that ushers in predators and getting rid of it or securing it could be all that it takes to significantly reduce predator populations on your land, which would prevent breaches of your coops.

How your coop was broken into will tell you the animal you are dealing with. Weasels and rats can squeeze through small holes, so there will not be much damage. Foxes and coyotes will make bigger holes in the fencing or weak points of your structure. Bears and wolves will cause massive destruction. Signs of their attacks will be very obvious. If entire birds are missing and no body parts are left while the coop is not damaged, your thieves are likely predator birds. Raccoons can open latches, so if you find your gates open, it is either these masked devils or other humans. Therefore, look at all the details of the breach with an understanding of predator behavior so you can know which solution to explore.

Chapter 9: Ethics and Best Practices

Ethics can get very complicated due to people having differing views on what is right and wrong, especially when it comes to animals. Different cultural contexts can dictate an appropriate way to treat non-human living beings. There are arguments on whether animals should be farmed at all, especially for meat, considering there is no way for an animal to consent to have its life taken. With all these intersecting dynamics to consider, the goal of acting ethically can be hard to achieve.

Ethics can get very complicated due to people having differing views on what is right and wrong, especially when it comes to animals.[18]

To form an ethical system that can be understood and embraced by most compassionate people, you have to delve into the science of animal behavior and psychology. Distressed or ill-treated animals will exhibit physical and social signs of not being well. Some indicators can be measured to determine animal well-being. Based on these, as well as the virtues of kindness and empathy, you can come up with principles that can align with how you should treat animals.

Through the exploration of how the actions of farmers impact poultry, some guidelines can be drafted for you to make sure you are acting ethically. Raising poultry is a huge responsibility, so you should make sure that you are doing it right. Your birds can give you so much, and since you cannot thank them with words, you should show them how grateful you are. Poultry farming ethics underpin the relational exchange you have with your birds. As the person responsible for every aspect of their lives, as well as their ability to reproduce, you should conduct a deep analysis of what would be the most appropriate setup and protocols to have so your birds can enjoy a full and healthy life.

Defining Poultry Ethics

Poultry farming ethics is all about maximizing the well-being of the animals in your care. Most people acknowledge the sentience of livestock. Animals can feel pain and experience suffering. Farming ethics, therefore, are concerned with eradicating all unnecessary suffering animals experience to live a comfortable life. Cultures across the world have developed standards of bioethics that align with the principle of harm reduction (Macer, 2019). In Ibaraki, Japan, many farmers expressed a deep empathy for their animals but found that they had to balance their caring with economic demands (Macer, 2019). Empathy and morality compel people to consider the treatment of the animals they raise, but that can come into conflict with profit motives, and it becomes quite complex.

The pursuit of maximizing how much money an individual can make has caused some horrific practices to become the standard around the world. Modern society requires walking a tightrope between commercial pressures and the ethical treatment of livestock. To find ways commercial poultry farming could implement ethical standards, Queens University conducted a study about how housing conditions affect the welfare of chickens (O'Connel, 2023). In Australia, no laws enforce the enrichment of housing environments for broiler chickens. This has resulted in the industry adopting farming methods that often cause the animals harm and distress. The large-scale research of Queens University included 40000 chickens (O'Connell, 2023). They found that the simple introduction of windows, perches, and other environment-enhancing equipment significantly reduced aggressive behavior and anxiety while improving the health and physical conditions of the birds (O'Connell, 2023). Even with a profit-motive driving your farming activities, actions can still be taken to reduce harm.

Ethical farming is built on the foundation of having compassion, kindness, and awareness to make changes that improve the lives of your poultry. As much as you are utilizing your birds for meat, eggs, feathers, or companionship, you cannot promote an exploitative relationship where your livestock gain nothing. Most farm animals are selectively bred into existence, which means it is a human choice that their species exist in the numbers that they do. Since people choose to selectively breed animals, it is their responsibility to maximize the physical and psychological well-being of the animals they bring into the world.

If you broadly define poultry farming ethics, they can be described as frameworks that outline the rights of farm birds and the obligations of farmers based on the societal virtues of respect, empathy, compassion, and fairness. Ethics can be a personal commitment, or it could be enforced by law and regulatory bodies. Ethical codes and regulations should be adjusted according to scientific data and new information on what is needed to increase the well-being of livestock. To be an ethical farmer, research what is best for the well-being of your poultry in terms of the changes you need to make to the operation you run, all while advocating for broader shifts in the industry.

Acknowledging that your animals are having a conscious experience that is entirely different from yours but still impactful enough is the beginning of having empathy for animals. Whether you are raising poultry for eggs, feathers, or meat, your animals, on the basis of being able to experience suffering and pleasure, should be given the best life you can reasonably provide. Not many would argue that animal lives have the same value as human lives, but it is essential to acknowledge that they have some intrinsic value, even if it is not the same as a person's. When you work with poultry, you start to see that their experiences, emotions, psychology, and social dynamics are layered and complex. They are not mindless drones just running around; they are engaging with the world with their own form of intelligence.

Poultry ethics can be broken down into a few basic categories:

- Poultry have the right to nutritional food and adequate water.
- Poultry should be allowed to live comfortably in an environment that protects them from injury.
- Poultry should be protected from disease and treated for any ailments or injuries they have.
- Poultry should live in conditions free from emotional and psychological distress.

Every decision you make on your farm should align with these four principles. Once you explore each one, you'll find that there are many subsections to unpack. These principles often overlap, which creates multifaceted solutions. For example, if you combine the principle of providing nutritional food with poultry's right to live comfortably, you may conclude that allowing your birds to feed freely in an open pasture is the most ethical option.

When you farm poultry for profit, food, or as a hobby, you take full responsibility for the welfare of your animals. This gives you a lot more control to make ethical decisions that a mere consumer can't. Poultry meat purchased in stores has labeling that affects consumer decision-making based on morality. However, what the consumer believes is true is often different from the reality on the ground. For example, people may prefer to buy free-range chickens over battery-farmed birds. However, the "free range" label could be misleading because it refers to chickens not kept in battery cages. Free-range chickens can still be kept in dangerously overcrowded conditions. Running your own farm gives you the most moral decision-making power compared to the average consumer.

Acting ethically towards animals is the responsibility of every person on the planet, but once you start raising poultry, you take on additional obligations. Not all birds are the same. You do not raise chickens in the same way you raise ducks or turkeys. Therefore, ethical actions are catered to the unique position and structure of your farm. You have to deeply understand your animals so that you can make the correct choices for their well-being. Ethics are not always black and white and often fall into grey areas, especially when it comes to livestock, because so many cultures have wildly varying views on what is right or wrong. Although some clear ethical standards should be upheld, your values will determine how you align with them in the small details of your operation. To measure whether your farm protocols adequately ensure the well-being of your animals and provide them with dignity, you must assess the impact of your actions.

The Impact of Choice

The choices you make for your birds will affect the quality of their entire lives. Sometimes, a misunderstanding of what your choices cause can result in you taking a path that exponentially increases the suffering of your animals. Various species of poultry have complicated social hierarchies, biology, and psychological processes. Small actions could have a huge impact on your birds. If you do not understand the impact of your actions on their physical and emotional well-being, you could take paths that leave your beloved animals in constant distress.

When compassion and kindness are not the foundation of your farm, it is easy to slip into a spiral of inhumane activities. For example, turkeys do not thrive in overcrowded conditions. If turkeys do not have enough space, they become violently aggressive. Having aggressive turkeys in a small space leads to many fights as the birds get into each other's way. Commercial turkey farmers usually keep the birds in lower light because it reduces their aggression, which adversely affects their eyes, causing defects and blindness. Turkeys can also become cannibalistic in crowded conditions. The constant fighting and cannibalism cause some farms to remove their beaks to reduce injury. The first unethical practice of overcrowding directly caused two more unethical actions, namely, damaging the turkeys' eyes with low light and mutilating their bodies to make fights less deadly. Cruelty is a slippery slope that exponentially multiplies negative outcomes.

Sometimes, consumer demand facilitates unethical choices for farmers. Foie gras is the French delicacy of fatty duck liver. This dish is served in many top restaurants around the world and can be ridiculously expensive. The fatty liver comes from ducks kept in constrictive cages and force-fed through a pipe to achieve the flavorful liver texture that foie gras enjoyers love. As a poultry farmer, you could probably make a lot of profit by exploiting this niche market. Your choice to participate in the industry because of the consumer demand directly increases the suffering of ducks. You will need to weigh the ethics of valuing the comfortable life of your ducks with obtaining insane profits selling the high-class delicacy.

Ethics is not a zero-sum game and typically works with a sliding scale. Some practices are better than others, but that does not mean they are cruelty-free or even ideal. This becomes apparent when you look at battery-farmed chickens compared to their cageless alternatives. In battery cages, the cramped conditions prevent hens from exhibiting many of their natural behaviors, like nesting, perching, and dustbathing. This causes increased frustration and stress, which could lead to some physical symptoms like feather loss and a weaker body. Their cageless counterparts are allowed to spread their wings and move around freely, so in terms of managing emotional and psychological distress, this option is by all means superior.

This does not mean that cageless farming is ethical. Many of the same practices that happen in battery farming are replicated in cageless farming. On egg farms, many breeders kill male chicks because they are not economically viable to raise. These chicks are often burnt alive, drowned, or even put into plastic bags to rot. Both cage-free and battery farms purchase chicks from breeders, where this unethical practice is the norm. Moreover, both cage-free and battery chickens have their beaks cut off and are usually slaughtered long before they reach adulthood. Therefore, although cage-free chicken farming is better, it is still not ethical.

If you were to choose between cage-free chickens or battery chickens based solely on ethical evaluations, you would probably go with the former, even though it is unethical when using a black-and-white lens. Furthermore, some practices that are considered to be morally correct today could be completely abhorrent in the next ten years based on new research that emerges and the direction in which society moves. The greyness of ethical dilemmas is unavoidable. Being too rigid in your ethical standards can hold you back in many ways. It can be frustratingly difficult to determine which path is the best option for raising poultry.

It is hard to make an immediate transition from unethical to ethical, considering that the concept of ethics can be so amorphous and abstract. You live in a world filled with questionable and downright immoral actions written into many of the systems and institutions that form society. When you start making ethical considerations, especially as they relate to farming, you will quickly notice that you must make gradual steps toward allowing your farm to align with the values of kindness and compassion. Some people may argue that the practice of raising animals is itself unethical, so reaching 100% purity in poultry farming may be an impossible pursuit. You must approach your ethics as a constant mission to align with your virtues and moral systems. Take an animal-centered approach where you value your birds beyond commodities as living beings. Work on transforming your yard into a turkey, duck, chicken, or guinea paradise by studying their behavior, observing their responses to the environment, and looking at their health outcomes.

When you look at birds that were raised in a healthy environment with a farmer who is deeply concerned about ethical practices and compare them to a factory farm that only cares about ethics as it relates to staying within the bounds of the law, the differences are stark. Many people see their neatly packed chickens on their plates, but they never get to see how they were treated while they were alive. It is reasonable to assume that if some people saw the treatment of animals on factory farms, they would think twice about the meat they purchase. Humanity as a collective is participating in a project to move the world to a more ethical place. This shows up in all the systems of law and morality that people embrace. One of the frontiers of improving the world is how people treat nature and animals. It is impossible to undo all the cruel practices that have been embraced as the norm with one backyard farm. The small changes you make in your life and the ideas you advocate for will push the farming industry into a more caring position.

Beyond the Backyard

The ethics you have on your farm do not stop at your gate. There is a whole industry and supply chain linked to all the actions you take on your farm, including sourcing your animals and acquiring feed. Where you buy your poultry from is crucial for embracing more humane ways of farming. It does not help to have a humane farm while you support breeders who have no regard for ethics. For example, some breeders that sell egg-laying hens kill the male chicks because they are not as profitable. Other breeders genetically manipulate broilers so that they can grow faster, but this has the adverse effect of the chickens developing deformities and chronic diseases. Unnecessary suffering begins where you get your animal from.

The next step in the poultry farming supply chain to consider is where you get your feed from. The life quality of your birds is not the only ethical concern you should have as a poultry farmer. If your values are based on compassion, you cannot ignore your environmental impact because there are a multitude of living beings directly impacted by how you engage with this planet. The grains grown to feed your chickens may have been produced using chemicals and practices that degrade the soil and destabilize local ecosystems. Therefore, growing your own feed or sourcing organic produce is a way to be ethical beyond the gates of your farm.

Your advocacy for the restructuring and improvement of the commercial farming industry is one of the most important things you can do to stretch your ethical arms beyond the confines of your property. Making changes in the way you raise poultry is powerful for spreading interspecies kindness, but you are only one farmer in a giant pool. To reform the industry, you need to get many more people on board with the vision of compassion that you have. Your activism is needed to change the minds of farmers stuck in the status quo of the industry and to apply pressure on lawmakers and regulatory bodies to enforce new rules for systematic change.

Although it is not always possible, try as best you can to source your animals and the products you use for poultry farming from local producers. The carbon footprint of sourcing locally is significantly lower than that of products that are shipped in. Moreover, you will likely support small businesses and local economies that keep mom-and-pop stores alive. If your ethics stem from your virtues, you should also extend them to your economic decision-making. The choices you make with your purchases impact the environment and society, so you should be mindful of what you buy and where you buy it.

You do not need to advocate for your feathered friends alone. Multiple NGOs, NPOs, and other activist organizations are already working toward making the world a better place for farm animals. You can also join online communities to amplify the message. It may seem daunting, but when you become active, your small contribution will add momentum to the movement, creating a rapid snowball effect. Every kind farmer should be an advocate for the well-being of animals. You may want to treat your animals right because you have a personal connection with them. Use that empathy as a motivating force because if you understand the bonds you have with your birds, you should be able to conclude that other poultry deserve the same. As long as there are birds who are not experiencing the anguish-free life you provide, your work is not done.

Chapter 10: Beyond the Basics: Rarer Breeds and Conservation

In this chapter, you'll delve into the fascinating world of some of the rarest poultry breeds. You'll find out about the intricacies that contribute to the rarity of these birds, learning their distinctive traits, captivating histories, and close encounters with extinction. Moving forward, you'll also explore the significance of conservation and the efforts it requires.

Meet the Rare Gems

1. Dong Tao

One of the most unusual chickens you will ever see is the Dong Tao, also referred to as the Dragon Chicken. They are quite big, and the roosters weigh over 12 lbs., whereas the hens weigh around 9 lbs. The Dong Tao features brilliant red wattles and ear lobes on a pea comb. The hens' feathers are off-white in color, while the roosters are red with black breasts. Their thick and scaly crimson legs can grow to the width of a man's wrist. Because the hens have a tendency to smash

One of the most unusual chickens you will ever see is the Dong Tao, also referred to as the Dragon Chicken.[19]

their eggs, mechanical incubation is typically used to raise the chicks. These breeds only lay eggs for 2 to 3 months and then rest for a while before getting back at it. This is why they are called the cyclical layers. They lay up to 60 eggs a year. This breed is calm, friendly, and good-natured. These uncommon chickens, which are prized as delicacies in Vietnam, were originally reared exclusively for royal consumption. These days, a pair of Dong Tao can for over two thousand dollars.

2. Sultan

Tab.41.

This rare breed can be found in three colors: blue, white, and black.[30]

A Sultan is a sight to be admired. The vulture hocks, long tail, dropped wings, muffs, head crest, large nares, and the V-comb are just a few of its exquisite traits. This rare breed can be found in three colors: blue, white, and black. White is the most well-known and easy-to-find breed. The blue variety is incredibly rare. These hens, which date back to the 14th century in the Ottoman Empire, were housed as decorative birds in the Sultan's residence. In Turkish, they are known as Serai Tavuk, which translates to "fowl of the Sultan's palace." The roosters can weigh up to 6 lbs, whereas the hens may weigh up to 4 lbs. They also come in even rarer bantam sizes! Seeing how they are poor layers, the hens can only lay two eggs per week. They make for wonderful house chickens and are purely ornamental.

3. Brabanter

This is one of the oldest breeds, dating back to around 1676. It was developed in the historic Brabant area, and that is where it gets its name. They are pretty small and weigh around 4 to 5 lbs. only. The hens may weigh even less. These are not like your typical birds. They have no wattles, large and wide nostrils, a beard, and a crest. They come in a variety of colors, which include cuckoo, gold, and silver spangled. They can lay up to 3 large eggs in a week and love to free-range. These birds are smart, friendly, calm, and shy. They are rarely, if ever, unhappy. It's fascinating to note that enthusiasts were able to save these hens from extinction at the beginning of the 20th century. However, they are still quite rare and in need of conservation efforts.

4. La Fleche

Its name, which means "arrow," comes from the French town of La Fleche, which is near Le Mans.[21]

La Fleche was an extremely popular table bird in the fifteenth century. Its name, which means "arrow," comes from the French town of La Fleche, which is near Le Mans. This chicken grows quite slowly and takes around ten months to grow enough to be sold. Its slow growth is the reason why this wonderful chicken has become so rare. They lay around three large white eggs per week, or 180 eggs per year on average. The species, known as the Devil species, has a peculiar appearance with a Vshaped comb. The roosters are about eight pounds in weight. The hens are too heavy for city living—they weigh more than 6.5 pounds. They also like to fly a little bit and roam freely. Although uncommon, this bird is starting to repopulate.

5. Old English Pheasant Fowl

The Old English Pheasant is a historic English breed of poultry.[22]

The Old English Pheasant is a historic English breed of poultry. They were made from various utility poultry varieties and were once fairly common on farms in Yorkshire and Lancashire. Many of these old types of pheasant fowl were absorbed into the Hamburg breed. Some bird enthusiasts searched around the country for ones that had not been absorbed. This is why, in 1914, the birds were named Old English Pheasant fowl to ensure that they were protected. They are energetic and flighty breeds that love to run wild and would not appreciate closed spaces at all. Their feathers are brown and black. The feathering acts as a camouflage and protects them from predators while they are free-ranging. These birds are good layers and produce around 3 to 4 eggs per week and around 160 to 220 medium-sized eggs per year. They are not very broody and make for wonderful mothers to their chicks. Due to its rare dual-purpose nature, this is an ideal bird for homesteads.

6. Breda

Tab. 19.

It appears in artworks dating back to 1660, where they are shown as farm animals.[28]

The Netherlands is home to the historic breed of Breda chicken. It appears in artworks dating back to 1660, where they are shown as farm animals. It is known by many names, including Crow heads, Kraaikops, and Guelderlands. They were quite popular in the US during the Civil War; however, they lost their popularity until they became completely extinct from the US in the 1800s. The Dutch maintained this breed, but its numbers were quickly declining there as well. This chicken is friendly and alert but calm. Free-ranging is one of its favorite things, and it prefers to stay around its house after its daily walkabouts. With its vulture hocks and feathery legs, the Breda stands erect. It has muscular thighs. It is capable of a fantastic standing leap when startled. Because it lacks a comb, it works well in chilly areas. Its head contains a few feather tufts, albeit they are not very noticeable. It features little red wattles and white earlobes. Its nares are large, just like the Brabanter.

7. Onagadori

Onagadori was first bred in the seventeenth century in the Kochi District of Japan. This rare breed is famous for its unusually long tail. In 1952, it was regarded as a National Natural Treasure of Japan. The longest tail recorded was an amazing 88ft long (27m). Only a rooster's tail is able to grow this long as the hen's feathering is similar to that of other chickens, and it will not grow that much. Sadly, only 250 chickens are estimated to exist now, and it is purely an ornamental breed. The hens lay over 80 to 100 brown eggs but are not sitters. Breeding it requires a lot of experience. You will only want to give this rare bird a chance if you're a seasoned breeder. Their coop and run must be big enough and should be kept clean. Its perches should also be placed high to protect its tail.

This rare breed is famous for its unusually long tail.[24]

8. Burmese

The Burmese bantam chicken is probably the rarest one in existence today. It has been staggering on the brink of extinction for decades now. It was considered extinct at one point until a small flock was discovered in the 1970s. It was not the most fertile bird, and it had to breed with other similar breeds. One of them is Barbu D'Uccles. This practice revitalized the breed, and the flock has continued to grow gradually. The Burmese are regarded as real bantams and have a single comb with a little crest of head feathers. The roosters weigh around 600g, and hens weigh over 500g. Their legs are bright yellow with feathers, and they have vulture hocks with white plumage. Their legs are unusually short, and it is caused by a "creeper" gene that also causes high mortality in embryos. That is also why this bird has become so rare. This breed is quite old, as is mentioned in one of Charles Darwin's books (The Variation of Plants and Animals under Domestication). The hens lay 3 small brown eggs each week and make for great mothers of broody. Overall, it is a friendly and quiet bird that makes up a great backyard flock.

9. Scots Dumpy

DUMPIES, BELONGING TO J. FAIRLIE, ESQ.

These birds originated from Scotland and are an endangered breed.[35]

These birds originated from Scotland and are an endangered breed. This breed gets its name from the creeper gene that gives them really short legs. They have also been referred to as Crawlers or Creepers. Unfortunately, this gene has caused many embryo deaths. Before a small flock was found in Kenya and brought back to the UK, it was believed that they had gone extinct in 1970. Scots Dumpys are a dual-purpose breed that loves to free range. It lays around 3 eggs per week and makes for excellent mothers. They consist of four color varieties: silver grey, black, cuckoo, and dark. Seeing how it's endangered, this rare breed is in severe need of protection.

10. Magpie Ducks

These active and docile birds are decorative, have great egg layers, and are known for their meat.[36]

Magpies were recognized in 1977 by the APA (American Poultry Association). They weigh 4 to 4.5 lbs. and lay medium to large white eggs. These active and docile birds are decorative, have great egg layers, and are known for their meat. They are also known for their white plumage, with a few specific marks on their crown and body (from the shoulders to the tail). Those markings are usually black and blue. Some breeders have developed other colors like chocolate and silver. It is important to note that their markings do not change colors when they mature; this allows the breeders to choose utility birds and breeding stock when they are young. If you are looking for breeding stock, select strong-legged and active birds that come from high-egg production families. Keep in mind that their ability to lay eggs and the size of those eggs are significantly influenced by high-producing families.

11. Jersey Buff Turkey

The Jersey Buff turkey is a rare, striking, buff-colored bird with black, white, and brown feathers. It originated from the mid-Atlantic region and is also known as the Buff Turkey. In 1874, the American Poultry Association (APA) approved this breed. They weigh from 12 to 21 lbs. The hens weigh about 12 lbs., whereas the toms can weigh up to 21 lbs.

These birds can be either docile or aggressive. The hens lay pale cream to medium brown colored eggs with spotting. The Buff Turkey is ideal for hobby or small-scale farms. They are mainly bred for meat production. It can be a costly bird. A 16 lbs. Jersey Buff Turkey can go for around $349.99. Its meat is in high demand.

12. Cotton Patch Geese

In most, the males are mostly white, whereas the females are mostly dove gray to brownish with white variances in their feathers.[27]

The Cotton Patch is a light to medium-sized, upright bird. It has an elongated body and is less rounded than other breeds like Pilgrim goose or Shetland. Cotton Patch geese have rounded heads, blue eyes, an orange-pink beak, and feet. It has a minimal paunch and, when present, a single lobe. In most, the males are mostly white, whereas the females are mostly dove gray to brownish with white variances in their feathers. The geese can lay up to 4 to 7 eggs per clutch. The eggs are large and white in color. The ganders can weigh around 9 to 12 lbs., whereas the geese weigh up to 8 to 10 lbs. These birds are great flyers, which helps them escape predators, but that may not be a great quality to some breeders. These birds are great foragers, and thanks to their small size, they can survive extremely hot weather.

13. Saxony Ducks

Saxony ducks are wonderful, easygoing birds that can adapt to all sorts of environments. Their eggs are extra-large and may be white or blue-green in color. They are large, all-purpose birds and can weigh around 6 to 8 lbs. One of their best qualities is their calm and docile nature. Saxony ducks are wonderful foragers and reduce the number of snails and slugs around.

Saxony ducks are wonderful, easygoing birds that can adapt to all sorts of environments.[28]

14. KellyBronze Turkey

KellyBronze Turkey has one of the most expensive meats and is greatly celebrated by celebrity chefs.[29]

KellyBronze Turkey has one of the most expensive meats and is greatly celebrated by celebrity chefs. It is sold for around $12 per pound, which means that a fully adult bird may cost around $300. It has delicate and moist meat. It takes half the time to cook than a regular turkey and is naturally juicy. If they are allowed to forage for themselves and roam freely, they'll produce that highly sought-after meat. It is a slow-growing breed and takes a long time to get to the right weight. Its maturity has a significant impact on the flavor. The hens lay eggs in spring and only lay for 10 weeks.

Conservation: Why It Matters

Conserving poultry breeds has multiple ecological implications. It is mainly related to environmental sustainability, biodiversity, and the preservation of genetic resources. Here is a list of some key considerations:

Environmental Sustainability

The poultry breed has evolved in different geographic areas and has adapted to various environments. There is a need to conserve these breeds in order to ensure that the industry remains resilient when it comes to environmental challenges like climate change. It is also essential to understand that some of these traditional breeds may have developed resistance to certain diseases. These traits can only be conserved if these species are taken care of.

Biodiversity Preservation

Conservation of various poultry breeds helps with maintaining a diverse genetic pool. This is especially important for fighting against illnesses, environmental changes, or other issues. This diverse group also contributes to the overall biodiversity in agriculture. It is extremely important for the broader ecosystem as these diverse agricultural systems support many other organisms like insects, plants, fungi, etc.

Sustainable Agriculture Practices

Native poultry breeds play a huge role in sustainable farming practices as they do not require any external inputs such as special diets or medication, leading to a sustainable and environmentally friendly agricultural system. Moreover, maintaining a variety of poultry breeds can prevent overreliance on certain highly specialized breeds. Diversity may be able to reduce the impact of large-scale industrial poultry farming.

Cultural and Heritage Conservation

Many poultry breeds have local and cultural significance. By preserving these breeds, you maintain the connection between people and their agricultural history. It also helps support local economies, especially in areas where the traditional breed has a significant impact on the livelihood of those communities.

Education and Awareness

You can highlight the importance of sustainable agricultural practices and biodiversity to create awareness among friends, farmers, decision-makers, and the public.

Getting Involved

You can also learn how you can help and make active efforts towards the conservation of the environment. It is a collective responsibility to take care of the wildlife habitat to ensure that all the threatened species are not harmed. Everyone must take conscious steps to ensure that their best interests are prioritized. Here's how you can get involved:

1. Learning about the Endangered Species in Your Region

The first step toward conserving the environment is learning about the amazing wildlife around you. You must find everything you can about the endangered species in your region and learn what makes them interesting and why they are so important. The natural world has provided you with benefits, including clean air, food, water, and even medicines. It is your duty to pay back and protect the environment.

2. Give Back by Volunteering

Try your best to visit and volunteer at wildlife parks. Protected spaces keep native wildlife, including plants, birds, and fish safe. The best way to protect endangered species is to protect the environment. These dedicated places create many wildlife-related jobs for thousands of people and help businesses support the environment.

3. Make Your Backyard Wildlife-Friendly

You should try your best to make your home a safe space for wildlife. Keep your garbage cans closed. Lock your pets in at night and feed them inside to avoid attracting wild animals. You must also make an effort to disinfect the bird baths to avoid disease transmission. Sadly, a large number of birds die as a result of collisions with windows. You can also reduce the number by putting decals on your windows.

4. Native Wildlife Rely on the Native Plants

You should try your best to allow native plants to fully grow. You can pollinate your plants by attracting bees and butterflies. Unfortunately, the spread of non-native species has significantly impacted the native populations around the globe. These species are usually invasive and compete with the native species for habitat and resources. They can also force the surrounding native species into extinction.

5. Avoid Pesticides

Although insecticides and herbicides can keep your backyard healthy and looking great, their contents are extremely detrimental to wildlife. These chemicals take a long time to degrade and may build up in the soil, affecting the food chain. Predators like owls, coyotes, and hawks can also get harmed if they consume poisoned prey. Keep in mind that amphibians are especially vulnerable to these pollutants and can greatly suffer if exposed to high levels of pesticides.

6. Drive Responsibly

Drive carefully and under the speed limit to avoid harming wild animals. Roads are especially dangerous for wildlife.

7. Recycle

Pay attention to what you consume, and always recycle. Make an effort to buy recycled and sustainable products to reduce your carbon footprint. Never buy furniture made from wood procured from rainforests. Also, the mineral used in cellphones and other electronics is mined in gorilla habitats; this is why it is important to recycle your mobile phones and other appliances. Also, try to limit the use of palm oil as tiger habitats are being destroyed to make more room for plantations.

8. Do Not Interfere with Wildlife

Interfering with wildlife by shooting, trapping, or forcing into captivity is illegal and can lead to endangered species going extinct. If you come across someone doing any of those things, contact the local wildlife enforcement office.

9. Do Not Buy Products Made from Endangered Species

This goes without saying, but never buy anything made from an endangered species. Going on trips abroad is an exhilarating experience, and it makes you want to collect souvenirs. However, avoid anything made from tortoise shells, coral, or ivory. You should also never buy products made from endangered species like tigers, sea otters, polar bears, crocodile skin, and parrots.

10. Protect Habitats

Wildlife habitats are being destroyed rapidly, which poses a major threat to many species. The best way to protect threatened species is by protecting where they live. They should have access to resources to raise their young and find food and shelter. Petition the local authorities if you hear of any oil and gas drilling, logging, and overgrazing near wildlife.

Conclusion

Taking the first step to start a poultry farm may not be the most difficult, but it is the most daunting. Jumping into the unknown will always be scary. You now have the basic knowledge you need to get started. Remember, you need to match the birds you want to raise to your property. Not every fowl will do well in all environments. You then must set up adequate housing that caters to all their needs. For example, if you are raising ducks, you need a body of water nearby. If you have chickens or turkeys, they need ample space to move around and places to perch.

From nutrition to the health and wellness of your animals, you are well prepared to embark on this amazing journey. Whether you are farming poultry for food or just as a hobby, dealing with livestock is not child's play. Once your farm becomes productive and you get that first feather harvest or gather that initial dozen eggs, the joy you will feel is unrivaled. However, the life of a poultry farmer has a lot of ups and downs. You need to brace yourself for a wild ride. A disease could spread through your flock, or a predator could rip through your cages. You must be resilient and prepared enough to take some hits along the way.

Farming can never be selfish. You are dedicating your time and effort to the well-being of helpless animals. Compared to domesticated dogs and cats, the connection that can be cultivated for other species is often underrated. As you spend time with your birds, you will begin noticing their behavior and unique personalities. You might even develop a bond with a few that will become your favorites. This bond should inspire you to act within the bounds of ethical practices and even take steps for the sake of conservation. Given that Earth supports all life, you should care for it like you care for your birds. If you are breeding protected species, remember that there is a big responsibility on your shoulders. You also need to make sure that you function within legal frameworks to stay out of trouble.

Transforming your homestead, yard, plot, or commercial farm into a poultry paradise will take a lot of elbow grease. Getting down into the dirt is exciting and can awaken something primal in you. If you look after them well, your birds will respect your efforts and return the favor bountifully. Good luck on your poultry adventure, and take the time to refresh your mind with the tips and techniques you find throughout this book whenever you feel lost or confused.

Part 2: Livestock Guardians

How to Use Llamas, Donkeys, Dogs, and More to Safeguard Your Herd and Property

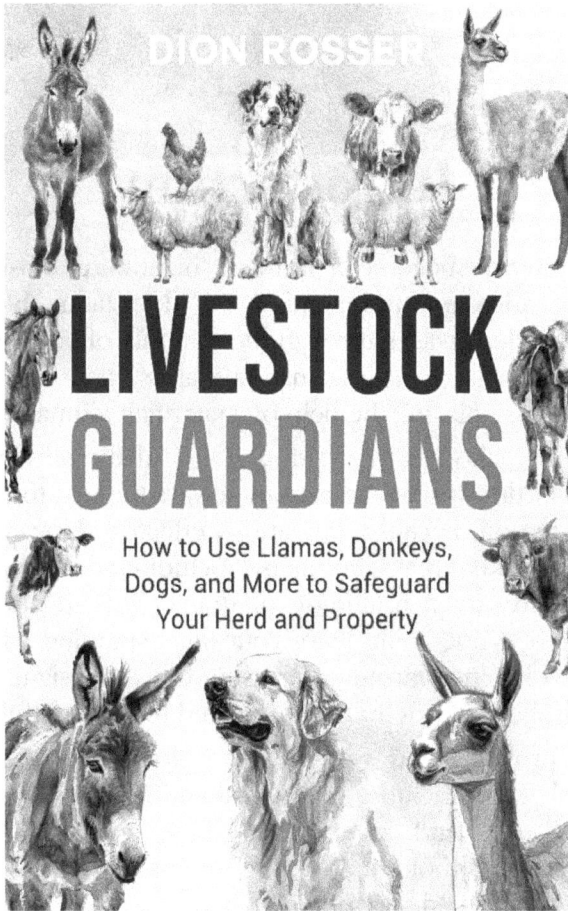

Introduction

Predators can quickly become a farmer's nightmare. Losing an animal here and there adds up, never mind the devastating blows when an unwelcomed intruder ravages through the majority of your flock. Farmers are fighting an eternal battle against predators, and one of the most humane solutions is enlisting the help of a guardian animal.

Pictures of the galloping guard dog across idyllic hills bring nostalgic visions of simpler times. Dogs or cats are always the first to come to mind, and with good reason, because they are so effective. However, numerous animal species make great guardians, including donkeys and llamas. Furthermore, there are a multitude of dog breeds to choose from, so deciding on the best one could leave your head spinning. Moreover, dogs can quickly devolve into intruders, causing the most significant risks for your livestock if they are not trained and cared for thoughtfully.

This book provides you with all the information you need about guardian animals. This includes the ethical and legal considerations – and which breeds, species, and conditions are best suited for the homestead, the farm, or the smallholding you are building. Choosing a guardian animal blind can be disorienting. Therefore, the guiding light of theoretical information and practical tips is presented to lead you to a successful farm.

Some methods of predator control, like poisoning or trapping, can be inhumane and cause undue suffering. Poison can make the environment around you toxic, and it will kill animals that it was not meant to kill, while traps can keep a predator in prolonged pain. Although livestock guardians attack and kill predators, they are a more humane option because they keep predators away, which will maintain their population in the wild.

Man, meeting nature does not have to be disastrous. By creating a cohesive system that includes your guard animals, you can build an ethical and productive farm that meets and surpasses regulatory standards and is eco-friendly. The bonds you create between your flock and guard animals are the mutually beneficial relationships that highlight how humans and nature can coexist productively. The fulfilling journey of setting up your farm in a way that keeps your animals safe and maximizes their well-being will reward you both mentally and financially.

Following proper guidance lets you rest easy knowing your animals are protected. Acquiring the skills and knowledge this book provides you will make you a much better farmer. From medical considerations to nutrition and habitat, all the bases are covered to make you the best guardian animal owner. Do not hesitate. Dive into this book and unlock your full potential as a livestock keeper. You are your animals' first line of protection, but that does not mean you don't need some assistance along the way. The perfect helping paws or hooves are right at your fingertips if you are curious enough to to go deeper into the world of livestock guardians!

Chapter 1: The Guardian's Role

This chapter discusses the essential role of guardian animals in protecting livestock and property and how they contribute to overall security. You'll find a brief overview of the historical use of guard animals, which essentially started with the domestication of wolves and the initiation of dogs into police and military systems. You'll explore the evolution of guard animals' role over time, discovering the advantages of this predator management method. Finally, you'll learn about ethical and legal considerations regarding the use of guard animals.

The Historical Use and Evolution of Guardian Animals

Around 40,000 years ago, humans noticed incredible potential in wolves. This animal is strong, intelligent, and able to hunt. They realized that wolves would become more trainable, friendly, and receptive to humans by domesticating them. This would allow the domesticated animal to use its territorial and hunting instincts to guard humans and keep their belongings safe. Like modern dogs, wolves have always used barking to warn their pack about imminent danger.

Around 40,000 years ago, man domesticated wolves.[80]

Early research suggests that humans separated wolf pups from their packs and trained them to do several tasks. However, this theory is unlikely because the animal is virtually untrainable. Unless they managed to socialize the pups when they were as little as 19 days old, the animals would've never responded to them. Training a young animal is also taxing; it's unlikely that hunter-gatherer early humans – whose only goal was survival – would've taken the time needed for this process.

Another theory was that food waste and other paraphernalia left around humans' early settlements attracted wolves to the area. Wolves are naturally inclined to scavenge, hunt, and look around for food. While these settlements would've undoubtedly made a desirable food source, wolves are also naturally scared of humans and potential sources of danger.

Whenever a wild animal senses the presence of a human or another potentially dangerous entity, their "flight distance" instinct kicks in. This instinct refers to each animal's instinct to allow a source of perceived danger to approach them before they flee. It is reasonable to believe that wolves with weak flight distances were eventually domesticated since having a weak flight distance means they are more sociable than their counterparts. They were more likely to engage with humans and spend more time physically near them. While this theory is unconfirmed, it has been supported by scientific experiments regarding the domestication of foxes.

Mesopotamian Dogs

Regardless of the technicalities, dogs, as everyone knows them today, exist because humans in different corners of the world recognized the potential of wolves. Proof of humans using dogs as guardians goes back to ancient Mesopotamia. Native legend and folklore tell about large animal breeds guarding local livestock. Not only does Mesopotamian art feature dogs abundantly, but they're also generally known to have protected homes and livestock from predators, especially smaller wolves. Dogs were also carved into protective amulets.

The Revered Dogs of Ancient Egypt

Dogs were also sacred to the ancient Egyptians. They held religious significance because they were associated with Anubis, the god of the dead. Anubis was depicted as having a human's body and a dog's head. Dogs were also commonly kept as pets because of their protective nature and hunting abilities, and they were also a great source of companionship. Ancient Egyptians formally mourned the passing of their dogs, which further signifies their reverence.

The First Official Use of Guardian Dogs

Ancient Greek mythology is perhaps the most solid proof of the protective role of dogs at the time. According to lore, Hades, the god of the underworld, employed Cerberus, a three-headed dog, to guard the gates of his realm. The world-renowned Athenian philosopher Plato also frequently employed dogs as philosophical examples. He highlighted their natural roles as hunters and loyal protectors and explained in his work, *The Republic*, that intelligent animals can easily distinguish between friends and foes.

The Molossians, the ancient Greek tribe that lived in Epirus, are known for their role in breeding Molossus dogs. The Molossus breed was used to guard pastures and homes, and while it is now extinct, it's the ancestor of the Mastiff breed. The dog breed also served as a personal guardian and was even sometimes deployed on the battlefield alongside warriors.

Roman Molossers

Ancient Romans also commonly used guard dogs to protect their homes and belongings. Archeologists found evidence in the ancient city of Pompeii hinting at the role of dogs in the Roman Empire. One artifact was a mosaic artwork featuring a massive black dog and text translated into

"Beware of the Dog." Similar warning pieces, along with the remnants of a dog that was chained to a temple, were also found.

As the Roman Empire expanded and cultural practices spread to different parts of the world, the idea of using guardian dogs also became more popular. Romans introduced Molossers to the areas they conquered, which led to breeding more Mastiff dogs around the region. At this point in time, however, people didn't know the difference between different dog breeds.

The German Rottweiler

Having a dangerous reputation and being notorious for their incredibly powerful bites, German Rottweilers are among the most popular guardian dogs today. They were among the earliest guard dog breeds to ever exist. They were historically utilized to herd livestock and protect their owners' prized belongings. While it is considered a dangerous breed, the Rottweiler makes a good guardian animal because it can form bonds and companionships with humans and other animals, can be controlled, and is highly intelligent.

German Rottweilers are among the most popular guardian dogs today.[81]

Similar dog breeds were also commonly used to protect homes and property. The Italians also trained the Cane Corso breed to protect and herd livestock and hunt predators. Molosser-type dogs were generally used for entertainment, such as dogfighting and bullbaiting. While these activities are highly unethical, they highlight traits such as controlled aggression and tenacity, which are necessary in guarding animals.

The Emergence of More Dog Breeds

During the 19th century, more dog breeds, including the German Shepherd, emerged. Scientists and breeders were breeding dogs to develop breeds that ultimately carried all the traits they desired within a dog. Some strove to create entirely new breeds, while others simply wanted to enhance existing ones.

In the 1920s, for instance, the Argentinian Dr. Antonio Nores Martinez wanted to create an excellent hunter who could serve as an effective family guardian. He cross-bred several breeds, including Bull Terriers, Mastiffs, Great Danes, and even the Cordoba Fighting Dog – which no longer exists – until he created the Dogo Argentino. This dog was banned in the UK due to its high levels of aggression.

The creation of the Doberman Pinscher, which remains one of the most effective protection dogs today, is another interesting story. The development of this breed all started when a German tax collector was desperate for a guardian animal to accompany him at work. He cross-bred Beaucerons, Greyhounds, Rottweilers, German Pinschers, and Weimaraners to come up with the perfect guard animal for his needs.

The Development of Police Dog Programs

As more dog breeds were recognized, the police and military recognized the potential within certain driven, highly protective, tenacious, and intelligent dog breeds. Police departments in different parts of the world started conducting dog training programs in the early 1900s. The most common breeds used in these programs were the Belgian, Dutch, and German Shepherd dogs.

Recognizing the Opportunity for Training Dogs

The incredible role that police and military dogs play garnered the attention of many people, probing the question of whether guardian dogs could be employed for similar purposes in the private sector. Over the last few decades, the idea of using a guardian dog or other protective animal has become more systemized.

People seek out different types of dogs for distinct purposes, such as family, property, or livestock protection. Dogs are among the most popular guardian animals because they are relatively easy to train. When working with dogs, you can reinforce desirable behavior and get them to abandon negative ones. Training and guidance, combined with the natural bond they'll build with you, your family, and your livestock, will allow them to perform their roles effectively. The breed's temperament also influences how fit they are for their intended purpose.

The idea of using other animals, such as llamas, alpacas, donkeys, and even ducks, to protect certain types of livestock from specific types of predators is also growing more popular today.

The Advantages of Using a Guardian Animal as a Predator Management Method

Guardian dogs and other animals like llamas, alpacas, and donkeys have been used for centuries to protect livestock and property from predators, trespassers, and other potential threats. Depending on the nature of the guardian animal and the livestock they protect, guardians, especially dog guardians, often view the livestock they protect as companions. They learn to protect them out of care, which is something that the livestock also recognizes and responds to.

Why Do Guardians Protect Livestock?

Other guardian animals (like alpacas, donkeys, and llamas) often don't care about the livestock they protect. They would rather protect the flock because they either despise a potential predator or perceive it as an unknown source of potential danger. Training a guardian animal requires you to socialize it with the livestock it will be protecting. The socialization process allows the guardian to familiarize itself with the flock or herd. This way, the livestock becomes acceptable to the guardian and is no longer perceived as potentially dangerous or uncomfortable. However, when an unknown predator approaches, the guardian animal will lean into their instincts and react accordingly.

Regardless of whether the guardian animal protects the livestock out of care or mere familiarity, it will get the job done. That said, understanding the differences between each species' mechanisms to protect livestock will allow you to choose the right animal for your needs. Using livestock guardians is one of the few non-lethal predator management methods, which is why it's becoming increasingly popular. It encourages species to coexist, crucial for sustaining a healthy ecosystem. Using livestock guardians also reduces the need for lethal and brutal predator control methods.

How Does It Work?

Using guardian animals like dogs is an effective control method because the animal signals their presence instead of killing predators. Signaling refers to using scent and vocal communication to mark an animal's territory. When potential predators like foxes and wild dogs recognize that the guardian inhabits a certain location, the predators will avoid going there so a conflict doesn't occur. If the predator decides to ignore the signal and head over to the marked territory anyway, the guardian animal will show signs of aggression and attack the predator in case it persists. The livestock knows that if it flees, the predator will perceive it as a more attractive target, which is why it simply gathers behind its guardian, allowing it to do its job.

When employed correctly, guardian animals can prove to be very helpful at protecting predators, as well as animals like kangaroos and deer. While they successfully get rid of predators without killing them, they don't push them into nearby lands. Predators often free the marked territory altogether, which creates a safe space for the livestock to graze and wander around.

Things to Keep in Mind

When considering getting a dog or another guardian animal to protect your livestock, many worry that the guardian might harass or even harm the flock. This, however, isn't true. This predator control method is effective when landowners ensure that there are enough guardian animals for the size of the property and the number of livestock. They must also consider the nature of the terrain, the type of vegetation, the predator species and numbers, and the type of terrain and livestock.

Remember that your guardian animal is a living entity, not a robot. Just as all employees need healthy work environments and appropriate compensation, your animal needs to be rewarded for its efforts. It needs to be trained and guided so it can thrive at its job. You should neither treat the animal as a house pet nor neglect it altogether. You must ensure the guardian animal's physical and psychological needs are met. Providing the guardian animal with proper care ensures its health and longevity and allows it to do its job effectively.

Remember that, at first, you'll have to invest a lot of time, effort, and money into your guardian animal. Your investments, however, will pay back over time with less predator threats and more peace of mind. If you decide that you no longer need the guardian animal, you can also sell it for profit later.

When choosing a guardian animal, you should know that each has *its own limitations.* Some animals require more training and maintenance than others. Others require more support and positive reinforcement. If you need a quick fix to your problem, you shouldn't opt for a dog because they require a lot of training and support. For instance, if you're searching for a low-maintenance guardian animal, then a guardian donkey wouldn't be your safest bet.

The rewards you can reap from keeping a guardian animal don't come at a small price. This is why, when exploring your options, you should consider the amount of initial time, effort, and financial investment you're willing to make and the level of maintenance and support you're willing to provide the animal over time.

Ethical and Legal Considerations

If you plan on owning a guard animal, remember that the animal might be considered dangerous by law, depending on your location and the type of animal. For instance, guard dogs, even after retirement, are considered dangerous under the Domestic Animals Act of 1994. You must comply with certain regulations and conditions when keeping a guard animal; otherwise, you'll likely be subject to penalties for non-compliance.

Note that the following regulations can vary depending on where you live, so check with your local authorities before acquiring a guard dog. However, the following are the most common rules and non-compliance penalties:

- If your guardian dog attacks someone, you can get jailed for 5 to 10 years under the Crimes Act of 1958.

- You must notify the authorities about the location of your guard animal.

- You must follow the applicable enclosure requirements.

- You should always keep the animal collared, on a lead, and muzzled when accompanied outside the property.

- If you plan on selling or putting the animal up for adoption, prospective buyers or adopters must be notified that the animal is dangerous. This must be stated in writing as well.

- If the animal owner is under 18 years old, the owner's guardian will be considered the legal owner of the animal.
- Some guard animals must be implanted with an ISO microchip in accordance with the applicable regulations.
- The responsible authorities must be provided with the chip's ID number, alongside other required information.
- Guard animals must always wear a prescribed, reflective collar that can be recognized from a distance. The collar is usually red and yellow and between 20 and 30 mm wide.
- You must put up signs alerting visitors and passers-by that you're keeping a dangerous animal on your property. The signs must be clear, durable, reflective, and placed on all property entrances.
- If your dog is not guarding a non-residential property, it must be kept in a secure enclosure that prevents it from escaping.
- Only the legal owners of the animal must have access to the enclosure.
- The enclosure must be spacious, granting the animal enough room. It must also be supplied with a roof, a drain, a weatherproof sleeping area, walls, and a gate with a lock.
- Check with your local authorities about the details and requirements for the enclosure construction. The usual requirements for a dangerous dog's fence, however, are that it must be at least 2.63 feet tall and made of timber, brick, iron, concrete, or any other strong material mixed with chain mesh. You should regularly maintain the enclosure to ensure it's not weakened or damaged over time, compromising your dog's safety or granting them a way to escape. All the gates must be locked while the dog is on guard.
- You must notify the local authorities if your dangerous pet goes missing, gets adopted or sold, or its owner changes for any reason, or if you move into another home or relocate the pet. *In most cases, you must inform the relevant entity within 24 hours of these changes.*

After reading this chapter, you should better understand what it means to have a guard animal protecting your property or livestock. Guard animals can be a great, non-lethal method of predator control when utilized correctly. The effectiveness of this technique depends on your choice of animal and how well it suits your personal goals and resources, along with how it bonds with and protects your livestock and the type and number of predators in the region. There are also some ethical and legal concerns that you must keep in mind when getting a guard animal. This way, you'll avoid getting into trouble and ensure your animal is psychologically and physically prepared to fulfill its role effectively.

Chapter 2: Predator Behavior and Control Strategies

In these intricate ecosystems, predator behavior plays a pivotal role in shaping the dynamics of natural communities. Predators are an integral ecosystem component, exhibiting a fascinating array of behaviors honed by evolutionary processes to ensure their survival and success as hunters. From intricate hunting strategies to establishing territories, predator behavior is a complex interplay of instinct, adaptation, and environmental influence. This chapter explores the fundamental aspects of predator behavior, seeking to uncover the mysteries of how these creatures navigate their environments, select and pursue prey, and establish their roles within the delicate balance of ecosystems.

Fox preying on a mole.[32]

Common Predators to Know

Arctic Fox (Vulpes lagopus)

Arctic foxes have thick fur that changes color with the seasons, helping them blend into their snowy surroundings. They have a compact build and a bushy tail for balance. Furthermore, these animals are highly adapted to cold environments. Arctic foxes are known for their intelligence and resourcefulness. They are opportunistic omnivores, scavenging for food when necessary - and primarily feeding on small mammals, birds, and insects. They use their keen sense of hearing to locate prey beneath the snow, then pounce to catch it. These foxes can be expected visitors if you live in areas with heavy snowfall.

Bengal Tiger (Panthera tigris tigris)

Bengal tigers are large and muscular, with a distinctive orange coat marked by black stripes. They have powerful jaws and retractable claws. Solitary by nature, Bengal tigers are territorial and can be nocturnal and diurnal. They are strong swimmers and climbers. Tigers are ambush predators, relying on stealth and strength to get close to their prey before launching a powerful attack. Their preferred prey includes deer, wild boar, and sometimes larger animals like buffalo. These tigers can feed on livestock being raised near their habitat.

Golden Eagle

Golden eagles are large raptors with distinctive white heads, tails, a pointy beak, and sharp talons. They have powerful wings for soaring. Known for their keen eyesight, bald eagles are opportunistic hunters and scavengers. They are often found near large bodies of water. Bald eagles primarily hunt fish, using their powerful talons to snatch prey from the water. They also feed on livestock, waterfowl, and scavenged carrion. You can always expect bald eagles and other flying carnivores to attack poultry, rabbits, and other smaller animals they can easily hunt.

Cheetah (Acinonyx jubatus)

Cheetahs are slender and built for speed, with distinctive black tear stripes on their face. They have a lightweight frame, long legs, and a flexible spine. They are the fastest land animals, capable of reaching up to 75 miles per hour. They are primarily solitary, with males forming small groups called coalitions. Cheetahs rely on incredible speed and agility to chase down prey, mainly small to medium-sized ungulates like gazelles. Their hunting strategy involves stalking and a sudden acceleration to catch their prey. They are a potential predator of animals like sheep, goats, and cattle raised near their habitat.

Komodo Dragon (Varanus komodoensis)

The Komodo dragon is the world's largest lizard, with a robust build, scaly skin, and a long, muscular tail. Their saliva contains bacteria, making their bites potentially deadly. Komodo dragons are solitary and territorial. They are skilled climbers and swimmers despite their large size. These opportunistic predators prey on various animals, including deer, birds, and smaller dragons. If livestock is present within their territory, a Komodo dragon won't hesitate to make your livestock their next meal. They use their powerful jaws and sharp teeth to deliver a lethal bite, and their venomous saliva aids in incapacitating prey over time.

Snow Leopard (Panthera uncia)

Snow leopards are adapted to cold, mountainous environments. They have a thick, fur-covered tail for balance, large paws for walking on snow, and distinctive rosette markings on their fur. Snow leopards are elusive and solitary, well adapted to the harsh conditions of high-altitude regions. They are known for their excellent leaping and climbing abilities. These animals primarily prey on blue sheep and other mountain ungulates. They use their powerful hind limbs to make incredible leaps and ambush their prey from above. If you raise livestock in mountainous regions with lots of snowfall, you can expect snow leopards if their habitat is nearby.

Snow leopards are elusive and solitary.[33]

Red Fox (Vulpes vulpes)

Red foxes have a slender body, a bushy tail, and distinctive red fur. They are adaptable, found in various habitats, and are referred to as opportunistic omnivores. They are known for their intelligence and ability to thrive in both urban and rural environments. Red foxes have a diverse diet, including small mammals, birds, insects, and fruits. They use their keen senses, agility, and stalk-and-pounce hunting techniques to catch prey.

Spotted Hyena (Crocuta crocuta)

Spotted hyenas have a robust build, powerful jaws, and a distinctive hunched back. They have a unique social structure with a matriarchal hierarchy. They are highly social and live in clans. They are known for their vocalization and often compete with other predators for food. Spotted hyenas are skilled scavengers and hunters, preying on various animals, including wildebeests and zebras. They use cooperative hunting techniques to exhaust and bring down larger prey.

Various other predators can potentially feed on domestic and livestock animals. These include snakes, coyotes, skunks, bobcats, raccoons, and hawks.

Predator Identification

Predator identification is crucial for implementing effective protection measures, as it allows for targeted conservation efforts and the mitigation of potential conflicts. Here are some general guidelines to enhance predator identification.

In-Depth Study of Field Guides

Acquire and thoroughly study field guides specific to the geographical region of interest. Pay attention to detailed descriptions, illustrations, and range maps for each predator species. Understand variations in physical characteristics based on age, sex, and season.

Comprehensive Training and Workshops

Attend specialized training sessions or workshops conducted by wildlife experts. Participate in hands-on activities, including specimen examination and practical field exercises. Engage in discussions on the nuances of predator identification, emphasizing distinguishing features.

Online Resources Exploration

Explore reputable online resources provided by wildlife organizations and research institutions. Utilize multimedia content, including videos, images, and interactive tools. Familiarize yourself with digital databases and citizen science projects contributing to species identification efforts.

Engagement with Local Experts

Establish connections with local wildlife experts, researchers, and naturalists. Arrange field visits or guided tours with these experts to gain real-world exposure to predator habitats. Seek mentorship to refine your observational skills and receive personalized guidance.

Mastery of Tracks and Signs

Develop a deep understanding of tracks, scat, and other signs left by predators. Engage in tracking courses to enhance your ability to interpret these signs accurately. Practice distinguishing between similar-looking tracks and recognizing patterns that indicate specific species.

Behavioral Analysis

Study the behavioral ecology of different predators. Understand nuances in hunting techniques, communication methods, and social structures. Observe captive animals to witness behaviors that might be challenging to observe in the wild.

Technological Integration

Embrace technology, including the use of camera traps and trail cameras. Learn how to set up and maintain these devices effectively. Familiarize yourself with image recognition software and understand its limitations and strengths in predator identification.

Identification of Key Indicator Species

Identify and deeply understand key indicator species relevant to the ecosystem. Explore their ecological roles, habitat preferences, and interactions with other species. Use these indicators to gauge ecosystem health and identify potential threats to predators.

Systematic Documentation

Develop a systematic approach to documenting predator observations. Include detailed notes on behavior, location, and environmental conditions. Capture high-quality photographs and record audio if possible. Share your observations through scientific channels, online platforms, or local conservation initiatives.

Predator Control

Predator control refers to managing and mitigating predators, typically through human intervention, to minimize their impact on livestock and property. This practice is essential for safeguarding agricultural interests, protecting domestic animals, and maintaining ecological balance. The primary goals of predator control are to reduce economic losses, ensure the safety of domestic animals, and prevent potential conflicts between wildlife and human activities. Several reasons underscore the importance of predator control.

Livestock Protection

One of the primary reasons for predator control is to safeguard livestock from predation. Predators like wolves, coyotes, big cats, and bears may threaten domestic animals like sheep, cattle, and poultry. Reducing the impact of predators helps maintain the livelihoods of farmers and ranchers who depend on livestock for income.

Economic Considerations

Predation of livestock can result in significant economic losses for farmers and ranchers. Besides the direct loss of animals, predation can lead to decreased productivity, lower reproductive rates, mental health issues in farm animals, and increased costs associated with additional security measures. Effective predator control minimizes these economic impacts.

Human Safety and Property Protection

Certain predators, especially those living near human habitats, can threaten human safety and property. For example, large predators may enter residential areas searching for food, potentially leading to conflicts. Predator control measures help mitigate these risks and promote coexistence between humans and wildlife.

Conservation of Endangered Species

Predator control is not solely about eradicating predators; it often involves carefully managing their populations. This is crucial for conserving endangered or threatened species by addressing conflicts with human activities. Balancing predator populations with the needs of local communities contributes to overall biodiversity conservation, eradicating the population from a habitat that would otherwise disrupt the food chain and the ecosystem.

Ecological Balance

Uncontrolled predator populations can disrupt ecological balance. In some cases, overpopulation of certain predators can lead to declines in prey species, affecting vegetation and other ecosystem components. When implemented responsibly, predator control helps maintain a healthier balance within ecosystems.

Livestock Industry Sustainability

The sustainability of the livestock industry is closely tied to effective predator control. By mitigating predation risks, farmers and ranchers can maintain stable and profitable operations, contributing to the sustainability of the agriculture sector.

Ethical Considerations

While predator control is sometimes necessary for practical reasons, ethical considerations are essential. Using humane and ethical methods to minimize harm to predators and non-target species is necessary. Balancing the needs of human livelihoods with the ethical treatment of wildlife is the key to effective and sustainable predator control.

Predator Control Plan

Creating a predator control plan requires a thorough understanding of the specific circumstances, including the types of predators involved, the nature of the environment, and the community's or stakeholders' goals. Here's a step-by-step guide with corresponding examples to help tailor a predator control plan to specific circumstances:

Step 1: Assess the Situation

In a region where coyotes threaten livestock, assess the specific risks by considering the size of the coyote population, the types of livestock present, and historical predation patterns.

Step 2: Identify Target Predators

Determine whether the main concern is large predators like wolves, smaller predators like foxes, or a combination of both. Tailor the control plan based on the specific predators causing issues.

Step 3: Understand Local Ecosystem Dynamics

In an area with a delicate ecosystem, consider the potential impacts of predator control on non-target species and ecological balance. Assess how changes in predator populations may affect prey species and vegetation.

Step 4: Set Clear Goals and Objectives

Define specific goals, such as reducing livestock losses by a certain percentage or promoting coexistence between predators and livestock. Clear objectives help measure the success of the control plan.

Step 5: Choose Appropriate Control Methods

Depending on the circumstances, control methods could include non-lethal measures like improved fencing, guard animals, or deterrents. If lethal measures are deemed necessary, choose methods that are humane and targeted, such as selective trapping or shooting in specific situations.

Step 6: Consider Non-Lethal Alternatives

Explore using deterrents like sound or light devices, guardian animals (e.g., llamas, dogs), or modifying livestock management practices (e.g., changing grazing patterns) to reduce predation without harming predators.

Step 7: Implement Monitoring and Evaluation

Establish a system to monitor the effectiveness of control measures and adjust the plan accordingly. This might involve regular surveys of predator populations, tracking livestock losses, and assessing changes in ecological indicators.

Step 8: Involve Stakeholders and the Community

Engage with local farmers, ranchers, conservationists, and other stakeholders to gather insights and address concerns. Community involvement fosters a collaborative approach and increases the plan's chances of success.

Step 9: Educate and Raise Awareness

Conduct workshops, training sessions, or informational campaigns to educate the community about predator behavior, the importance of coexistence, and the rationale behind specific control measures.

Step 10: Adaptability and Flexibility

Be prepared to adjust the control plan based on evolving circumstances. For instance, if a new, non-lethal technology becomes available, consider integrating it into the plan to improve effectiveness.

Step 11: Legal and Ethical Considerations

Ensure that the control plan complies with local and national regulations. Consider the ethical implications of control methods and strive to use approaches that minimize harm to predators and non-target species.

Step 12: Documentation and Reporting

Keep detailed records of control activities, outcomes, and any unexpected consequences. Regularly report findings to stakeholders, funding agencies, and regulatory bodies to maintain transparency.

Following these steps and tailoring each aspect to the specific circumstances can enable you to make a predator control plan and effectively address the challenges while considering the ethical implications of predator management. The key is to strike a balance that protects human interests and wildlife conservation.

Non-Lethal Predator Control Strategies

Improved Fencing

Reinforce existing fencing or install predator-specific barriers to prevent access to livestock. It's a humane method as it keeps predators away without harming them. Installing these fences won't be an issue for local authorities and is a minimal method that aids habitat preservation.

Guardian Animals

Introduce trained animals like dogs, llamas, or donkeys to deter predators from approaching livestock. Your livestock won't be bothered as these animals have natural deterrent instincts to stop predators from coming nearby. Getting trained dogs for protection won't be an issue. This positive approach to predator control promotes coexistence without direct harm to predators.

Deterrent Devices

- Use devices emitting sounds, lights, or odors to discourage predators from entering an area. You won't be harming predators with these gadgets while ensuring the domestic animals stay protected. However, before using any of these devices, please contact the local authorities, as there are restrictions for using specific deterrent devices. Although this method effectively keeps predators at bay, these devices can also create disturbances for other wildlife.

Livestock Management Practices

Implement strategies like changing grazing patterns or providing night penning to reduce predation risk. Executing this method will be possible through a change in livestock management practices where you reduce the exposure of the prey to the predators.

Lethal Predator Control Strategies

Selective Trapping

Use traps to capture specific predators, allowing for their release or euthanasia. There are mixed opinions about trapping, and regulations must be followed in most regions.

Culling

This is the controlled reduction of predator populations through targeted removal. It's a controversial practice and must be conducted ethically with the involvement of relevant authorities. If the predator is a wildlife species, go through the wildlife management laws and the rules you must comply with. Eradicating predator populations in a specific area can potentially disrupt the balance of the ecosystem.

Aerial Shooting

Employ aircraft to shoot predators from the air. This method is mainly used for large predators when attempts for ground capture fail. A dart gun is used to inject a sedative into the animal, making them unconscious and enabling their safe capture. Before using this method, you will need a special permit or a heads-up from the local authorities.

Toxicants/Poisons

You can also use chemical substances to poison predators. This method is considered inhumane and controversial, as it kills the predators in an inhumane manner, puts other animals at a higher risk of secondary poisoning, and can significantly disrupt the ecosystem.

Monitoring and Adaptive Management

Regularly assess the effectiveness of control strategies and adjust them based on results. With regular monitoring, you'll naturally minimize potential risk and improve your existing strategies if any discrepancy comes up.

Public Education and Outreach

Inform and engage the public about the rationale and methods of predator control. You can educate your neighbors and community members about the methods of predator control, establish their necessity, and determine the positive effects they will have on every species involved when done the right way.

Implementing a combination of these strategies while carefully considering ethical, legal, and environmental factors can contribute to effective and responsible predator control while minimizing negative impacts on ecosystems and wildlife. Regular assessment, community involvement, and adherence to ethical standards are essential for the success of any predator control program.

Integrated Predator Management

Integrated Predator Management (IPM) is a holistic approach that combines a variety of strategies to manage and mitigate the impact of predators on livestock, wildlife, and ecosystems. The key principle of IPM is to use a combination of non-lethal and lethal methods in an integrated and adaptive manner, considering the ecological, economic, and ethical aspects of predator control. This approach aims to achieve maximum effectiveness in reducing predation while minimizing harm to non-target species and maintaining a balance in the ecosystem.

Real-Life Examples of Successful Integrated Predator Management

Yellowstone National Park, USA

The reintroduction of gray wolves into Yellowstone in 1995 led to a shift in the ecosystem. To address conflicts with local ranchers, a combination of range riders, guardian animals (such as dogs and llamas), and targeted lethal control was employed. Integrating non-lethal and lethal measures contributed to reduced livestock predation and facilitated the coexistence of wolves and ranching communities.

NamibRand Nature Reserve, Namibia

In NamibRand, where cheetahs were preying on livestock, a combination of guard dogs, improved fencing, and community engagement initiatives were implemented. Non-lethal measures significantly reduced livestock losses, fostering a more positive relationship between the local community and the cheetah population.

France – Pyrenees Mountains

In regions where brown bears were preying on sheep, an integrated approach included guardian dogs, electric fencing, and compensation programs for affected farmers. Outcome: The combined measures led to a reduction in bear-caused livestock losses, contributing to both predator conservation and the protection of livestock.

Australia – Livestock Guardian Dogs

Livestock guardian dogs, such as the Kangal and Maremma breeds, are employed to protect livestock from foxes and dingoes. These dogs have successfully reduced predation on sheep and other livestock without resorting to lethal control, demonstrating the effectiveness of non-lethal methods.

IPM recognizes the importance of maintaining ecological balance by considering the broader impacts of control measures on non-target species and ecosystem health.

With its multifaceted and adaptive approach, Integrated Predator Management demonstrates that effective predator control can be achieved while promoting coexistence and minimizing negative impacts on predators and ecosystems. Success stories from various regions emphasize the importance of tailoring strategies to local circumstances and involving communities for sustainable and responsible outcomes.

Chapter 3: Choosing the Right Guard Animal

A comprehensive assessment of protection needs is a pivotal starting point in safeguarding livestock and property. This foundational chapter aims to enlighten you on the significance of this evaluation, emphasizing its role in informed decision-making when selecting guard animals and crafting protective strategies.

Before exploring guard animals and protective strategies, it's imperative to recognize the essence of conducting a thorough assessment. This process serves as the foundation upon which adequate protection is built. It involves tapping into factors like the type of livestock, geographical location, prevalent threats, and specific vulnerabilities unique to the property. Protection isn't a one-size-fits-all endeavor. Each livestock species demands a tailored approach. It starts with an assessment that includes understanding these threats, whether predatory wildlife, opportunistic thieves, or environmental challenges is paramount. Geography also plays a pivotal role in determining protection needs. The challenges faced by livestock and property in different regions vary significantly.

This chapter lays the groundwork, developing an understanding of the critical role played by a thorough assessment in devising effective protection plans. Armed with this foundational knowledge, you will be better equipped to navigate the nuanced world of livestock and property protection as you progress through the book.

Understanding Livestock Dynamics

To comprehensively understand the protection needs of your livestock, start by dissecting each species' behaviors, habits, and specific requirements. Cattle, for example, operate within a social hierarchy and may require protective measures that consider their herd dynamics. Sheep and goats, known for their flock mentality, might need different strategies. Poultry, with diverse breeds and foraging habits, demands a nuanced approach. Delve into the intricacies of their daily routines, feeding habits, and interactions to tailor protection that aligns seamlessly with their unique needs.

Cattle operate within a social hierarchy and may require protective measures.[34]

Property Dimensions

Beyond livestock specifics, the physical layout of your property plays a critical role in designing adequate protection. Evaluate the size of your property, noting features like natural barriers, open spaces, and secluded areas. Identify potential hiding spots for predators or areas where livestock may congregate. This scrutiny enables the strategic placement of guards and aids in designing fencing that complements the existing layout. An in-depth assessment of these physical dimensions provides the groundwork for a protection plan harmonizing with the terrain.

Geographical Insights

Geography forms the canvas upon which your protection strategies are painted. Assess the terrain – whether your property spans hilly landscapes, flat plains, or includes water features. Consider the climate, understanding temperature ranges, precipitation levels, and seasonal variations. Factor in regional nuances, such as nearby wildlife or prevalent environmental challenges. This comprehensive understanding guides decisions on guarding animal selection and implementing protective infrastructure that is seamlessly woven into the natural environment.

Microclimate Considerations

Identifying microclimates adds another layer of precision to your protection plan. Identify areas on your property that may experience unique weather patterns or temperature variations. Recognize spots that may be more prone to extreme conditions. Tailoring protection to these microclimates ensures that your strategies are practical and adaptable to the specific nuances of your property's climate. This granular approach enhances the well-being of your livestock by acknowledging and accommodating localized variations.

Documenting Vulnerabilities

Analyze your property critically to identify vulnerabilities in your existing protection measures. Look for potential weak points in fencing, areas prone to erosion, or access points for predators. Documenting these vulnerabilities serves as a roadmap for strategic fortification. This proactive approach minimizes risks, whether it involves reinforcing fences, implementing deterrents, or redesigning specific areas. It strengthens the overall robustness of your protection plan.

Evaluating Your Existing Protection Measures

As you safeguard your livestock and property, rigorous evaluation of your existing protection measures is imperative. This reflective process ensures that your current strategies are practical and aligned with your environment's evolving needs and challenges. Here's a step-by-step guide to aid you in this critical self-assessment:

Fencing Infrastructure

Begin by closely examining your fencing infrastructure. Assess its integrity, height, and material. Identify any signs of wear, damage, or potential weak points. Evaluate whether the fencing aligns with the specific needs of your livestock and property layout. Consider the type of predators in your region and assess whether your current fencing is a sufficient deterrent. Conduct periodic checks to ensure ongoing effectiveness.

Lighting Systems

Evaluate the lighting systems implemented on your property, especially in areas crucial for livestock and property protection. Adequate lighting not only deters potential threats but also aids in surveillance. Assess the coverage, brightness, and reliability of your current lighting installations. Consider whether they effectively illuminate vital areas and potential blind spots. Optimal lighting enhances overall security and can be a valuable deterrent during nighttime hours.

Alarm Systems

If you have alarm systems in place, scrutinize their functionality and coverage. Test the alarms periodically to ensure they are in working order. Assess whether the alarm systems cover critical areas and are equipped to detect potential threats promptly. Evaluate the responsiveness of your monitoring or response mechanisms tied to these alarms. A robust alarm system serves as an early warning mechanism, providing a crucial layer of protection.

Surveillance and Monitoring

Consider any surveillance or monitoring systems integrated into your protection measures. This could include security cameras, motion sensors, or other technological aids. Evaluate the coverage and clarity of your surveillance systems. Ensure that monitoring is consistent and that potential blind spots are addressed. Embrace technological advancements that align with your protection needs, enhancing your ability to detect and respond to threats effectively.

Integration of Guard Animals

For those incorporating guard animals into their protection plan, evaluate the effectiveness of their presence. Assess whether the selected species align with the specific threats in your region. Observe their behavior and interactions with livestock. Gauge whether they contribute to a sense of security and act as a deterrent to potential predators. The symbiotic relationship between guard animals and other protective measures is pivotal for a holistic defense strategy.

Response Protocols

Evaluate the response protocols that are in place. Assess whether you have clear and well-communicated action plans in case of a security breach. Review the coordination among individuals involved in responding to threats. Ensure that everyone on your property knows their roles and responsibilities during such situations. Regularly conduct drills to practice response protocols and address any areas needing improvement.

Regular Maintenance

Lastly, consider the maintenance aspect of your protection measures, regularly scheduled inspections, and maintenance checks for fencing, lighting, alarm systems, and other components. Address wear and tear promptly and replace or upgrade equipment as needed. A proactive approach to maintenance ensures that your protection measures remain reliable and effective over time.

Noise and Disturbance Analysis

Consider the potential impact of noise and disturbance on the functionality of your protection measures. Noise, whether from nearby construction, machinery, or natural elements like storms, can compromise the effectiveness of alarms or the vigilance of guard animals. Assess the decibel levels and frequency of these disturbances and strategize ways to mitigate their impact on your security systems.

Vegetation Management

Evaluate the role of vegetation in your protection infrastructure. Overgrown bushes or trees can compromise the visibility of security cameras and provide hiding spots for potential threats. Regularly assess and trim vegetation to maintain clear sightlines and eliminate potential blind spots, ensuring that natural growth does not hinder your protective measures.

Multi-Layered Approach

Assess how well your protection measures work together in a synergistic, multi-layered approach. Ensure that the various elements – fencing, lighting, alarms, and guard animals – complement each other to create a robust defense system. Consider potential gaps or overlaps in coverage and fine-tune your strategy to achieve optimal synergy among the different layers of protection.

Neighbor Collaboration

Explore collaboration with neighboring properties to enhance collective security. Evaluate the possibility of sharing a communication network or coordinating protection efforts. Open communication with neighbors can foster a sense of community protection, enabling a quicker and more effective response to potential threats that transcend property boundaries.

Adaptability to Emerging Threats

Anticipate and assess how well your protection measures can adapt to emerging threats. Stay informed about new predator species in the region, evolving environmental conditions, and technological advancements that could impact your defense strategies. Develop a proactive mindset that allows your protection plan's continual evolution to address emerging challenges effectively.

Accessibility for Emergency Services

Evaluate the accessibility of your property for emergency services. Ensure that entrances are marked and paths are easily navigable. This consideration is crucial for facilitating a swift response from emergency services in case of incidents requiring their intervention, thus contributing to your livestock's overall safety and well-being.

Livestock Identification Measures

Assess the adequacy of your livestock identification measures. This includes ear tags, microchips, or other identification methods. Clear and compelling identification is essential for managing your livestock. It plays a crucial role in recovery efforts in the unfortunate event of theft or loss.

Wildlife-Friendly Measures

Evaluate whether your protection strategies consider the well-being of local wildlife. Implement measures that deter threats to livestock while minimizing harm to native species. This could involve using wildlife-friendly fencing or deterrents that specifically target potential predators without causing harm to non-threatening wildlife.

Cybersecurity Measures

If you have technologically advanced protection systems, assess their vulnerability to cyber threats. Implement robust cybersecurity measures to safeguard against unauthorized access or tampering. Regularly update software and firmware to address potential vulnerabilities and stay ahead of evolving cyber threats, as digital systems used for livestock management and security systems can be a potential target.

Legal Compliance

Ensure that your protection measures comply with local regulations and zoning laws. This includes adhering to any restrictions on fencing height, lighting, or the use of guard animals. Legal compliance avoids potential legal issues and ensures your protective measures align with community standards and regulations.

By meticulously exploring these facets in extreme detail, you gather information and develop a comprehensive understanding, which is the bedrock for informed and tailored protection strategies. This depth of insight positions you to navigate the complexities of livestock and property protection with precision and adaptability.

Clarifying Specific Protection Needs

In pursuing a robust defense strategy, the clarity of specific protection needs becomes paramount. Each step in this process requires a nuanced understanding, allowing for the precise tailoring of defenses to mitigate identified risks. Let's delve into the details:

Prioritize Critical Areas

Initiate by meticulously identifying and prioritizing critical areas on your property. These could range from vulnerable entry points to zones with high livestock concentration or areas susceptible to environmental risks. This strategic prioritization forms the foundation for targeted resource allocation. For prioritized critical areas, elevate the fortification of fencing and physical barriers. Choose materials and designs that align precisely with identified threats. Heighten the structure to a level that acts as an effective deterrent against predators.

Evaluate Livestock Concentration

Identify areas where livestock concentration is pronounced. These spaces demand heightened protective measures. Consider strategies such as reinforced fencing, increased lighting, or advanced surveillance to fortify these zones against potential threats.

Identify High-Risk Zones

Scrutinize the landscape to identify high-risk zones based on the previously assessed vulnerabilities. Dense vegetation, uneven terrain, or proximity to natural habitats could elevate risks. Tailoring defenses in these zones employs strategies like vegetation clearance and specialized fencing.

Customize Protection for Specific Livestock

Precision is critical when customizing protection for each type of livestock. Recognize the unique vulnerabilities and behaviors associated with different species. Craft tailored strategies that address the distinct challenges posed by each livestock category.

Employ Advanced Surveillance in High-Risk Zones

High-risk zones demand a sophisticated surveillance approach. Deploy advanced technologies like infrared cameras or sensors with an extended range. This technological investment enhances monitoring and provides early detection capabilities, especially in areas susceptible to environmental challenges.

Integrate Guard Animals Strategically

Strategically position guard animals based on the prioritized critical areas. Optimize their locations to cover zones effectively. Rotation of guard animals may be necessary to maximize their impact on deterrence, aligning with the ever-changing landscape of potential threats.

Monitor Environmental Changes

Maintain a vigilant stance toward environmental changes that may impact protection needs. Seasonal variations, migration patterns of potential threats, or alterations in vegetation should prompt adaptive adjustments to your defense strategy.

Invest in Targeted Technologies

Invest strategically in technologies specifically designed to counter identified risks. This may include specialized alarms, tracking devices for high-value livestock, or technologies tailored to mitigate environmental risks. Precision in technology investments ensures optimal resource utilization.

Evaluate Natural Barriers

Conduct a comprehensive assessment of the natural barriers present on your property, such as rivers, cliffs, or dense forests. Understand their potential as deterrents for unauthorized entry or predators. Simultaneously, evaluate how these features might create challenges or opportunities for your livestock as well as potential threats. Consider factors such as ease of access for wildlife or the impact of terrain on visibility.

Implement Biosecurity Measures

Integrate a robust biosecurity system to prevent the introduction and spread of diseases within your livestock. This involves implementing strict quarantine protocols for new animals, conducting regular health checks, and ensuring proper waste disposal practices. Evaluate the effectiveness of these measures in maintaining the health and well-being of your livestock while considering factors like disease prevalence in your region.

Enhance Communication Systems

Upgrade your communication systems to ensure swift and effective coordination during emergencies. This may involve investing in reliable two-way radios, mobile phones with consistent coverage, or community alert systems. Evaluate the reach and reliability of these systems while considering factors such as terrain and potential interference.

Utilize Smart Technologies

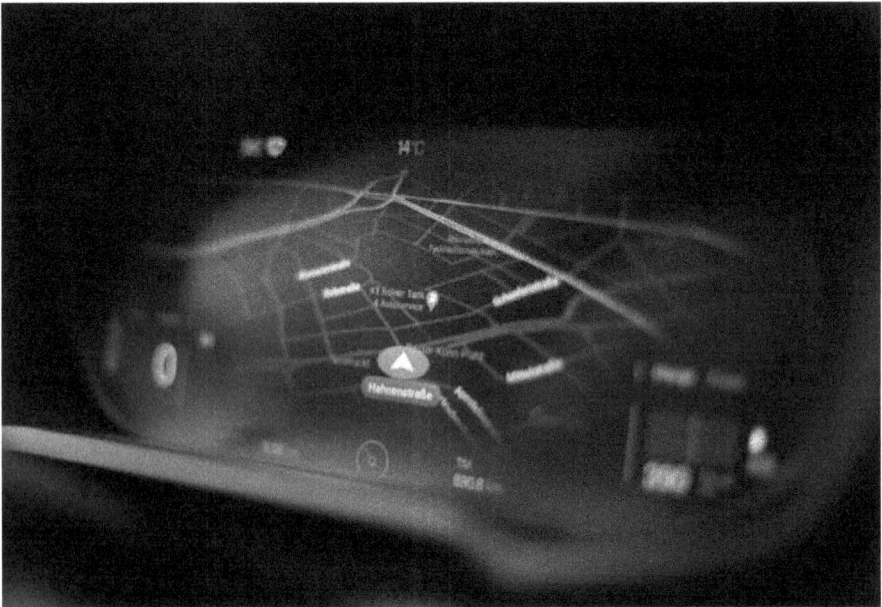

A GPS tracking device can help you monitor your livestock's movements.[85]

Explore the integration of smart technologies to enhance your overall security measures. Consider employing GPS tracking devices for your livestock to monitor their movements in real-time. Additionally, assess the feasibility of using drones for aerial surveillance, providing a bird's-eye view of your property. Evaluate the practicality and effectiveness of these technologies in your specific context.

Investigate Local Wildlife Patterns

Gain a deep understanding of your area's local wildlife patterns and behaviors. This knowledge is crucial for crafting defenses, considering interactions between domestic animals, wildlife, and potential predators. Evaluate how wildlife behaviors might impact your livestock and adapt your protective measures accordingly. Consider factors such as migration patterns, feeding habits, and potential conflicts.

Establish Secure Storage

Create secure storage facilities for valuable equipment, feed, and other essentials. Assess the design and construction of these storage areas, considering factors such as durability, accessibility, and resistance to tampering. Evaluate how these secure storage spaces contribute to property security and protection against theft or damage.

Engage in Continuous Training

Promote ongoing and comprehensive training programs for individuals involved in livestock management. This includes educating them on response protocols and providing continuous training on identifying potential risks and implementing preventive measures. Evaluate the effectiveness of training programs through regular assessments and feedback mechanisms.

Investigate Animal Theft Prevention Measures

If livestock theft is a concern, take specific measures to prevent such incidents. This could involve implementing identification methods, such as microchipping or unique markings, to make stolen animals easily traceable. Evaluate the success of these prevention measures by tracking incidents and recovery rates.

Develop Relationships with Authorities

Establish and nurture relationships with local law enforcement and animal control authorities. Evaluate the effectiveness of these relationships in creating a collaborative approach to addressing security concerns. Assess the support and insights authorities provide to enhance overall livestock and property security.

Monitor Weather-Related Risks

Consider and monitor weather-related risks that might affect your livestock and property. Develop strategies to safeguard against flooding or extreme weather events, including elevated platforms for shelter or flood-resistant enclosures. Evaluate the resilience of these strategies in the face of varying weather conditions.

Invest in Training for Guard Animals

Provide specialized and ongoing training for guard animals to enhance their effectiveness as protectors. This could include obedience training, exposure to various environmental conditions, and reinforcement of desired protective behaviors. Evaluate the impact of training on the behavior and performance of guard animals through regular assessments.

Explore Insurance Options

Investigate insurance options that cover losses related to livestock and property security. Evaluate the terms and coverage provided by different insurance plans, considering factors such as the financial impact of potential security incidents. Assess the reliability and responsiveness of insurance providers in the aftermath of security-related losses.

Understanding these factors enables you to thoroughly understand the nuances and intricacies of implementing these protection measures. This detailed evaluation forms the basis for a comprehensive and adaptive defense strategy tailored to your unique context and requirements.

Chapter 4: Livestock Guardian Dogs: Breeds and Traits

This chapter introduces you to livestock guardian dogs, exploring the different breeds and the traits that make them effective in protecting livestock and property. It explains why these animals are great livestock guardians, why breed selection is crucial when choosing livestock guardian dogs, and how certain breeds are better suited to specific environments and livestock. The chapter also provides a list of the most well-known guard breeds used as livestock guardians (along with their characters and temperament) and tips on choosing the right breed based on specific needs, climate, livestock, and more.

Dog as guardian.[86]

The Importance of Livestock Guardian Dogs

Using guardian dogs to safeguard livestock is the most effective way of keeping predators like carnivores (both four-legged and winged) or other dogs at bay. In practice, dogs are typically used for guarding smaller animals, like poultry, and ruminants, like goats and sheep, as these are more vulnerable to predators due to their size. However, some dog breeds can also work with large-bodied livestock, like horses and cows.

Livestock guardian dogs have a few characteristics in common, including living and moving around the herd or flock. They're also larger in size and easy to work with, meaning they get along with the animals they are guarding, their owners, and other guard dogs, if there are any (large farms typically necessitate more than one livestock guardian dog). They have been bred to protect and avoid hurting the animals they guard, even if they're hungry or being attacked by them. At the same time, they're usually unfriendly with other animals, including stray and kept dogs that wander into their territory. A good guardian dog keeps even the neighbor's dogs and cats away, which is particularly good for protecting poultry. They also watch over the livestock's behavior, which can alert them of the presence of predators and other threats.

Even if you have unwanted visitors that won't harm your farm animals, they can still damage your property and steal food from your animals. Livestock guardian dogs will prevent this from occurring. They are independent thinkers, meaning they won't look for commands but take the action they are trained to take immediately upon noticing a potential threat.

Other benefits of using dogs as livestock guardians include an increase in profit (with fewer losses due to predators, animal husbandry becomes more profitable), proactive protection instead of mitigating damages, elimination of the need for other, more costly control measures, like traps and hunting, reducing the likelihood of the livestock coming in contact with wild animals carrying illnesses, and longer effectiveness at lower investment in labor and time.

Livestock guardian dogs are particularly effective with larger flocks and herds (keeping them for small groups may not be as cost-effective) in areas with high predation rates. When trained and cared for properly, canine guardians represent an excellent investment, especially for safeguarding small animals.

The Most Popular Livestock Guardian Dog Breeds

Not all dogs can become livestock guardians. Different breeds possess predator-specific traits that make them more effective at deterring particular types of predators. Below, you'll find the most popular livestock guardian dog breeds, their core characteristics, and information about socialization, livestock compatibility, and health.

Great Pyrenees

The Great Pyrenees is one of the largest dog breeds.[87]

One of the largest guard dog breeds is the Great Pyrenees, which originates from the French and Spanish royal courts. Due to its calm and regal demeanor, this canine is most commonly used for protecting sheep. However, because it's always looking for action, it can work well with smaller animals, too – the more it has to walk around following them, the better. At the same time, Great Pyrenees are incredibly gentle and patient dogs, so you won't have to worry about them trampling poultry and young livestock. They're also perfect for family-owned farms as they are great with children, too.

Tall and built like a miniature horse, this dog has a long, double-layered, white fluffy coat and double dew claws on its rear limbs. They thrive in colder climates and can't stand higher temperatures because of their fine, wooly undercoat. They are also prone to hip dysplasia (abnormal tissue growth), especially if one or both of their parents had the condition.

Anatolian Shepherd

Anatolian Shepherds are known for their intelligence and loyalty.[38]

Known for their intelligence and loyalty, Anatolian Shepherds are the embodiment of the perfect guard dog. They're naturally independent and calm but tend to bark excessively when they perceive a threat. This usually occurs when predators get too close; otherwise, these canines won't draw attention to themselves. If they do, you can be sure they're doing their job of protecting your animals and property. They can be paired up with livestock of all sizes, and you can be assured they'll keep them safe while you tend to your other responsibilities on your farm/house.

The Anatolians are large and muscular dogs with short fur, which means they fare well in hot weather. You can leave them alone with the herd or flock for several days, and they'll be fine. They have very few health issues, but they require intensive training. You have to be assertive when training them so they can learn what's required of them. Otherwise, they'll act independently, and although they're unlikely to hurt the livestock, they might damage your property in their overzealous attempt to chase away a perceived threat.

Komondor

Komondors are muscular canines.[89]

Like the Anatolians, Komondors are muscular canines, which make them perfect for guarding large livestock or using them in areas where larger predators represent a frequent threat. Instead of barking, they launch into action and chase away predators or other intruders that wander onto your property. Their sheer size alone can be enough to deter small nuisances and for the livestock to respect them. They're very energetic, so they are recommended for larger territories where they can run around and actively safeguard larger herds or flocks of farm animals.

Komondors have a thick, white coat that is prone to matting. Still, it keeps them warm in the chilly winters in colder climates (they originate from Hungary). The unique appearance of their coat also helps them blend in well with sheep, which is why they are most commonly used for protecting these ruminants. Komondors require intensive training and socialization with the livestock before they can be trusted to safeguard them. Once the Komondor familiarizes itself with the herd or flock, they are tasked to protect, along with the territory, a strong bond is formed, and they'll go to great lengths to protect them. They are characterized by strong health and lengthy and active life.

Caucasian Shepherd Dog

Caucasian Shepherd Dogs were used to safeguard livestock.[40]

Hailing from Russia, the Caucasian Shepherd Dog was once used to safeguard livestock from large predators like wolves and bears. These are increasingly territorial canines with exceptional guard instincts. Once they perceive a threat, they'll take it on with confidence, so you won't have to worry about the safety of your livestock while busy with other tasks.

With their thick, double-layered fur, these dogs thrive in colder climates and aren't meant to be out in the sun all day in hot weather. They have strong bodies, which makes them excellent protection against predators, but they're gentle enough not to harm small livestock. Still, in practice, they are typically used for guarding large or medium-bodied ruminants. They have few health issues and can live between 10 and 11 years.

Maremma Sheepdog

Maremma Sheepdogs have a muscular build.⁴¹

The Maremma Sheepdog is a breed with rich, white fur and a muscular build meant for safeguarding livestock from predators of all sizes. While protecting the farm animals and bonding with them very easily, this canine won't hesitate to attack intruders. They are known to be particularly protective of young animals – and even remain wary of their owner's actions around youngsters. They're the perfect option for protection against four-legged predators like coyotes and foxes because they won't let themselves be outsmarted by these cunning creatures. The Maremmas are also suspicious and will sense a threat by observing the farm animals' behavior. They alert the intruders by barking loudly, ensuring they are heard and discouraging them from advancing into their territory.

They're perfect guards for sheep, especially if the animals are kept outside during mild and moderate winters. They also like to work in groups as they are very social, so they can be employed alongside other livestock guardian dogs. They have few health issues but are prone to hereditary hip dysplasia.

Kuvasz

The Kuvasz has Hungarian origins.[42]

Like the Komondor, the Kuvasz also has Hungarian origins. They are fierce and strong canines, always ready to protect their territory and herd/flock. They form strong bonds with the owner and the livestock. While they won't hesitate to take action against a perceived threat, they aren't completely independent. They thrive with regular guidance and commands. At the same time, they are somewhat more challenging to train because they tend to establish a leadership position at an early age. For the same reason, they are best employed alone (without other guard dogs) or with canines they've been socialized with since puppyhood.

The Kuvasz are excellent choices for ranches and farms with large livestock breeds. They won't tolerate the aggressive behavior of other species, including farm animals like poultry, but they won't harm them inadvertently. They have a corded white coat specifically developed to blend in with goats and sheep that they have been used to guard since ancient times. They tolerate all temperatures fairly well and typically enjoy good health.

Akbash

The Akbash is smaller than most canines used for livestock protection.[45]

Like many other livestock guardian dogs, the Akbash has white fur, albeit varying in length. They're also smaller than most canines used for livestock protection, often slenderer than stout. Still, they're known to be excellent guards against predatory carnivores like wolves. Along with their name, which translates as "white head," these dogs hail from Turkey.

They are independent but require a fair bit of socialization before becoming efficient guardians and good companions to their herd or flock. They'll keep a vigilant watch once they familiarize themselves with their territory and companions. They're non-herding, making them suitable for safeguarding cattle and sheep in a smaller territory. They don't have many health issues and can serve for a long time in most climates.

Tosa Inu

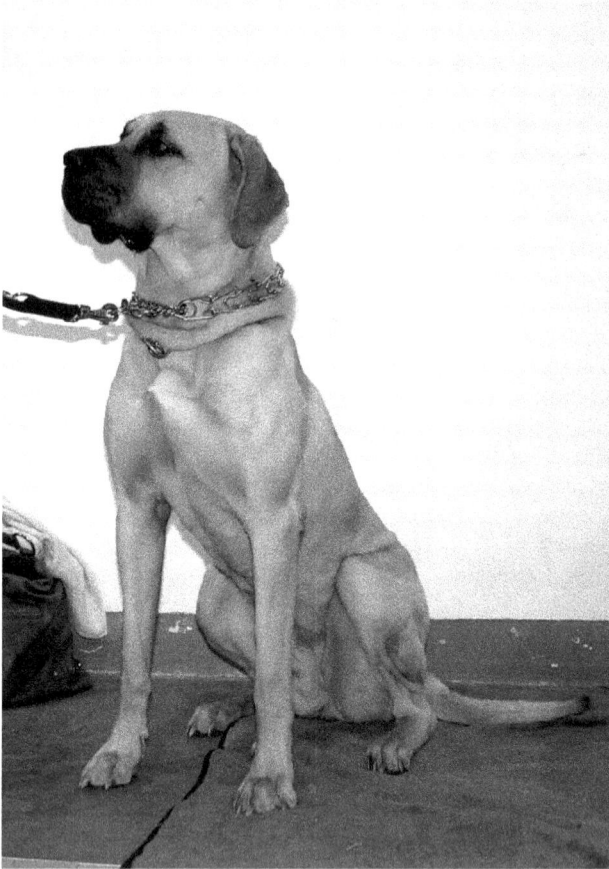

Tosa Inus can reach up to 130 pounds."

Unlike the previous breed, the Tosa Inu is much larger and can reach up to 130 pounds in weight. One of the biggest advantages of a dog this size is that they can become more vigilant as they don't require as much exercise as smaller breeds. Despite their intimidating presence (handy when they need to scare off intruders), they're gentle with their herd or flock. At the same time, their exceptionally high prey drive will ensure that no predator will endanger your livestock or property. Moreover, they require direction, and despite loving to guard passively, they don't like to be without a task.

Unlike other guardian breeds, the Tosa Inu isn't aggressive toward people. Their short, light-brown fur makes them suitable for all climates. They're, however, prone to developing joint issues and bone diseases, along with cancer.

Tibetan Mastiff

The Tibetan Mastiff has an imposing presence."

With their body weight reaching up to a staggering 160 pounds, the Tibetan Mastiff has an imposing presence. Like the previous large canine breed, this one also has a short coat and a short tail. Requiring moderate exercise levels, these make excellent herd dogs for herds and flocks of all sizes. They thrive in colder climates because, despite being short, their fur is relatively dense. However, they can withstand moderately warm temperatures as long as they don't need to run around all day.

Tibetan Mastiffs are incredibly territorial, making them the perfect guard dog. They'll sense intruders from far away and launch into action to protect your farm animals and property if needed. Despite their high prey drive, they're gentle giants when it comes to their herd or flock, and they socialize well with their owners (including small children). They are prone to having eye issues and hereditary conditions like hip and elbow dysplasia.

How to Choose the Right Livestock Guardian Dog Breed

If you are wondering how to choose the right breed based on your needs, livestock, and climate, here are a few tips to help you make an informed decision.

Determine Your Needs

The first step in finding an adequate guard dog is determining your needs based on the animals you keep and where you keep them. Do you have predominantly large livestock, like cattle or horses? If so, you'll need a low-energy dog. However, suppose you have smaller animals or ones that need to be herded. In that case, a high-energy canine will thrive on running around. By contrast, these dogs won't be a good fit for indoor guarding as they'll get bored, inattentive, or aggressive. Also, consider how much space the canine guardians will need to cover. If you have a large farm with multiple pastures, you'll likely need several dogs – in which case, opt for ones that work well in groups. Answering these and other questions regarding your requirements and conditions will help you find the canine that best matches them.

Think about Your Guard Dog's Needs

Another crucial aspect to consider is all your canine guard's needs. While most livestock guardian dogs thrive on being independent workers, some require more attention and care than others. Some dogs can be left alone to guard for days, and you'll need to provide them with enough food and water for this time. These are great if you live away from your farm and can only visit on certain days. Other dogs are more social and thrive better if they interact with their owner daily. Think about your climate. Guard dogs live outside, but if you live in a climate with unstable weather or exceedingly warm temperatures, your canine protector will need some sort of shelter from the elements.

Research the Potential Breeds and Dogs

Once you have your needs and the condition down, you can research the different guard dog breeds to narrow down your choice. Here, consider *training*. Some breeders train guard dogs for exact purposes. However, you'll still need to take care of socializing your canine on your property and with the animals it will be guarding and working alongside (if you have multiple guard dogs). Depending on what type of animals you have, you might also have to think about specialized training for tasks like herding, for example. Consider how much you are willing to invest in training (some dogs require far more training than others) before opting for one breed or another. When you find the right breed, you can proceed to look for the individual dogs. Remember, not all dogs will be suitable for becoming livestock guardians despite their breed being known as protectors.

Is Roaming an Option?

While livestock guardian dogs can be trained to stick to a fenced-in territory, some are more prone to roaming. High-energy dogs will prefer to cover a larger distance when looking for prey, and if you have a small farm, this might take them outside your property. Besides causing potential issues with neighbors, this can also be problematic if they refuse to stay inside the small area you placed them in alongside the herd or flock they are supposed to guard. If you want your canine guardians to remain in small pastures, opt for a non-roaming breed that will be satisfied with passive protection measures, like watching for signs of predators from livestock behavior.

Consider the Canine's Temperament

While most livestock guardians are characterized by a calm temperament, those requiring higher activity levels might become anxious or aggressive in small spaces. At the same time, you don't want your guard dog to be shy or cower in front of other animals, especially if you need them to protect against predators. *Prey drive* is a dog's instinctive characteristic to find, pursue, and capture another animal. Most livestock guardian dogs are bred not to have a strong prey drive so that they can guard farm animals instead of hunting and hurting them. However, some canine guardians will still instinctively pursue other animals that are encroaching or threatening to encroach on their territory. This can be a good thing for keeping predatory carnivores at bay. In this case, investigating whether a threat exists (as most canines with a low prey drive do) isn't enough. They need to actively engage against the intruders. If you live in an area with a high prevalence of predators, you'll need a dog with a high prey drive but one that won't harm your livestock. Here, the goal is to find a balance between calmness and alertness. However, if you don't have many predators in the area and your main concern is to have a herding dog that eventually scares away critters that might damage your property and carry diseases, then you'll need a more mild-mannered dog with a lower prey drive to avoid them biting or chasing the farm animals.

Barking is another factor to consider. Do you want your canine guard to alert you of a threat to your livestock with intense barking but then wait for your orders unless the intruder attacks? If not, then you need an independent thinker who leaps into action instead of just altering with barking or howling. Moreover, barkers might not get along with certain types of animals and might get even more agitated and confused. While being alerted to a threat is beneficial for the guard dog, creating confusion can make them more vulnerable to predators (for example, they might run in the opposite direction than where they are supposed to run and end up in an area where predators can get to them).

Look into the Dog's Interactions with the Livestock

Consider how you want the canine guardians to interact with your livestock. Do you want your stock to follow the dog's guidance when herding but not be afraid of the dog? If yes, look for a breed with a naturally imposing demeanor without being overly dominant. They should be cautious, but it is easy to socialize with farm animals. Some breeds prefer to guard from a distance and not be picked or accidentally stepped on by livestock. If you have to keep larger animals, you don't want a dog that will bite them if they accidentally prod and poke it. Likewise, some dog breeds prefer running around the stock territory, while others walk calmly with your livestock, quietly observing their behavior. The latter will also readily sleep next to the animals, so if this is something you need, look for breeds that don't mind interacting and socializing with their herd flock.

Chapter 5: Training, Feeding, and Care

This chapter will guide you through the fundamentals of LGD training. You'll understand what obedience or communication training is and why it's an essential precursor to socialization. You'll also find LGD training tips, tricks, core commands, and other commands to teach your dog. Then, you'll find out about the different nutrition options you can choose from and understand the factors that determine the type and amount of food your dog needs to thrive. Finally, you'll learn about veterinary and dental care, vaccinations, spotting signs of illness, parasite control, and grooming.

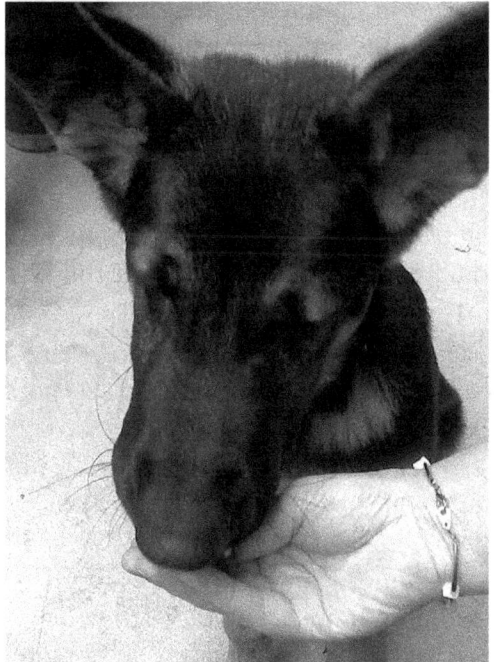

Guardian dogs require proper care.[46]

Training Your Livestock Guard Dog

The belief that guard dogs don't need to interact and bond with humans is a very common misconception. Like all others, livestock guard dogs crave to build companionship with their humans. While LGDs (livestock guardian dogs) are highly intelligent and capable of protecting livestock, even without constant supervision, they still turn to their owners for support, guidance, approval, and, most importantly, partnership.

Training LGDs is a long process. However, it shouldn't be too hard to do with the right techniques and tools. If you choose the right breed for the intended person, it should respond to your efforts as long as the training sessions are fun, light, and interesting.

Obedience (Communication) Training

When training an LGD, you must start with obedience training before introducing it to the livestock it protects. This will set it up for success in its role as a guard dog and ensure that it responds to your commands and engages in desirable behaviors. Obedience training is integral for healthy connections and interactions and the safety of your dog, livestock, and people.

Guard dogs are usually very large and powerful. If they're not obedience trained, any sudden movement or action they make could put others in danger. Imagine your large Mastiff jumping up on a child (even with the intention of playing with them). If you can't get the dog to listen to you, it would probably hurt that child.

It could also endanger itself if it doesn't listen to your commands. For instance, if the dog attacks a predator and you notice that the animal is trying to get away, the dog won't respond if you command it to "come" or let go. The predator, in that case, could hurt your dog. In some cases, LDGs that have never witnessed birth could kill newborn livestock, mistaking them as potential sources of danger. This is another situation where obedience training comes in handy.

Building a strong bond is both a foundation and an outcome of obedience training. If you want your dog to listen to you, you must invest time and effort into building a strong relationship with it. You must create a partnership where you both care for, respect, and look out for each other. Your dog will reciprocate how you treat it and what you feel for it.

Many dog trainers suggest that "obedience training is a dated term, and that the word 'obedience' should be replaced with 'communication.'" You should never approach your dog from a place of power and control. Instead, think of it as a way to teach your dog how to work with you and an opportunity to learn how to work with it. By maintaining the mindset of partnership and communication, you will eventually get the dog to obey you.

Positive Training Techniques

Positive training methods require you to reinforce desirable behaviors rather than using punishment and shame to deter your dog from undesirable behaviors. Using praise words, play breaks, and treats and making training sessions feel more like play will allow your dog to perceive training and obedience as fun and rewarding rather than dutiful and overbearing.

When training your dog, you should be mindful of its needs and behaviors. For instance, if it's engaging in unusual behaviors or barking more than usual, you need to show concern. Check if there's something it's barking at, pat it, and reassure it. Responding to your dog's needs and concerns will be perceived as a sign of care and respect, further strengthening your bond and enhancing the effectiveness of your training efforts. Not only is using positive training methods highly effective, but it's also the only ethical and humane way to treat your dog.

Tips and Tricks for Training Your Dog

1. **Release All Pent-Up Energy.** If your dog is excited and all worked up during the training session, then you're going to struggle to teach them anything. Ensure they've had enough time to exercise and play so they're calmer and less hyper when you start.

2. **Create a Distraction-Free Zone.** Most dogs are very easily distracted by any sound, object, or even smell that they find interesting. Dogs, especially those that have never been trained, usually find it hard to learn new things. Training them in a place where they're likely to encounter various external stimuli doesn't make it any easier for them. Choose a distraction-free environment for your training sessions for more fruitful learning experiences.

3. **Most Importantly, Enjoy.** Dogs are naturally playful creatures. They respond and engage with things that they perceive as fun. Your training sessions should be fun and feel like play rather than a chore. Use this as an opportunity to bond with your dog and

spend some quality, fun time together.

4. **Set Up a Reward System.** You need to use rewards to reinforce good behavior by giving the dog something it wants whenever it responds to one of your cues. Getting to know your dog allows you to determine which reward it wants the most. Some dogs prefer treats, some love to play with their favorite toy for a few minutes, and for others, pats, belly rubs, and a few praise words will do the trick.

5. **Know When Breaks Are Needed.** Chances are that your efforts will backfire if you resume training your dog when you're both clearly frustrated. Sometimes, both of you should take a break for a few days. When you're on break, however, avoid making any cues or commands to your dog; if it doesn't respond, you'll have to return to training it. You should also always try to end your session with success.

6. **Try Your Commands in Different Settings.** If you've successfully gotten your dog to "come," for instance, in the backyard, you have to try to get it to respond to the command in the park, on the porch, or inside the house. Some dogs don't understand that their response to a given command doesn't depend on the context or setting, so you should test out their responses in different places.

7. **Introduce Distractions.** If your dog successfully responds to your commands in different settings, you need to gradually introduce distractions to the context. You must ensure that your dog listens to you even when it finds something more interesting to do or explore. Remember that as a livestock guard, your dog will be surrounded by multiple distractions, so this step is essential. Once you complete its basic obedience training, you have to work on training it in a busy park, around other people and animals, and around livestock. You should also train it even when it's still hyperactive and hasn't had the chance to release its excess energy. Your training is successful when your dog responds to you no matter how it feels and regardless of its surroundings.

The duration of the training depends on how responsive your dog is. However, in most cases, you'll have to consistently train your dog for several months before it's ready to guard livestock. Don't give up, and remember that no matter how impossible it may feel, all dogs are trainable if you invest the time, effort, and consistency they need.

Expect your dog's learning pace to vary across different commands. It may pick up on some in just a few days and take weeks to learn from others. Avoiding frustration and staying patient is the key. You should also be mindful of when you stop or decrease the rewards. You have to do it when you're certain you won't lose your ground.

The 6 Core Commands

Several commands come in handy for a livestock guard dog; however, the 6 most important ones are:

1. **Look at Me.** This command is very helpful and usually easy for dogs to learn. It can set you up for success in the rest of your training because it encourages your dog to look at you and focus on what you have to say. You can use this command as a distraction if you need it to stop doing something it shouldn't do. It also allows you to (usually) get its attention regardless of the situation.

2. **Sit.** This command is necessary for your dog to learn before you can teach it to "stay." It is easier for dogs to learn to stay when they're already sitting down.

3. **Stay.** Teaching your dog to stay is crucial because, in many cases, it's the only way you can get it to back away for its safety or stop it from hurting others.

4. **Come.** Like the "stay" command, "come" can be used to stop your dog from harming itself or others. It is often a safer solution to the problem as well.

5. **Leave It.** This is another command that can both protect your dog and the livestock. If you notice a predator trying to get away or your dog mistakenly attacks livestock (newborn or new livestock), you can safely ask it to leave the animal alone.

6. **Off.** Another easy command you can teach your dog is asking them to get off if they jump on you or others. Many dogs stop jumping on people entirely if their owners repeat this command enough for them to understand that this is something that they shouldn't be doing.

Other helpful but not essential commands include stand, down, and shake. Some people also ask their dogs to bark on demand through a "speak" command. This command can actually help enhance the dog's protective instincts, encouraging it to bark when something goes wrong.

Duration and Challenges

While there are general guidelines you need to follow when training your LGD, you have to keep in mind that the training process is not one-size-fits-all. Like humans, each dog has a unique personality that makes it more responsive to certain types of training on command. While some friendlier and naturally protective dogs are more inclined to bond with and guard livestock, others might need more time to understand what's asked of them. This also applies to your livestock. Some will easily adapt to and respond well to the dog's presence. In contrast, others will initially show signs of aggression toward the dog.

Every livestock and LGD owner experiences unique challenges throughout the process because the situation solely depends on how the animals deal with each other. The socialization process is the most crucial step. It is where most problems arise and when you have to be the most patient and creative in finding solutions. You should also know that the training process requires a lot of trial and error until you figure out what works best for your dog.

The best part is that if you decide to acquire and train more dogs later on, you will face significantly fewer challenges. You will be more experienced and prepared, and the puppies will be more responsive because they'll naturally model the trained LGD's behaviors. In many cases, the older LGDs correct the younger puppies, making your only responsibility overseeing and monitoring the process.

When thinking of getting an LGD, you should also consider getting more than one dog. LGDs work best in packs, are likely to exhibit significantly fewer behavioral issues and experience training challenges when working in groups. Most importantly, one dog cannot effectively control predators and protect your entire ranch. The exact number of guard animals you need, however, depends on the size of your ranch, the number and type of livestock you own, and the nature of surrounding predators.

Feeding Your LGD

Suppose you've been reading into LGD care and feeding for a while. In that case, you've probably noticed that the greatest debate regarding LGD nutrition is whether you should opt for commercial or raw food. Many professionals suggest that LGDs should be fed raw food since they're descendants of wolves. In contrast, others argue that domesticated dogs have entirely different dietary needs and digestive systems, calling for a more varied and balanced diet. There is no solid right or wrong approach to how you should feed your dog as long as it's healthy and getting all the nutrients it needs to thrive.

Commercial Dog Food

Most LGD owners prefer to feed their dogs high-quality commercial food (some people also recommend grain-free types), as it contains the right balance of proteins, fats, carbohydrates, vitamins, and minerals. This is a good place to start, and you can always change your mind and try different diets further down the road. Make sure, however, to consult a vet before making any substantial differences.

Numerous commercial dog food brands are on the market, ranging from highly affordable to extremely expensive choices. Unfortunately, dog owners have found time and time again that you get what you pay for in terms of quality and nutritional value. Cheap brands will not satisfy your dog's nutritional needs, always leaving it hungry and fatigued. You'll end up having to feed it more, which can cause the dog to become overweight. Even when this happens, your dog will still be nutritionally deprived. Use very large and durable bowls to feed your dog.

Feeding Amounts

You can switch between a few high-quality brands so your dog doesn't get bored after a while. Adult dogs should generally be fed twice daily, while puppies require an additional meal. That said, some dog owners prefer to feed puppies around 4 times a day until they're at least three months old. While these are generic insights, you should consult your vet because they'll better understand your dog's unique needs. The exact amount of food that a dog needs depends on their weight and activity levels. Older, pregnant, and lactating dogs and those with health conditions require specific feeding requirements, too.

If you have many dogs on your ranch, feeding each of them twice a day can be a very daunting task. This is why many ranch owners prefer to free-feed their LGDs. If you must do that as well, try to keep a watchful eye on your dogs' eating habits, as well as their weight, to make sure that they're not putting on more weight than what is considered healthy.

If you plan on putting your dog on a raw diet, you should also consult your vet on how to safely implement it and ensure that your dog meets its nutritional needs. Some brands offer frozen, dried, and dehydrated raw food options for dogs, which are considered convenient and easy to serve.

Healthcare and Routine Care

Veterinary Care

- Adult dogs should get an annual veterinary examination (at least).
- Puppies (up to 4 months old) should see the vet every 3 to 4 weeks.
- Dogs over 7 years old should get at least 2 veterinary examinations a year.

Signs of Illness

Dog owners can easily sport signs of illness by observing changes in their dog's behavior. You should take your dog to the vet if you notice changes in appetite, activity levels, urination frequency, itchiness, lameness, or more obvious signs of illness.

Vaccinations

Dogs have to be vaccinated just as people do. Follow up with your vet to stay on top of your dog's routine vaccinations to protect it against diseases. Rabies, distemper, and parvovirus are considered core vaccines. However, depending on the environmental and regional circumstances, your dog might need additional vaccines.

Parasite Control

Tapeworms, roundworms, whipworms, and hookworms are among the main intestinal parasites that dogs can develop. These parasites can severely damage the animal's digestive system and hinder its ability to absorb the nutrients it needs. The best way to detect whether your dog has an intestinal parasite is to get a fecal sample tested at least once a year. Make sure to clean up your dog's feces frequently, as some parasites can be transferred to humans and other animals.

Some parasites, like heartworms, which are often fatal, are transmitted through mosquito bites. Dogs can also contract external parasites like mange mites, fleas, and ticks. You can use specialized body sprays as preventative measures to protect your dog.

Dental Care

Feeding your dog dry food, offering certain chew toys, and brushing its teeth regularly will help keep its gums and teeth healthy.

Grooming

You should brush your dog's hair regularly to get rid of tangles, remove small objects that might've accidentally gotten caught up in it, and remove shed hair. Mats and tangles can irritate your dog's skin, making them more likely to develop infections. You should also bathe your dog with pet shampoo periodically. Consult your vet regarding how often you need to wash your dog, as excessive washing can irritate skin.

This chapter serves as a mini-guide on how to train, feed, and care for livestock guardian dogs to ensure their well-being and effectiveness in protecting your livestock. Now that you've read it, you understand why training, nutrition, and care are crucial for your dog's success in their guardian role.

Chapter 6: Troubleshooting LGD Behaviors

In this pivotal chapter, you'll explore Livestock Guardian Dog (LGD) behaviors, recognizing them as the linchpin in adequately protecting livestock and property. The emphasis here extends beyond addressing behavioral challenges solely for the functionality of LGDs; it resonates with the fundamental understanding that their well-being is inexorably linked to their proficiency as guardians. This chapter navigates the identification and understanding of behavioral issues. It intricately outlines methods to effectively address and resolve these challenges.

Take the time to understand your guardian dog's behavior.[47]

Conducting a Thorough Assessment

When navigating Livestock Guardian Dog behaviors, conducting an assessment is crucial. This multifaceted process involves keen observation, baseline establishment, trigger identification, health evaluation, and analysis of interactions with both humans and livestock. Here are the steps you can take to conduct a thorough assessment.

Observational Techniques

To initiate this process, observe the LGD in its natural environment. Witness the intricate dance of its interactions with livestock, noting its demeanor and actions. Observe how it responds to potential threats, displaying alertness, aggression, or fear. Document regular behavioral patterns, including territorial marking, patrolling routes, and social interactions with humans and other animals.

Establishing Baseline Behaviors

Creating a baseline is pivotal for identifying deviations that may signal underlying challenges. Document the LGD's typical daily activities, including patrolling, resting, and interacting with livestock and humans. Understand the dog's sense of territory, noting its territorial behaviors and how it marks and defends its space. This baseline serves as a reference point for recognizing changes in behavior.

Identifying Triggers

Triggers play a significant role in influencing LGD behavior. Identify environmental changes that might act as triggers, such as new wildlife, construction, or alterations in the landscape. Record the LGD's reactions to these potential triggers, noting whether it responds calmly or displays signs of stress or aggression. This understanding aids in addressing the root causes of undesirable behaviors.

Health and Physical Examination

The integration of health into the assessment process is crucial. Collaborate with veterinary professionals to conduct a thorough physical examination, ensuring the LGD is in optimal physical health. Address any health issues that might influence its behavior, recognizing that pain or discomfort can manifest behavioral changes. A holistic approach encompasses both physical and mental well-being.

Analyzing Interactions

Evaluate how the LGD interacts with both humans and livestock. Assess the bond quality between the LGD and its caregivers, ensuring consistent and positive communication. Examine the LGD's interactions with livestock, looking for signs of stress or aggression and evaluating its effectiveness in protecting the herd. The dynamics of these interactions provide profound insights into the LGD's performance and challenges.

Behavioral Deviations

Identifying deviations from established baselines is vital. Record any changes in behavior, such as increased aggression, withdrawal, or altered patrolling patterns. Document when these behavioral deviations occur – whether related to specific times of the day, seasons, or events. This nuanced understanding helps pinpoint challenges and aids in tailoring targeted intervention strategies.

Developing a Customized Intervention Plan

Upon identifying challenges, empower yourself to develop a tailored intervention plan. Address each identified challenge individually, focusing on triggers and underlying causes. Emphasize gradual interventions to avoid overwhelming the LGD, ensuring consistency in reinforcing positive behaviors. This customized approach acknowledges the uniqueness of each dog and situation.

Holistic Well-Being

Recognize the importance of holistic well-being for LGDs. Consider mental stimulation as a vital component, including activities that engage their intelligence and instincts. Create an environment that fosters emotional fulfillment, ensuring a content and balanced LGD. Holistic well-being contributes to adequate protection and the overall quality of life for the LGD.

Ongoing Monitoring

Highlight the dynamic nature of LGD behaviors and the need for ongoing monitoring. Encourage continuous assessment to track the effectiveness of interventions and note any evolving behavioral patterns. Stress the importance of adaptability in strategies, as LGD behaviors may evolve, requiring adjustments to the intervention plan. This cyclical approach ensures sustained effectiveness and a responsive guardian.

Common Behavioral Issues

- ## Aggression Toward Humans

Territorial Instincts

Livestock Guardian Dogs (LGDs) exhibit a robust territorial instinct rooted in their evolutionary history as protectors. This behavior manifests as aggression towards humans perceived as intruders in their designated territory. This instinct is vital to their protective nature but requires careful management to ensure appropriate boundaries.

Fear or Anxiety

Aggression stemming from fear or anxiety is a complex aspect of LGD behavior. It often traces back to insufficient socialization during the critical developmental stages. LGDs not exposed to various environments, people, and stimuli may perceive humans as threats, triggering defensive aggression. Understanding these fear-based responses is crucial for addressing the root cause.

Protecting Resources

Resource guarding, including aggression to protect valuable resources, is ingrained in LGDs. This can extend to food, shelter, and favored areas within their territory. Recognizing and managing resource-based aggression involves creating an environment that minimizes competition and stress and develops a harmonious coexistence between the LGD and humans.

- ## Aggression Toward Livestock

Poor Socialization

Inadequate socialization during the formative stages of an LGD's life can result in aggression towards livestock. Without exposure to various animals during their early development, LGDs may view livestock as unfamiliar and potentially threatening. Addressing poor socialization involves gradual introductions and positive reinforcement to build trust.

Stress or Fear

Changes in the environment, handling procedures, or unexpected events can induce stress or fear in LGDs, leading to aggression towards livestock. Understanding the triggers and sources of stress is essential for developing strategies that alleviate anxiety, creating an environment where the LGD feels secure in its role as a guardian.

Maternal Instincts

Female LGDs may display protective aggression, particularly during breeding seasons or when safeguarding their young. This maternal instinct is a natural behavior rooted in ensuring the safety and well-being of the herd. Managing aggression related to maternal instincts involves providing a supportive environment in order for the LGD to fulfill its protective role without compromising safety.

• Barking Behavior
Territorial Defense

Excessive barking is a tool for territorial defense – a fundamental aspect of an LGD's role. Understanding that barking is a form of communication to establish and defend territory is crucial. Effective interventions allow the LGD to fulfill its protective duties and minimize excessive noise in residential or shared environments.

Lack of Stimulation

Boredom is a common trigger for excessive barking in LGDs. These intelligent and active dogs require mental and physical stimulation. Implementing enrichment activities, interactive play, and varied stimuli can alleviate boredom, address the root cause of the excessive barking, and promote a more contented LGD.

Communication

Barking is a natural means of communication for LGDs. Increased barking may signify heightened awareness of perceived threats or a need to communicate with humans or other animals. Deciphering the nuances of their communication cues enables owners to respond appropriately, fostering a more profound understanding between humans and LGDs.

• Predator Apathy
Lack of Training

Apathy towards potential predators can result from insufficient training. LGDs need to be trained to recognize and respond to specific threats. Implementing consistent and positive reinforcement training techniques enhances their ability to discern between friend and foe, ensuring effective predator control.

Health Issues

Physical discomfort or health problems may compromise an LGD's ability to perform its guardian duties effectively. Apathy may be a symptom of an underlying health issue. Regular veterinary checkups, promptly addressing health concerns, and adjusting the LGD's responsibilities during illness contribute to overall well-being.

Overfamiliarity with Livestock

LGDs raised alongside livestock from an early age may become less responsive to potential threats, especially if they perceive the livestock as part of their social group. Overfamiliarity involves balancing companionship with a vigilant stance towards potential predators, preserving the LGD's protective instincts.

• Roaming Behavior
Lack of Boundaries

Roaming behavior often results from inadequate fencing or unclear territorial boundaries. Establishing clear boundaries through secure fencing is crucial. Creating a defined territory helps the LGD understand its limits, reducing the likelihood of wandering and promoting effective territorial control.

Hormonal Influences

Unneutered or unspayed LGDs may roam in search of mates during breeding seasons. Addressing hormonal influences through spaying/neutering is a proactive measure to mitigate wandering behavior, ensuring that the LGD remains focused on its protective responsibilities.

Socialization Issues

Dogs that lack proper socialization may roam in search of companionship or stimuli. Introducing positive socialization experiences and ensuring that the LGD has adequate interaction with humans and other animals help address socialization issues, reducing the motivation to roam for social fulfillment.

• Fearful Behavior
Lack of Socialization

Fearful or timid behavior often stems from insufficient exposure to diverse environments, people, and stimuli during the critical socialization period in a dog's early life. Gradual exposure to positive experiences and a supportive environment aids in building confidence and addressing the root cause of fear-based behaviors.

Traumatic Experiences

Past negative encounters, abuse, or traumatic experiences can lead to persistent fear and timid behavior. Rehabilitation involves rebuilding trust through patient and positive interactions. Creating a safe and predictable environment supports the emotional well-being of LGDs recovering from traumatic experiences.

Genetic Predisposition

Some LGDs may have a genetic predisposition toward timidity. While genetic factors play a role, proactive socialization and positive reinforcement can help mitigate inherent tendencies. Understanding the interplay between genetics and environmental factors is essential for tailoring behavioral interventions.

Anxiety or Stress

Changes in the environment, routine, or the introduction of new elements can induce anxiety or stress, leading to increased marking behavior. Addressing the root cause involves identifying stress triggers and implementing measures to create a stable and secure environment, promoting emotional well-being.

Hormonal Influences

Intact males may engage in more frequent marking behavior, especially during breeding seasons, influenced by hormonal changes in reproductive activities. Spaying/neutering can mitigate hormonal influences, providing a more consistent and controllable behavior pattern.

Understanding these common behavioral issues and their nuanced root causes is pivotal for implementing effective intervention strategies. Tailoring solutions to address the specific underlying issues contributes to behavior modification and the overall well-being and effectiveness of Livestock Guardian Dogs in their protective roles.

Behavior Modification Techniques

Initiating behavior modification begins with a thorough assessment. Observe the specific behaviors causing concern, identifying triggers, contexts, and patterns. Documenting these observations provides a baseline for addressing challenges.

Positive Reinforcement Training

Utilize positive reinforcement to encourage desired behaviors. Reward the LGD for exhibiting appropriate responses to stimuli or situations.

Consistency in rewarding positive behavior fosters a deeper understanding of expectations.

Desensitization

Gradually expose the LGD to stimuli that trigger undesired behaviors – pair exposure with positive experiences or rewards to create positive associations. Slowly increase intensity or proximity as the LGD becomes more comfortable, reducing adverse reactions.

Establish Clear Communication

Consistent verbal and visual cues are essential for effective communication. Reinforce commands consistently, ensuring that the LGD understands and responds reliably. Clear communication enhances the bond between the owner and the LGD.

Controlled Socialization

Gradual exposure to new people, animals, and environments helps build confidence and reduce fear. Facilitate positive interactions during socialization to create positive associations. Monitor reactions and adjust the socialization pace based on the LGD's comfort level.

Environmental Enrichment

Provide mental and physical stimulation through toys, puzzles, and interactive activities. Rotate toys regularly to maintain novelty and prevent boredom. Engage in activities that simulate the LGD's instincts, such as scent work or puzzle-solving.

Consistent Boundaries

Clearly define and reinforce territorial boundaries. Use fencing and visual cues to help the LGD understand its limits. Reward adherence to boundaries with positive reinforcement, reinforcing a sense of security.

Addressing Fear-Based Behaviors

Identify and avoid triggers that induce fear. Gradual exposure to fear-inducing stimuli and reassurance and rewards for calm behavior reduce fear-based behaviors. A supportive environment is crucial in addressing fear.

Professional Guidance

Seeking assistance from experienced trainers or behaviorists for specific challenges is valuable. Professionals can provide tailored strategies based on the LGD's needs, ensuring a comprehensive and informed approach to behavior modification.

Behavioral Analysis

Conduct a detailed analysis of the LGD's behavior, considering past experiences, traumas, or environmental changes. Understanding the root cause facilitates targeted interventions.

Use of Deterrents

Introduce deterrents for undesirable behaviors, such as excessive barking. Devices emitting sounds or vibrations can discourage behaviors without causing harm.

Interactive Training Games

Incorporate interactive training games to stimulate the LGD mentally. Puzzle toys or games that require problem-solving engage their cognitive abilities.

Variety in Commands

Introduce a variety of commands to keep training sessions interesting. This prevents monotony and ensures the LGD remains attentive and responsive.

Scheduled Playtime

Designate specific periods for playtime and interaction. Structured play helps release excess energy and reinforces positive behavior.

Calming Techniques

Learn and implement calming techniques, such as a massage or gentle stroking, to soothe the LGD during stressful situations.

Preventive Measures

Begin socialization during the critical developmental period. Introduce the LGD to various environments, people, and animals to prevent fear-based behaviors from developing.

Environmental Assessments

Regularly assess the LGD's living environment for potential stressors or changes. Minimizing environmental stressors contributes to stable behavior.

Supervised Socialization Events

Arrange supervised socialization events with other dogs or animals. Controlled interactions provide positive experiences and enhance social skills.

Consistent Exposure

Regularly expose the LGD to various sounds, sights, and smells to prevent fear or anxiety associated with novelty.

Positive Handling Techniques

Implement positive handling techniques to build trust. Gradual acclimatization to handling ensures the LGD remains comfortable in various situations.

Routine Mental Challenges

Create routine mental challenges, such as hiding treats or toys, to stimulate the LGD's problem-solving abilities and mental agility.

Adjustable Training Intensity

Modify training intensity based on the LGD's responsiveness and energy levels. Tailoring the training regimen prevents fatigue and maintains enthusiasm.

Diversified Play Equipment

Introduce a variety of play equipment, like agility obstacles, to keep physical activities diverse and enjoyable for the LGD.

Consistent Verbal Reinforcement

Use consistent verbal reinforcement throughout the day to acknowledge positive behavior. Verbal cues contribute to reinforcing established commands.

Sensory Stimulation

Incorporate sensory stimulation through different textures, surfaces, and environments. Engaging multiple senses enriches the LGD's overall experience.

Structured Rest Periods

Establish structured rest periods within the daily routine. Adequate rest supports mental well-being and behavioral stability.

Flexible Training Schedule

Maintain flexibility in the training schedule to accommodate the LGD's energy levels and adaptability. A flexible approach ensures training remains enjoyable.

Regular Exercise

Provide ample opportunities for physical exercise in order to prevent boredom and excess energy. A well-exercised LGD is less likely to engage in undesirable behaviors.

Health Checkups

Schedule regular veterinary checkups to address any potential health issues. Physical discomfort can contribute to behavioral problems, so maintaining good health is essential.

Consultation with Professionals

Consult with experienced trainers or behaviorists for guidance. Professionals can offer personalized insights and strategies based on the LGD's unique characteristics, ensuring a holistic approach to behavior management.

Implementing these behavior modification techniques and preventive measures creates a comprehensive strategy for fostering positive behavior in Livestock Guardian Dogs. Recognizing the individuality of each LGD and making adjustments based on their responses and progress is essential for successful behavior modification. Seeking professional guidance adds an extra layer of expertise to addressing specific challenges effectively.

Ethical Responsibility

Livestock Guardian Dogs (LGDs) are indispensable protectors, but their well-being and humane treatment are equally paramount. Responsible LGD ownership entails a commitment to lifelong care. Recognizing the ethical responsibilities of LGD ownership ensures a holistic and humane approach.

Commitment to Lifelong Well-being

Owning an LGD is a lifelong commitment. As guardians, owners must pledge continuous care, addressing their companions' evolving physical and emotional needs throughout their lives.

Ethical Breeding Practices

Supporting ethical breeding practices is essential. This involves prioritizing health and temperament over profit and avoiding patronizing breeders who compromise the well-being of their dogs.

Adequate Living Conditions

Providing suitable living conditions is fundamental. LGDs deserve shelter, comfortable bedding, and a designated space that caters to their needs, promoting a sense of security.

Balanced Nutrition

Prioritize a balanced and nutritious diet. Collaborate with veterinarians to determine the optimal diet based on age, size, and activity level, ensuring their overall health.

Regular Veterinary Care

Scheduled veterinary checkups are non-negotiable. Regular visits allow for preventive care and early intervention, safeguarding the LGD's health and well-being.

Mental Stimulation

Recognize their intelligence and working nature. Provide mental stimulation through activities, toys, and interactions, preventing boredom and promoting mental well-being.

Socialization and Positive Reinforcement

Prioritize positive reinforcement and gentle training techniques. Continuous socialization efforts contribute to a well-adjusted and confident LGD, enhancing their overall welfare.

Prevention of Cruelty and Neglect

Uphold a zero-tolerance policy for cruelty and neglect. LGD owners must actively report signs of abuse or neglect within the community to protect all dogs' welfare.

Respect for Natural Behaviors

Acknowledge and respect the dog's natural behaviors. Avoid punitive measures that may compromise their well-being, fostering a harmonious, ethical owner-dog relationship.

Adaptation to Individual Needs

Recognize that each LGD is an individual with unique needs. Tailor care and training strategies to accommodate their distinct personalities, ensuring a customized approach to their well-being.

Consideration of Retirement

Plan for the LGD's retirement. Ensure a comfortable and peaceful transition as they age, acknowledging their contributions and providing for their changing needs.

Integration into Family Life

Integrate LGDs beyond their working duties into family life. Fostering a bond based on companionship and mutual respect enhances their overall well-being.

Humane End-of-Life Decisions

Face end-of-life decisions with compassion. Make decisions prioritizing the LGD's comfort, minimizing suffering during their final stages, and ensuring a dignified farewell.

Ethical LGD ownership encompasses a profound commitment to these remarkable animals' welfare, health, and happiness. Responsible owners are pivotal in setting ethical standards within the broader LGD community.

Chapter 7: Llamas as Guardians

If someone told you that a llama watches their sheep, you might think it is a dry, absurd dad joke. There is no need to force a chuckle because they are probably serious, but you can wait for the punchline if you'd like. Don't be fooled by the llama's cute and awkward appeal because these animals make brilliant guardians. They are not what you'd typically believe a guardian animal to be because they are grazers, not predators. However, llamas are powerful and territorial creatures that form deep bonds with the livestock that they protect. Furthermore, since llamas aren't predators, you do not have to worry about them mauling your livestock like cats or dogs.

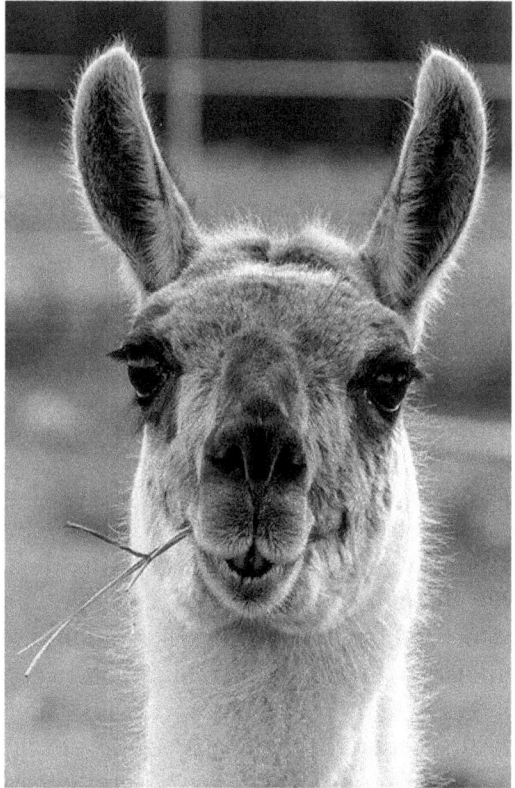

Llamas can be guardians.[48]

Llamas can graze alongside many species, increasing their time under their watchful eyes. In the right conditions, llamas are the perfect caretakers. Llamas are not excessively expensive and are relatively easy to maintain. Considering their effectiveness as guardians against numerous predator species, your pockets will be smiling at you. Their bulky, fur-covered, 400-pound body towering over your other animals is like a walking battle station looking to bite, kick, and stomp any intruder that crosses the line. This fox chaser will have the unwanted snackers running for the hills at top speed to avoid their ferociousness.

Llamas are generally calm and trainable, so you can keep them around children if you are careful, alert, and informed. They can develop a bad temper if they are mistreated, so you must care for them ethically for your safety and their well-being. Llamas, especially when young, are susceptible to many diseases, so you must ensure that you take the right medical precautions while remaining vigilant of signs of infection. Your fuzzy companion can keep you entertained for hours with their good looks and affection as a pack animal while they stay on duty, keeping your livestock guarded. So, give these cuties with their trendy haircuts a chance because their competence as a guardian may surprise you.

Physical and Behavioral Characteristics

Seeing a llama in a picture and seeing one in real life are two different experiences. The body of a llama is about four feet tall, but their long neck takes them up to about six feet. They can weigh anything from about 250 to 450 pounds, but generally, like with many other mammal species, the females are smaller. This is why people opt for sterilized males because they are bigger and less aggressive than a testosterone-filled giant.

Llamas are brilliant livestock guardians because they are naturally aggressive towards foxes, coyotes, and dogs, which are common enemies for poultry, sheep, and goats. Having their eyes on the side of their head gives them a 360 view that can spot a predator approaching from a distance. They thrive in high-altitude environments because of the hemoglobin levels of their blood and can run up to 40 mph, so you will not beat them in a foot race. The diseases they develop are usually nutrition-based because they have strong immune systems to fight off many contagious pathogens. Therefore, what you feed them is crucial to get the most out of your llamas.

Llamas are known for spitting, but they rarely aim at people. This behavior is usually done as a dominance-establishing competition between males trying to be the alpha or when they are irritated. Llamas do not attempt to escape their enclosures; they eat the same food as sheep or goats. They also prefer structured shelters, like those of sheep, which is why they are so well-suited for each other. Llamas are used in the mountains of South America because they can carry a lot of weight up steep hills. Their padded feet have two toes that do not cause as much damage as the hooves of horses or donkeys do.

They live for about 15 to 20 years, so you can trust that they will be around and active for a long time. You do not have to worry about constantly replacing them or even breeding them. Despite their goofy appearance, llamas are athletic and can easily chase down a predator when they need to. They have long, pointy ears used to listen carefully to slight changes in their surroundings as well as to communicate their emotions or temperament.

Llamas have tough fur that protects against injuries and attacks from smaller predators. Although they look similar to alpacas, they are not quite as gentle and are also bigger. Farmers in South America often keep a few llamas in their alpaca herd to fight off unwelcomed guests. They anger quicker than alpacas and do not run away from a confrontation. Unlike dogs, llamas naturally take on the guardian role. Dogs need to be trained so they don't attack the herd, but llamas just fall in line without any instruction. When lambs are born, you'll notice that your llama will take on the babysitter role without being prompted. They are herd animals, so these collective behaviors are expected.

Not many animals are as uniquely suited for the guardian role as llamas. Their physical structure, coupled with their mentality, makes them overachievers as guards. They have six sharp and angled teeth that can do horrific damage if they penetrate flesh. Their long legs keep predators away from their vitals, and they can quickly trample them before they attempt to attack. They are brave, and in some cases, they will even charge at bigger animals, scaring them off with sheer audacity.

Role as Livestock Guardians

Llamas have two main weapons of defense: their huge bodies and shrill screams. As strong, fast, and agile as llamas are, they simply cannot fight everything. However, even in the cases where they see a clear loss coming, they will loudly neigh, alerting anybody within earshot of the pressing danger. Their fancy footwork makes easy work of foxes and coyotes, while their protective nature ensures no one is left behind.

The effectiveness of llamas as guardians can't be denied. A study was conducted by Iowa State University on 145 sheep farms in the United States (Franklin et al., 2012). The study measured the effectiveness of introducing llamas as guardian animals. There was a significant difference between when the llamas arrived and before they got there. The number of attacks on sheep dropped from 11% to 1%, with 50% of farmers claiming that they had experienced no attacks at all (Franklin et al., 2012). The llamas used a variety of strategies, like herding the sheep away from danger or charging at the predators, which included coyotes, dogs, foxes, and even bears.

The role of a guardian llama is to spot danger, warn the herd about an approaching threat, get the herd away from the danger, and, if need be, fight the predator. They have similar diets to sheep, so they will feed alongside your animals. They can be taken out into the pasture to graze with your flock. Unlike guard dogs that do not become part of the flock, as a grazer itself, the llama will insert itself into the group as somewhat of a fatherly figure, protecting its weaker children.

With its all-around vision, powerful sense of smell, and amazing hearing, your llama is there to keep a lookout for predators. They are most effective against medium-sized threats like dogs, foxes, and coyotes but do not do well against bigger predators like bears and lions. Their height of six feet is also an advantage because they can see further than the sheep and goats they typically protect.

Since they will spend a lot of time feeding and in the same area as your livestock, they will establish a natural connection with them that is difficult to break. You do not have to train them like you would a dog, but you can take some steps to maximize their effectiveness. For example, to ensure they establish a bond with your livestock, which makes them protective, you should place them in an adjacent enclosure first and then gradually introduce them to your flock.

The best animals to pair llamas with are sheep or goats. They do not match well with cows because the predators they fight against are not much of a threat to older cows and would usually target calves. A cow can provide the same protection to its young as a llama. They can still assist with chasing predators off and acting as a vigilant alarm. Still, they are just more suited for smaller livestock. Sheep are low-strata grazers, going deep into the soil to eat what the livestock may leave behind, while llamas are medium-strata grazers that take the top half of the grass, as well as browsers that eat from trees and shrubs, so they are not in direct competition for food with sheep.

Taking care of your llama will help it become the best protector it can be. For instance, llamas are sensitive to excessive heat, so you must ensure that there are many shady areas for them to rest in and that they have water to cool themselves down. You need to trim their toes so that they do not get foot rot, and they require regular sheering, which also helps manage the heat. Llamas are susceptible to many parasites, so you have to take the necessary precautions to prevent infection. They also need annual vaccinations against Clostridial Disease, delivered as a five-in-one dose. The meningeal worm is deadly for llamas, so you must deworm them regularly. This parasite is found in deer, so if you have a large deer population in your area, llamas may be the wrong choice for you unless you take precautions to keep deer away.

Pros and Cons of Using Llamas as Guardians

Environmental analysis is the first stage of determining whether llamas are the guardian animals for you. You must think about which kinds of animals you have and how the llama would function within that environment. A lofty, mountainous region is a tick in the llama's favor because they survive well in high altitudes. Llamas become attached to the animals they protect because they are driven by a natural urge. However, what they see as dangerous could affect how appropriate they are for the services you need. For example, llamas will ward off foxes and coyotes but will ignore the much smaller raccoons, skunks, and weasels, which is terrible if you are farming with chickens. Therefore, one of the major downsides of having a llama as a guard is that they do not gel with all kinds of livestock. Dogs may eat chickens, but you can train them to leave them alone and project them, whereas a llama will just ignore the threats to chickens without realizing they are putting the flock in danger.

A huge pro of keeping llamas on your farm is that they adapt to a multitude of climates. The hardy animals do not get hurt easily and will not succumb to weather changes. This resilience to climate, paired with how long they live, means the gorgeous beast will be in service for many years. Younger llamas are not suited as guard animals, so you should get one that is at least over two years old. Preferably, it should be a male that is neutered. Llamas function best as guardians when they are solo, but depending on the size of your flock, you may need more than one.

Llamas are an ethical option for predator control. You may ask how this makes sense since llamas will kill foxes, dogs, and coyotes without hesitation. However, the presence of a llama is usually enough to keep wildlife away from your animals, which means you will be killing a lot fewer foxes than if you had used less ethical measures like poison. Furthermore, poison can inadvertently harm creatures that you do not want to harm, and some foxes have become so smart that they avoid poison bait. Additionally, poison can deteriorate the soil, which, over time, will impact the indigenous plant life on your farm, throwing off the delicate balance of the natural ecosystem.

The similarity of the llama's diet with a sheep or a goat diet means that you can seamlessly introduce them into your flock without much maintenance when it comes to nutritional considerations. However, you must ensure that they have enough copper, zinc, and vitamin D in their diets if you do not want them to develop malnutrition-related illnesses. Llamas don't easily pick up contagious infections, so feeding them properly is half the battle. Furthermore, they should always have access to an ample supply of water to prevent urinary blockages or infections.

Legal Restrictions and Regulations

Llamas, much like dogs, are one of the oldest domesticated animals. In South America, some people say that there is evidence that these gorgeous animals have been living side by side with humans for over 4,000 years. This is why llamas are considered domesticated animals, like sheep and cows, for the most part. However, it is important to be mindful of what is legal in your region. Different laws and ethical standards are applied according to the country or state that you live in. Familiarizing yourself with these regulatory standards will ensure that you keep the authorities at bay and do not have to pay fines, lose your animals, or even spend time in prison.

Sometimes, the laws and regulations put on you when holding animals can seem like a lot. However, it is essential to remember that the bodies that create and enforce rules are there to protect you and your animals. Having standardized regulations ensures that animals will be provided with appropriate care while protecting humans from a variety of dangers, like zoonotic diseases. People's ethical standards differ depending on their morals, values, upbringing, and culture. Therefore, people draw the line for what is appropriate, safe, and cruel at different points. Individuals can't function with their own perceptions and knowledge base because it could lead to dangerous practices and animal mistreatment. Therefore, governmental bodies exist to make the rules and regulations clear for everybody.

Regulations are built on biosecurity and ethics. These rules will shift according to where you are situated. For example, in Western Australia, you need to register your animals and classify whether you are using them for commercial purposes. In New Zealand, the ethical concerns outlined in their regulations require you to provide your llamas with a constant supply of water and have a feeding setup that reduces waste. Furthermore, you must ensure that your llamas do not have access to materials they can mistakenly ingest that would cause them harm, like loose wires, building paper, electrical fittings, or shards of plastic. In the UK, you will need a CPH number and a HERD mark, and you will also need to register with the British Llama Society if you want to keep these animals legally. You will need an NLIS registration in Australia, the National Livestock Identification System.

You also have to consider your use of llamas in a broader sense because some places don't allow animals that llamas work the best with, like Arizona, which does not allow sheep to be kept. In America, different states have widely varying regulations, so you need to do your due diligence and conduct thorough research to ensure you are functioning within the barriers of the law. In Colorado and Georgia, you can own llamas and pets. In Idaho, the barriers to keeping llamas are minimal because you do not need any permit for domestic animals. Therefore, review what you can do in your region to determine whether llamas as guardian animals are the best option for you in the legal context you find yourself in.

Multispecies Grazing and When It Should Be Applied

Multispecies grazing is when you are keeping two or more different animals in the same pasture. They do not necessarily have to be grazing at the same time, but if they share the land in short intervals, it still counts as multispecies grazing. Using multispecies grazing can be good for the environment because the different habits of various species add to the area's biodiversity. You will most likely pair llamas with sheep or goats because they share a diet and protect each other from their common natural enemies.

Llamas' susceptibility to parasites requires you to use rotational grazing. The lifecycle of parasites, from eggs to fully grown, runs for a certain period. Rotational grazing is when you take your animals to different pastures at different times of the year so that your land can have time to recover and you can avoid the dangerous parts of the parasite lifecycle. Different regions have varying parasites, so you must research the common parasites in your area and the best rotation schedule to use so that your sheep, goats, or llamas don't get sick.

Horses and cows share parasites, while sheep and goats share parasites. Therefore, when applying multispecies grazing, you should pair sheep with cows and goats with horses. In the case of llamas, this kind of parasite management is not possible because they are guardian animals. You must monitor them to see if they are weak or fatigued because it could be a sign of parasite infection. If you feel your animals are sick, make sure to call the vet immediately because if you wait too long, it could end up being fatal.

As a protective guardian, llamas pair well with sheep. You can also use them for chickens, but they will not be as effective. They are even less useful for cows because one of their biggest benefits is their size, and cows are bigger than llamas. Furthermore, they would be unable to fight animals targeting cows. Introducing llamas into a complex system of multiple animals recreates the conditions of the natural world, and it is great for your plant life and the biodiversity of the ecosystem you inhabit. The use of llamas forces multispecies grazing because they are only effective if they spend a lot of time with the flock they watch over. Therefore, in addition to being one of the most captivating guard animals, llamas are an eco-friendly option.

Chapter 8: Training Your Llama

Now that you understand how llamas function as livestock guardians, you need some more details on how to train them so that you can maximize their effectiveness. Llamas are made for the role of guardians, but a few missteps can radically decrease their functionality. Therefore, you must be informed on exactly how to treat your llama so they can be seamlessly integrated into your flock and the daily routines of your farm or homestead.

Llamas can be kind, but they also have a terrible mean streak. Much of your training will be focused on managing their aggressive tendencies and mood swings. Llamas spit, bite, and kick when they are angry, which puts you, other people on your farm, and your animals in danger. Instituting the correct protocols and interventions can ensure that your llama stays calm and every other living thing on your property is safe, except for the predators.

Llamas require a lot of training.[40]

From choosing the right llama, considering factors like size, age, gender, temperament, and personality, to finding ways to introduce your animal to their flock - all the steps of training a llama are covered. These practical tips will give you the knowledge you need to be an expert guardian llama trainer and get the most out of your animal. How well your llama performs solely depends on the work you put into training it. It may seem intimidating at first, but by understanding a few basic principles, you can be put on the fast track to becoming a pro.

Getting your llama on the same page as you requires mutual respect and understanding. You will dive deep into the psychology of your llama to set yourself up as the leader of its flock. Furthermore, you will maximize its protective and territorial qualities so that it can serve you well as a guardian. Llamas are already natural guards, so it does not take much to get them in tip-top shape for peak performance of their duties. You just have to lead your llama in the right direction toward its destiny as an elite guardian animal that will keep your livestock safe from many kinds of predators like foxes, dogs, and coyotes.

How to Choose a Llama

Choosing the right llama is the beginning of training. The right temperament, size, and personality will weed out the unsuitable candidates. If you were a basketball coach, you would choose the tallest, strongest, fastest, and most athletic people to be a part of your team if they all had no previous basketball experience. You would test their hand-eye coordination and their reflexes as well. Similarly, you should choose a llama that is best suited to its role as a guardian. This llama selection process will determine the level of difficulty you experience when training your llama for guard duty.

The age of a llama is very important when making your initial selection. Ideally, you want a male between the ages of 18 months and two years old. Once you have found a male that's the appropriate age, watch how he behaves. The llama should be accustomed to being handled by people because you will need to trim their toes, transport them, as well as sheer them. Ask the breeder to walk the llama around, and if possible, bring along a dog to see how the llama reacts to it. Llamas instinctively hate dogs, but some who grew up around domesticated dogs will not see them as an enemy, only targeting unfamiliar invaders.

Many llamas are kept as pets. This means the llama you want to purchase may have been brought up alone and raised on a bottle. These types of llamas are terrible as guardians because they bond more with humans than other animals. The pack behaviors of llamas, which make them such brilliant guardians, are learned in the first few months of spending time with their mother. Therefore, your llama must be on its mother's teat for at least six months before you buy it. Llamas hone their protective instincts by spending time with other llamas or flock animals. A great sign that a llama is not attached to people is if it exhibits minimal curiosity upon seeing you and acts aloof.

The male you select must be gelded – which means castrated. Gelded males are safer to work with because they will not challenge you as the leader. Moreover, they will not attempt to mount your other animals, which could cause injury. The llama must be gelded before it is bred because doing it afterward does not erase the threat to you and your animals. Testosterone-filled males who have not been castrated can become a huge problem because of their unpredictable tempers.

Observe how the llama moves and interacts. You want a level-headed llama that is not overly confrontational. Therefore, the llama you choose should not be screaming or spitting at people. Assertive llamas will attempt to chest-butt you or will stand their ground instead of moving out of the way when you approach it. When a llama shows these headstrong behaviors, it is best to keep looking. More signs that you are dealing with an alpha that will challenge your position is if the llama aggressively protects its food and refuses to allow people to clean its manure.

Using a reputable breeder is advisable because it is more likely that they will be honest and provide you with a strong and healthy llama. Breeders typically have to register with various regulatory bodies. Find out which organizations govern the industry in your region and seek out breeders who are aligned with them. If you can find a breeder strictly dedicated to raising guardian llamas, go with that option because the additional money you pay will be worth it. A guardian llama will set you back about $500 to $1,500.

If other animals are on the breeder's property, keenly observe how the llama interacts with them. A guard llama should be alert and curious about changes in its environment. They should be gentle with the animals around them. If you have pet dogs, ensure they are comfortable around them because dogs are natural enemies. Watch if the llama attempts to break the fence or get past it because you do not need an animal that is prone to escaping. Check if the llama is protective of young members of the flock. A guardian llama will either embed itself in the middle of the flock or walk up to higher ground to see better, so any of these behaviors is a great sign for an eligible candidate.

Fundamental Principles of Llama Training

The training for guardian llamas is not extensive because you are tapping into their natural behavioral patterns to meet your requirements. Like people, llamas are individuals. What works for one llama may not have the same impact on the next. Spending time with your animals allows you to get to know them. You'll learn what your llama likes, how it responds to different commands, and what causes it discomfort or stress. Llamas are prey animals, so they can be jumpy and easily startled. Be gentle and move deliberately so as not to frighten your animal. Take your llama out on walks, helping it become familiar with the property and comfortable with you as its feeder.

Llamas are quick learners, which can be a gift and a curse. You must be careful of the actions you take when training your llama. It will be very difficult to undo the impact if you inadvertently create a negative connotation to something, whether it is an object or an animal. Work with your llama every day because repetition will ingrain behavior, and you will learn your llama's personality better. Once you understand your llamas' individuality, you can adapt your training to be personalized to what it responds to.

Patience and calmness are the names of the game. Llamas are skittish and can be easily startled. You do not want to scare your llama into disobedience. Furthermore, rushing through training can cause you to overlook key details. Therefore, take your time each day and set reachable milestones. Your llama will only be as good as the training you are willing to put in. Luckily, the only areas you need to focus on are transporting your animal, integrating your llamas into the flock, and reducing aggressive behavior that can hurt people or your livestock. These sections of training can be easily addressed with the right information and minimal effort.

Step-by-Step Instructions for Building Protective Behaviors

1. Pair your llama with the right animals. Guardian llamas are best suited for sheep or goats. Their size advantage over predators does not apply to cows because they are bigger. Furthermore, they eat a similar diet to sheep and goats, which is important because in order for the llama to bond with a flock, it must spend time together. Llamas do not pair well with chickens because they often ignore predators that are dangerous to poultry, like weasels and skunks.

2. Make sure the llama bonds with your flock. To establish a bond or introduce your llama to your flock, you can place it in an adjacent enclosure. The bonding period takes about a few days to a couple of weeks.

3. Use only one llama. The problem with using multiple llamas is that they will become protective of each other instead of bonding with your livestock. One llama can cover 300 acres and can watch 300 sheep. If you have too much land or too many animals for one llama to be effective, you must make sure that your guardians do not meet.

Positive Reinforcement Techniques

Llamas, like many other mammals, are food-motivated. The best positive reinforcement you can adopt is using food as a manipulation tool. As a guardian llama, you may have to lead your animal into various sections of your farm. Therefore, you will need to train your llama to be comfortable getting led into different places. Using positive reinforcement when transporting your llama will ensure the process runs smoothly. Immediately reward your llama with a delicious, sweet treat, like apples or carrots, when it displays behavior that you like. This will create a positive connection with the behavior, which will cause the llama to keep repeating the desired action.

Positive reinforcement works best when coupled with a regular schedule. Feed and groom your llama at the same time every day. This routine reinforces desired behaviors with repetition. So, take your llama out into the pasture in the morning and bring him back in the late afternoon, giving him a treat when he enters the enclosure and leaves the enclosure. This way, you create positive reinforcement of its daily routine. Llamas can be stubborn, so getting them to enjoy being transported will help you in the long run because the animal will not resist being moved.

Integrating a Guardian Llama

Integrating your llama means getting him used to your unique farm environment. On your farm, you may have a variety of animals and other people that your llama will come into contact with. Your llama needs to be accustomed to all the interconnecting parts of your land, including other humans that work with the animals. Therefore, if people are interacting with your llama, they must spend time with him so that the llama can be well acquainted with the person they will regularly be in contact with. To reduce aggressive behavior, the llama must know that either you or anyone else they work with are a part of the flock. Try to limit human interaction because you want the llama to protect the animals and not form powerful bonds with people; otherwise, it will end up recognizing humans as the ones that need protection.

Llamas are extremely territorial, as they are herd animals that usually need to compete for resources. Its territorial nature can cause it to hurt members of your flock by kicking or biting. They can be especially violent toward other llamas, particularly if they are both males. You should only have one guardian on your property at a time to stop the llama-on-llama violence. To prevent the llama from attacking your flock, you must introduce them slowly. Keep the llama in an adjacent pen where it can see and interact with the flock without coming in direct contact with them. Your llama should be feeding at the same time as your flock so that it can make the connection that it is part of them. Gradually begin allowing them to interact. In the first few weeks, you must watch them closely so that you can intervene if there is any trouble.

Another way to prevent fights or attacks is to keep your sheep or goats in a big area with your llama. Confined spaces are breeding grounds for aggression. If your llama has enough open space, then the likelihood that it will attack your flock is significantly decreased. Llamas also have a strong sense of smell that guides their actions. You can use scent to your advantage when integrating your llama. Place hay or other objects with your sheep's scent in your llama's temporary pen. This will get your llama accustomed to the animal's smell, which will ease the integration process when you allow them to start spending time together.

Your llama needs to know where it is allowed to go and the borders where its territory ends. Walk your llama along the fence of your pastures and enclosures for your flock. Correct the negative behavior of trying to cross over the fence by yanking the lead and yelling a "No!" command. Introducing the llama to its space is just as important as introducing it to its flock. Furthermore, as a guardian, your llama must be familiar with its surroundings so that it can more easily spot danger.

Llamas and dogs are natural enemies, so if you have canines, you must either keep them separate from your llamas or introduce them so your llamas can accept your pet as part of its flock. Allow your dog and llama to meet under careful supervision so that you have control over both your animals. Correct the behavior if any of them show signs of aggression. You may need to repeat this process multiple times because you are attempting to override a natural fear, which could take a lot of time and effort.

Practical Solutions for Dealing with the Most Common Challenges during Llama Training

Some of the main challenges that can arise when training your llamas are aggressive behavior, like challenging you or spitting, distress, being easily startled, and forgetting some of the training you have already done. All these factors can be remedied with immediate intervention. Llamas, like dogs, can be trained with a combination of hand signs and voice commands. The best way to get the llama to internalize these commands is by using food as a reward. Positive reinforcement, just like food rewards, works with getting your llama to display behavior that you like, but it can be a bit tricky when you want to break negative behavior.

The challenge of aggressive behaviors from a llama starts with the selection process when you choose a llama according to its temperament.

However, llamas that seem level-headed at first can become more aggressive due to an environmental change or a traumatic event. When fighting aggressive actions like spitting, screaming, or chest-butting, the main principle is to address the behavior immediately when it occurs. You cannot let this negativity slide even once because it will let the llama think that the way it is acting is fine. Llamas learn by hand gestures and commands, so you can put your hand up and sternly yell "no." Another option you can apply is firmly pushing against its chest while shouting "no." Some people use a water gun or a spray bottle as a repellant. You must repeat your "no" command every time your animal is aggressive so that it will be constantly reminded that the behavior is unacceptable.

Sometimes, it is not anger that causes undesirable behavior; it is distress. You can gently hold your llama to calm it down when it is feeling shocked, anxious, or stressed. Controlling stress responses is all about being mindful and not scaring the nervous animal. Remember that once a negative connection to an object is established, it will be nearly impossible to break. Therefore, during key times, like transporting and feeding, you must be extremely careful and prevent your llama from getting startled in these crucial moments.

Stubbornness is another behavioral trait that is common among llamas. Everything may be good in one moment, and in the next minute, you get zero percent cooperation. This is the perfect scenario to exercise patience. First, investigate what went wrong. The llama may have spotted something that made it uncomfortable, like a dog or a predator. If you have assessed that there is no perceived danger for the llama, you may need to use a little force. By no means does that equate to hurting your animal in any way. Training methods that cause harm are completely off the table because ethically treating your guardians is essential. Simply yank on its lead and shout your chosen command, such as "Yep!" or "Go!" At times, you may need your llama to move immediately, so getting it accustomed to such a command is crucial.

The seasons on your farm may necessitate the adoption of differing routines depending on the time of the year. Your llama may forget what it was taught in the previous season, so you may need to retrain it. Repetition is what allows the llama to internalize schedules and commands, so when the repetition is broken, it can easily lose what it had learned before. This is why training llamas requires you to have a lot of patience. You may find yourself having to retrain your animal multiple times a year, depending on how your schedule changes. Make time for an adjustment period when you are making shifts. Radical changes can cause a lot of stress for your llama, so be sure to respond according to its emotional condition.

Llamas are so well-suited for the position of guardian animals that they do not require much training. As long as you maintain a healthy physical and mental state for your animal, there should be no problems. You can make some corrections for aggressive behavior and for introducing the llama to your flock, but for the most part, your llama will automatically jump into its duties.

Chapter 9: Guard Donkeys

To make one thing clear, not all donkeys are like Eeyore. They are social and fun creatures, albeit a little stubborn. They are also guard animals that can protect your livestock. These nice-looking animals have an aggressive nature that usually comes out when they are threatened, making them the ideal guardians. Once your livestock see how donkeys protect them from harm, they will gravitate around them to feel safe.

This chapter covers the unique characteristics of donkeys, their protective nature, what makes them great guard animals, and the advantages of donkey guards.

Donkey as a guardian.[50]

Donkeys' Unique Characteristics

Every animal is unique in its own way. Most people would tell you dozens of facts about cats and dogs, but if you ask them about donkeys, they won't have much to say. Donkeys are extremely underappreciated, but they are amazing animals with some interesting qualities that make them fun to raise.

They Have Big Ears for a Reason

Have you ever wondered why donkeys have large ears? Many of them evolved in dry conditions, like in Asia and Africa. Their large ears expel the heat inside their body to regulate their temperature so they can withstand the hot weather and remain cool during the summer. They also boost their hearing capabilities so they can pick up on mating calls and when a predator is approaching.

Some Donkeys Are Very Small

Have you ever seen tiny donkeys? They are ridiculously cute, right? Some types of donkeys are really small. They are about three feet tall and are very common in Sardinia and Sicily. Interestingly, the shortest donkey in the world is 25.29 inches high. Although many small animals breed, the donkey's small size is natural.

Donkeys Are Stubborn

Donkeys are very stubborn animals. Sometimes, they plant their feet firmly on the ground and refuse to move from their place. Even if you try to pull them, they will not budge. Understand that they are not being jerks or dumb, as some people assume. In fact, they are very clever animals. If donkeys feel threatened or in danger, they will stay put to give themselves time to think if it's safe to keep moving. They are pretty smart, aren't they? This is unlike horses, which run away when they are afraid.

They Are Very Social Creatures

You will rarely see a donkey alone in the wild. Donkeys are social creatures that like to be in groups. It is in their nature since they usually live in herds and form strong and lifelong friendships with other animals. Two donkeys can form a close bond, which is called a "pair bond." They become very attached to each other, and they would suffer from stress, anxiety, loss of appetite, and discomfort if they were separated. So, it is better to adopt two donkeys to keep their spirits up and keep each other company.

They Are Hairy Creatures

Some donkey breeds are very hairy and look very pretty. One of the most popular types is the Poitou donkey, which originated in the French city of Poitou. These donkeys have long and thick hair and are usually very expensive.

Unique Voice

Donkeys have a distinct sound called "braying." Unlike zebras, horses, and other animals, donkeys can make this sound while breathing. They make the "hee" sound while inhaling and the "haw" sound while exhaling. They use their unique vocalization to communicate and connect with other donkeys. They are usually very loud, so they can call on other animals from a distance.

They use their unique vocalization to protect other animals by braying loudly to alert them of any potential dangers.

More Than Work Animals

Many people treat donkeys as just work animals. They depend on them for transportation or to guard their livestock because of their endurance, strength, and ability to adapt to tough conditions. However, there is more to donkeys than what meets the eye. They are sociable, intelligent, affectionate, loyal, and can form deep relationships with their owners. Your donkey will feel like family, not just a guard animal.

Adapt to Dry Conditions

Donkeys can survive and easily adapt to harsh and dry weather conditions. Their body can conserve water as their kidneys extract water from different organs, so they can stay hydrated for long periods of time.

They Are Light Sleepers

The next time you see a sleeping donkey, tiptoe around them, or you will disrupt their slumber. Donkeys are light sleepers and only nap for a couple of hours every night. However, they are usually cautious and alert during this time, so even while resting, they remain vigilant. They sleep while standing up but lie on their back or side when they need to rest.

Donkeys Are Therapy Animals

It isn't just cats and dogs that can be therapy animals; donkeys can be, too, thanks to their intuitive and gentle nature. They offer companionship and support to mental health patients and people with disabilities. They can sense when you are going through hard times or experiencing depression or anxiety.

Donkeys Are Fast Learners

Donkeys are intelligent, resilient, and pragmatic animals with a great memory. They are fast learners and can understand instructions quickly.

Male vs. Female

Male donkeys are called "Jacks," and female ones are called "Jennies," and each has their own fighting style. Jacks kick their enemies with their front feet, while Jennies use their hind legs.

Hormones

Female donkeys experience hormonal changes every month, which can lead to behavioral issues. They can either be very angry or super friendly. If you plan to raise Jenny, you should be understanding and patient during this time. You should also log her cycle dates on your calendar to be prepared every month. However, some female donkeys don't show any sign of behavioral changes during their cycle, and their temperament remains the same.

Protective Nature

It is a donkey's nature to protect other animals, like goats and sheep, from roaming dogs, coyotes, and other predators. They are territorial and will attack any stranger that invades their space. Donkeys are also very strong and are able to handle themselves against many strong animals. However, they are friendly and affectionate to human beings.

Female donkeys (or Jennies) are more protective than their male partners since their motherly instincts drive them to protect weaker and smaller animals and keep them safe.

Some people believe donkeys don't deliberately protect farm animals – they protect themselves and their territory. Whatever their intentions are, donkeys will keep your animals from harm.

How Donkeys Protect Their Flock

Donkeys don't always come to mind when people think of guard animals. In fact, you are probably wondering how a donkey can protect livestock. First of all, the donkeys should be present with the herd at all times. You can't just keep them with the animals for a few hours each day because you never know when a predator will attack. Donkeys also need to spend more time with the farm animals so they can bond together. This won't be hard for these social creatures who crave connections with other animals.

Donkeys rely on their unique hearing capabilities, which can make them detect noises from a distance, and their strong sight allows them to spot a predator from afar and take the necessary precautions before they attack. Sheep and other farm animals are very smart. They will quickly notice that the donkeys are their friends and allies and will seek their protection when threatened.

Donkeys scare their predators by letting out very loud brays and chasing after them to drive them away. This tactic should also get your attention and alert you that something isn't right so you can go and check on your animals. In most cases, you won't need to interfere, as the donkeys will confront the predator by themselves.

However, not all canines will retreat right away. In this case, the donkey will attack them by kicking them with their front feet, injuring or killing the predator. Male donkeys may also bite.

A donkey's strong herding instincts, aggressiveness, and natural dislike for predators make them ideal guard animals.

Advantages of Using Guardian Donkeys

Unfortunately, donkeys aren't as popular as guard animals as dogs are. People think they aren't strong or clever enough to protect their livestock. However, there are many reasons to consider guard donkeys.

Donkeys Are Always Alert

Thanks to their big ears and peripheral vision, donkeys are always aware of their surroundings and alert to any impending danger. Even when asleep, they are still alert and able to pick up any strange noise close or far away.

Territorial Behavior

Donkeys are very territorial, and their protective instinct results from this behavior. In other words, they don't protect the herd but their territory. If they feel someone invading their space, they will attack immediately.

Unlike dogs, donkeys don't patrol their area. They are already alert and can sense danger without moving.

Compatibility with Livestock Animals

Donkeys are compatible with sheep, and they bond easily with one another. Most donkeys happily protect sheep from predators. However, you should introduce both animals to each other early on and raise them together. Even if they didn't grow up in the same place, you can still teach your donkey to protect the herd by letting them live next to each other for two weeks. Significantly, the donkey and the sheep are compatible to avoid conflict. They won't protect an animal they can't tolerate. They are also compatible with horses, alpacas, llamas, goats, pigs, and other donkeys.

However, donkeys aren't compatible with farm dogs or any type of canine, so you should be very careful when introducing them to each other.

Guard Donkeys Aren't Expensive

Inexperienced guard donkeys aren't expensive, but you must train them. This will be easy since donkeys are clever and follow commands. Some won't even require training – you just let them socialize with your flock, and they will follow their protective instinct. You can buy a well-trained donkey, but they are more expensive.

Better Than Dogs

Training dogs takes more time and effort than training donkeys. They may also attack your livestock instead of protecting them. Guard dogs tend to bark a lot, unlike donkeys, who are fairly quiet unless they feel threatened. Most farm owners prefer to live in a quiet environment, and the barking can be off-putting. Dogs are also considered predators and won't be able to relate to farm animals. Donkeys, on the other hand, can relate to farm animals since they are both prey.

Donkeys Are Independent

Guard donkeys are very independent; they only need shelter, food, and water. They don't require constant care or attention. They also won't need expensive vet care since they aren't prone to injuries.

Protect against All Animals

Guard donkeys will protect almost all livestock, such as goats, sheep, and even chickens. Unlike with guard dogs, you won't have to worry about your donkeys attacking or eating any of your livestock.

They Live a Long Life

Your guard donkey will be with you for thirty years or more. Unlike other guard animals, donkeys have a long lifespan. They are also cost-effective since you won't need to buy a new one every ten years.

No Separate Accommodations

Being a guard, donkeys won't attack your animals; you can keep them in the same pasture with your livestock. This is another advantage they have over dogs, which require their own accommodations.

They Are Large

Most donkeys are large in size (between 300 and 500 pounds), so they will be able to handle different predators like foxes and coyotes. Stick to large donkeys and avoid miniature ones. They are nice to look at, but they won't protect your livestock from predators.

Their Braying Is Useful

Unlike dogs, a donkey won't bray all night or expect you to come to their aid. However, their very loud "hee-haw" sound is a clear sign that a predator is nearby.

Unfriendly to Canines

Donkeys don't get along with dogs or any type of canine, so they will be on guard if they see one approaching. Some donkeys don't have a problem with pet dogs, but many don't appreciate their presence.

They Are Ready for a Fight

Donkeys will never run away from a fight – they will stand their ground. They don't scare easily or get nervous in unfamiliar situations. They are curious, confident, and courageous in the face of danger. In fact, coyotes, foxes, and other small predators avoid confrontations with donkeys at all costs because they know they are tough fighters.

Calm Temperament

Donkeys are very calm animals and won't pose any threat to you, your family, neighbors, or other animals.

Real-Life Story

Amanda and her husband, Taylor, are fond of cattle ranching. They love their animals and consider them family. Standing among their cows, walking around, and braying are her beloved donkeys. Amanda said her husband didn't want dogs or horses on their ranch. She decided to prank him and get donkeys instead. To her surprise, Taylor came home one day with three donkeys. She realized that her husband had always loved donkeys and had plans to add a few to his ranch for a long time.

Amanda immediately fell in love with the donkeys because they were very affectionate and friendly. However, they weren't pets and should be kept with the cattle to guard them. Amanda said raising the donkeys was easy, and they got along very well with their cows. They followed the herd around and ate and drank with them. The donkeys protected the cows and their calves from roaming dogs and coyotes. Amanda and her husband agree that donkeys are the perfect guard animals. They have been with them for seven years and have only lost one cow to coyotes.

Amanda and Taylor entrust their cattle with the donkeys all day while they are at work. Every day, they appreciate their little helpers more and more.

Caring for a Guardian Donkey

If you want your donkeys to stay healthy and live with you for a long time, you should take good care of them and pay attention to their feeding, shelter, and health.

Feed and Care

You should leave fresh water for your donkeys all day. Check it throughout the day and refill it when needed. One donkey requires 10 to 25 liters every day. You should add mineralized salt to their diet. Read the ingredients on the feed packaging or check with the district agriculturalist to find which minerals are missing from their food. To protect your animals from mineral or vitamin deficiency, find ways to add them to their diet, like giving them supplements.

During the winter, feed your donkeys high-quality hay. Avoid legume hay since it is high in protein. Brome grass and meadow grass are your best options. Feed pregnant and nursing donkeys 50 percent alfalfa and 50 percent Timothy hay. Feed male guardian donkeys grains and give them supplements to increase their energy levels. Avoid supplements made for poultry, pigs, or cattle, as they can be toxic to them.

Health

Donkeys require regular deworming and vaccinations. Deworm them three to six times every year. You can do this yourself using a paste warmer or get a professional to do it for you. If you suspect your donkey has parasites, call your vet right away to get them the proper vaccinations.

Proper hoof care is necessary for guard donkeys. Trim and clear out their feet every month. If you neglect hoof care, they will grow to a very large size and cripple your animal.

Donkeys also require dental care, so make sure to get their teeth checked twice a year.

Shelter

Donkeys prefer warm climates, but they can adapt to the cold if they are provided with enough food and a warm and safe shelter. Donkeys can't stand the rain since their coat isn't waterproof, so they are left cold and wet, which can lead to various diseases like bronchitis and pneumonia. Make sure their shelter protects them from the rain. You should also remove the snow from their coat during the winter. Keep your donkeys in the barn during the winter and only let them out on warm days. In the warm weather, they will only need an open-front shed bedded with dry straw.

Pasture

Let your donkeys graze coarser pastures, but avoid lush ones since they can increase their weight and cause other serious health issues. Allocate your donkeys one acre of pasture every month.

Donkeys are intelligent and strong animals that can protect your cattle against any threat. They have unique skills that can make them sense their enemies from a distance. Although there are different guard animals, donkeys have many advantages that make them a great choice.

Mankind has been depending on donkeys for centuries. They have used them for transportation, to guard their animals, and even to eat their meat and drink their milk. These faithful companions make life much easier, and they never ask for anything in return. Make sure to give them a loving home and a warm shelter during the cold. Take care of their health and protect them just like they protect you and your livestock.

There are still more things to discuss about donkeys, like how to choose the right one for you and how to train them. Head to the next chapter to find out all this information and more.

Chapter 10: Choosing and Training Your Donkey

Now that you know everything about guard donkeys, you are probably considering bringing one home to protect your livestock. However, you can't just choose any donkey. You have to go through a process to find the right one for you. Afterward, you will need to train them so they can become the best guard animal there is. Understandably, this is easier said than done.

This chapter provides expert tips and practical techniques for the donkey's selection and training process.

Training guardian donkey.[51]

Selecting Guard Donkeys

There are a few things to consider before choosing a guard donkey, like age, breed, temperament, and gender. You don't want to bring a donkey home only to realize they aren't a good fit. Follow these tips to select the ideal guard donkey for you.

Age

Choose a donkey that is – at most – three years old because sheep and other cattle get along better with younger animals. Remember, the older the donkey, the harder the introduction will be. They will also be playful, and they will run around with the sheep and bond together. Some people prefer donkeys that are six months or younger to raise them with the herd. However, an animal that age won't be a good guardian. Older cattle may also bully them or play roughly with them.

Gender

Jenny and her foal (young donkey) are ideal for guarding donkeys. Females have motherly instincts and are natural protectors. However, the Jenny will be enough if you don't want more than one donkey. Geldings have also become very popular in the last few years because of their calm temperament. Avoid intact Jacks (unneutered males) because of their aggressive nature and tendency to be violent with people and cattle. Pregnant Jennies aren't a good idea since they will focus more on their newborns and ignore the livestock. If your flock is attacked, they will only defend their newborns with no concern for the safety of the other animals.

Size

Stick with large or normal-sized donkeys. However, some people don't prefer very large donkeys as they are hard to handle. There is no denying that they will scare off predators, but you should consider if it is worth the hassle. Choose a size of about 44 inches.

Avoid miniature ones because they are too small and don't have the physical strength to guard a flock. A small donkey won't be intimidating or scare predators. Your herd may also be attacked by a pack of animals, so you need a big enough donkey to fight them off and scare them away. A miniature donkey will still fight them because it's their nature, but they will get seriously injured or even killed.

Breed

All donkey breeds, like Mammoth, Australian, and Irish, can be guard animals. Just make sure you choose a healthy and sturdy one.

Temperament

Avoid donkeys with an aggressive nature, as they aren't easy to handle. Remember – you want a donkey that will protect your animals, not one that is easily agitated and can hurt them. Choose an even-tempered donkey that you feel safe leaving your flock with all day.

Flock Size

Donkeys can only guard a small flock of about 100 animals or less if they are scattered across the land. However, a donkey can guard about 200 sheep if your flock grazes on one pasture. So, you should consider getting more than one donkey if you have a large flock.

Other things to look out for:

- Good attitude
- Straight legs
- Good conformation

Where to Find a Guard Donkey

- "Adopt, don't shop" applies to guard animals as well. You will find many rescue donkeys in specialized organizations. They are usually tested with goats and sheep to assess their guardian skills. You can return the donkey to them if things don't work out. However, if things do work out, you will be giving a worthy donkey a loving home - and a job!

- You can also find donkeys in livestock auctions or a mule and donkey breed association.

Training Guard Donkeys

After choosing your donkey and bringing it home, you should start training it. You can get an experienced guard donkey, but they are usually more expensive. If you want to save money, learn to train your animal yourself. Luckily, this will be easy since donkeys are very clever animals.

Basic Principles of Training Guard Donkeys

The main principles of training animals are behavior correction and positive reinforcement. Your donkey's negative behavior should be corrected right away so they understand that there are consequences to their actions. Positive behavior should also be rewarded.

Positive reinforcement is one of the most powerful training techniques, as it can shape or change your donkey's behavior. It usually involves giving rewards like praise, treats, or anything your donkey enjoys. They will most likely repeat the positive behavior in order to keep getting the rewards.

Training your donkey or any animal requires a lot of patience. You are teaching your donkey to adopt new behaviors, but they are bound to make mistakes and return to their old ways, so you need to be patient with them. Getting your donkey to repeat the same behavior isn't always easy, even with them being clever. You may sometimes feel bored or frustrated, but you must exert self-control. You lose control when you lose your temper, which confuses the donkey. Always remain firm and calm, and you will see real results in no time.

Obedience Training Techniques

Instructions:

1. If your donkey is hyper or acting out, training them will be very difficult. They won't be able to focus and learn something new. So, before you start, let them do a couple of exercises to get into a better and calmer state.

2. Remove all distractions. Teaching an animal something new is already tricky, so try to eliminate anything that can affect their concentration. It is better to train them in a low-key environment.

3. Make the technique fun. It should feel like playing, not work. Enjoy your time with your animals, and take the opportunity to know them better.

4. Decide on a reward system and make sure it is something your donkey responds well to, like treats or praise.

5. Reward them with treats or praise when they follow your commands. If they don't obey, be patient, and keep trying... they will eventually get it.

6. Take a break whenever you start to feel tired or frustrated. The break can be a couple of hours or a few days. Be patient with yourself and your donkey.

Stopping Bad Behavior

- Don't punish your donkey because many animals don't understand the concept of punishment. It can do more damage than good.

- When your donkey misbehaves, walk away from them. Donkeys that are bonded with their owners will not want to lose the attention you give them. They will try to rectify their behavior to regain your bond and trust.

- You can also withhold something they like from them, just like you do with a child. For instance, if they bite or fight with the cattle during mealtime, withhold their food from them until they correct their behavior. When they do, reward them with positive reinforcement, like treats or food.

Positive Reinforcement vs. Treats

Treats are effective, but you can't reward your donkey for every good behavior. This will teach them to act favorably only to get something in return. They will come to expect treats each time and may act out if you don't give them any. So, use treats only on occasions and when you want to correct very bad behavior, like biting. Stick with positive reinforcement instead, like petting, scratching, praise, or positive talk.

Train Your Donkey in a Small Area

Training your donkey in a small area will put you in control of the situation. This will prevent them from running or hiding. It will make things easier since you will be able to limit distractions, so your donkey will only focus on you.

More Training Tips

- Your donkey will learn something new every time you interact with it.

- Donkeys don't understand the difference between good and bad behavior. Their behavior is either effective or ineffective for them.

- Donkeys learn activities related to their natural behavior faster. It takes them longer to learn things that are unnatural to them and detached from their nature, like traveling in a trailer, holding their feet up for hoof cleaning, pulling a cart, and being ridden or driven.

- Start with teaching your donkey relatable behavior, like getting food or walking next to you.

- Using positive reinforcement when teaching your donkey natural behavior will make it easier to teach them unnatural ones.

- Never discipline your donkey or punish them; they will get angry and stop cooperating.

- Don't use sticks when interacting with them; instead, use carrots.

- When they don't follow directions, switch to another familiar activity.

Patrolling

Donkeys don't patrol the area – they usually look for any threat within their flock. Although this behavior isn't in their nature, you can train them to patrol. For instance, you can take them on walks to discover the area so they get used to it and know it's safe. You can also ask someone to make a sound in the distance and take your donkey to investigate. This will teach them to patrol the area when they hear a strange sound. Use positive reinforcement or teats to reward them for patrolling.

Alertness and Responding to Threats

Although donkeys are naturally alert, you can still train them to boost this behavior. Reward your donkey whenever it brays or exhibits any guarding behavior at any sign of danger. This teaches your donkey to be more alert to predators and threats.

You can use the same technique to train your donkey to respond to threats. As donkeys are territorial, they will naturally be protective over the livestock. Use treats or positive reinforcement whenever your donkey responds to threats; this encourages that behavior more.

Socializing Your Donkey with Your Livestock

Introduce your donkey to your cattle right away to initiate the bonding process. The donkey will only exhibit protective behavior when they feel the sheep is part of their flock. Raise Jenny and her foal with the cattle.

Weaned foals can be left alone with the cattle.

There are other steps you should take to help your donkey socialize with your livestock. Understand that this won't always be a simple process. Some donkeys are prone to territorial behavior, and it can take them a while to accept other animals. Depending on the donkey, the introduction can take an hour or a few days. However, the bonding process takes about five weeks. Make sure to have someone with you while making the introduction in case the donkey or the herd reacts unfavorably.

Instructions:

1. Let the donkey stay in the same barn as your livestock for two weeks, but separate them with a fence.

2. After the two weeks, bring them to the same pasture and put a fence between them. Give them time and space to sniff each other so they can become familiar with one another's scent, but keep an eye on them.

3. You can lead the donkey around the flock with a rope so they can smell one another. Repeat this until they accept and trust each other.

4. Feed the donkey with the cattle so they can bond. The donkey will also feel that it's a member of the herd.

5. Once they accept each other, allow the donkey to run around on the pasture. In time, the cattle will seek the donkey whenever threatened.

Signs the Donkey Isn't Reacting Favorably

- Lunging
- Biting
- Ears pinned
- Head down
- Chasing
- Ears pulled back
- Flared nostrils
- Whiteness around the eyes.
- Exposed teeth

Expect some minor fights, but this isn't any cause for alarm. They are just getting to know each other. Only intervene if they start to act aggressively. However, don't stand between them. Create a distraction so they would pay attention to something else. Don't introduce them to each other right after the fight. Give them more time to get used to each other's scent, then try again. Remember – donkeys are stubborn, so things may not go as you planned. Don't let this discourage you, though. Since donkeys are also social creatures and love bonding with other animals, they will eventually get along. Just give them time.

Get Your Donkey to Trust You

It isn't enough that your donkey trusts the cattle – they should trust you, too. Creating a strong bond between you and your guard animal will make training much easier.

Instructions:
1. Visit their area a few times a day.
2. Stand there and don't approach them.
3. If they approach you, pet them or give them a treat.
4. Try standing a little close to them while monitoring their body language.
5. Retreat if they look uncomfortable.
6. If they come to you again, give them another treat.
7. Repeat this every day until they learn to trust you.

Introducing Donkeys to Predators

You can't bring a coyote to your farm and let it hang around your livestock. Your safest option is a dog.

Instructions:
1. Put your dog on a leash and bring it to the donkey to make the introduction. The donkey should be tied or held.
2. Keep a distance between them, but make sure they can still see each other.
3. Approach the donkey slowly with the dog.
4. Use commands like stay, wait, stop, sit, come, etc., to control your dog if the donkey acts out.

5. If the dog seems interested or curious about the donkey, stop approaching and give your dog a treat.

6. Take another step while monitoring your dog. If they remain calm, give them another treat. If the dog or the donkey seems scared, calm them down.

7. When both are calm, approach gradually while keeping an eye on both of them.

8. Once you get close to the donkey, allow them to sniff each other. Do this for a couple of seconds, then retreat and give each animal a treat.

9. Repeat this process until they become familiar with each other. Make sure to keep both of them leashed so you can remain in control and protect them from harm.

10. Once they seem comfortable, remove the leash and let them interact.

Safety Tips

- Monitor their interactions at all times because your dog may bite the donkey or get too close to it, making the donkey uncomfortable.

- If the donkey gets irritated or agitated, it might kick the dog and seriously injure it. Keeping an eye on both of them will guarantee everyone's safety.

Safety Measures

You need to keep yourself safe when training your donkey. Donkeys may not react favorably to training, so you should be prepared for anything.

Handling a Donkey

- When approaching a donkey, speak in a calm voice to get their attention.

- Don't approach them head-on or from behind, or they may consider you a threat. Instead, approach by their shoulder.

- Gently touch their neck and keep touching them so they are aware of your location.

- Stand by their side to protect yourself from getting kicked.

- Keep it on a leash if it is prone to kicking or aggression.

Safety Precautions

- Monitor your donkey's body language during training sessions and take a few steps back whenever they seem uncomfortable. Remember, donkeys are clever animals that may kick or bite you from behind to take you by surprise.

- Training sessions should be in spacious areas so you can easily get away whenever they show any sign of aggression.

- Avoid sudden moves or raising your voice. Speak calmly and use a gentle touch to prevent agitating them.

- Aggression is a sign of fear, so try to be understanding.

Common Challenges

Charging

When a donkey is angry or threatened, it can charge at you or another animal. If your donkey is about to attack, walk away from it. Stand across the fence until it calms down and realizes that you are not a threat. Luckily, charging isn't a common behavior among donkeys.

Kicking

Donkeys have very strong kicks, which is one of the reasons why they are great guard animals. If they kick you or an animal of your flock, they can cause serious injuries. Kicking is a sign of aggression, so treat the situation with caution.

- Leave them alone for a few hours until they calm down.

- Find what triggered their aggression and deal with it. For instance, if they are afraid of another animal or person, separate them from each other.

Biting:

Biting is another sign of either aggression or fear. They will either bite you or the flock they are supposed to protect. For instance, they may bite and toss smaller animals or birds like baby pigs, chickens, or ducks. They may also bite you if you are making them do something against their will. You can change this behavior by using the tips in this chapter.

Snorting

Snorting is a sign that your donkey doesn't want to be bothered today. They are either mad about something or want to be left alone. Give them some space, then check on them.

Flaring Nostrils, Pinned-Back Ears, and Pawing at the Ground

These are all signs of aggression. Your donkey may act this way because it feels threatened. Before you react, make sure that there aren't any predators nearby. Try to find what triggers this behavior. If it is afraid of another animal, separate them, wait until they calm down, and make gradual introductions again.

More often than not, your donkey's aggression is a sign of fear. You must eliminate whatever triggers these emotions and make them feel safe. When you become familiar with their behavior, you will know whether they are acting out or scared. Use any of the tips in this chapter to rectify their behavior. Remember to always be calm and patient with them and treat them like children.

Conclusion

Now that you've explored the details of livestock guardians on all levels, you are ready to begin your journey with these protective beasts. Do not rush to make any decisions. Take your time and consider all the aspects of your land and the animals you are raising. The right guardian can keep your livestock safe, but the wrong choice can increase your stress. Taking on a livestock guardian as part of your farm family is not a small decision to make. Think long and hard about whether you are ready for the responsibility and how introducing this animal to your livestock will help you. Do not wear rose-tinted goggles when assessing your farm, and be completely honest with yourself so that you can make the most beneficial decision for you and your livestock.

Take the calculated steps to first check which predators are plaguing your land and how they behave. Then, consider which guardian species or breed best aligns with your individualized context. Whether you choose dogs, donkeys, or llamas, it will all depend on your specific contextual environment. Consider how big the predators you are facing are and how the guardian responds to them. When you have replayed every possible scenario in your mind multiple times and looked at your farm through a microscope, you will be ready to take the next step and identify a guardian animal.

You are crafting an artificial ecosystem with the animals you introduce to your farm. The animals you bring together must create a seamless dance of cooperation. There may be hiccups and conflicts along the way, but as the head of the ecosystem you created, you can intervene when necessary. You are the choir conductor who creates the melody of your farm. Carefully analyze the fine details of your biodiverse approach to farming so that you can easily respond to any challenge or required change.

Be mindful of your environmental impact. The earth, which includes your farm, provides you with literally everything. Leave the planet in a better condition than you found it so that future generations can thrive. Using livestock guardians is already a step in the right direction because it is superior to more detrimental methods of predator control, like poisoning. It is not about humankind conquering nature but rather about building an environment where both can symbiotically coexist.

Raising a guardian animal is a big responsibility. There are countless care considerations you must make, like nutrition, parasites, and medical concerns. Your guardian is doing an important job, so the least you can do is make sure that their well-being is optimal. You must care for your guardians so they can help you care for your other animals in a beautiful balancing act of nature. Predators can be the downfall of a farm, so a good guardian is intrinsically tied to your success as a farmer. Therefore, you must do all you can to ensure they are emotionally, physically, and mentally at ease.

Here's another book by Dion Rosser that you might like

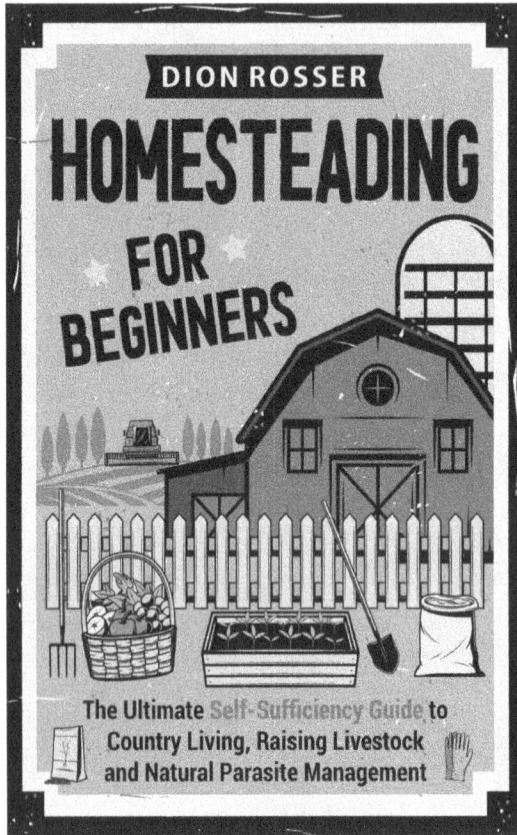

DION ROSSER

HOMESTEADING

FOR BEGINNERS

The Ultimate Self-Sufficiency Guide to Country Living, Raising Livestock and Natural Parasite Management

References

10 Facts about Geese. (2019, April 9). FOUR PAWS International - Animal Welfare Organisation; #organization. https://www.four-paws.org/campaigns-topics/topics/farm-animals/10-facts-about-geese

10 Fun Facts about Chickens. (2022, March 26). BC SPCA. https://spca.bc.ca/news/fun-facts-about-chickens/

10 Incredible Duck Facts. (n.d).AZ Animals. https://a-z-animals.com/blog/incredible-duck-facts/

10 Turkey Facts. (2020, September 28). World Animal Protection. https://www.worldanimalprotection.us/blogs/10-turkey-facts

15 Management Tips for Better Poultry Performance Potential. (2018, June 21).Alltech. https://www.alltech.com/blog/15-management-tips-better-poultry-performance-potential

7 Benefits to Raising Backyard Chickens. (2022, October 31). Strombergs. https://www.strombergschickens.com/blog/7-benefits-to-raising-backyard-chickens/

7 Therapeutic Benefits of Birdwatching. (n.d.). Careuk.com. https://www.careuk.com/company/care-uk-campaigns/bird-watch/7-therapeutic-benefits-of-birdwatching

Ajaero, T. M. (2018, February 8). How to Care for Baby Chicks After they Hatch. ProfitableVenture; Profitable Venture Magazine Ltd. https://www.profitableventure.com/care-for-baby-chicks-hatch/

Amorvet is a Poultry Feed Supplement Manufacturer. (2023, July 27). Amorvet. https://www.amorvet.com/blogs/poultryfeedsupplement/

April. (2022, April 18). 5 Most Expensive Turkey Breeds. The Hip Chick. https://thehipchick.com/expensive-turkey-breeds/

Are Treats for Chickens Good for your Flock's Health? (n.d.). Raising Happy Chickens. https://www.raising-happy-chickens.com/treats-for-chickens.html

Atapattu, S., & Baker, A. (n.d.). SOLID BROILER MANAGEMENT Training Manual. https://pdf.usaid.gov/pdf_docs/pa00mgpt.pdf

Basic Duck Care. (2020, February 17). Cornell University College of Veterinary Medicine. https://www.vet.cornell.edu/animal-health-diagnostic-center/programs/duck-research-lab/basic-duck-care

Basic Poultry Nutrition. (n.d.). Extension.org. https://poultry.extension.org/articles/feeds-and-feeding-of-poultry/basic-poultry-nutrition/

Benefits of Poultry Feed Supplements. (2021, January 12). Shivam Chemicals Limited. https://www.shivamchem.com/blog/benefits-of-poultry-feed-supplements/

Berg, C. (2002). Health and Welfare in Organic Poultry Production. Acta Veterinaria Scandinavica, 43(Suppl 1), S37. https://doi.org/10.1186/1751-0147-43-s1-s37

bestnestbox.com. (2015, August 12). Interested In Raising Chickens? Here Are Some Common Myths About Chicken Farming, Debunked: Part 1. Bestnestbox.com. https://bestnestbox.com/blogs/news/common-myths-about-chicken-farming-debunked-part-1

bestnestbox.com. (2015, August 15). Interested In Raising Chickens? Here Are Some Common Myths About Chicken Farming, Debunked: Part 2. Bestnestbox.com. https://bestnestbox.com/blogs/news/interested-in-raising-chickens-here-are-some-common-myths-about-chicken-farming-debunked-part-2

Bird Food Guide: An Insider's Guide to the Ideal Avian Diet. (2012, April 7). Lafeber® Pet Birds.

Branaman, J. (2018). Cage-free vs. battery-cage eggs. The Humane Society of the United States. https://www.humanesociety.org/resources/cage-free-vs-battery-cage-eggs

Brian. (2015, March 11). 5 Common Misconceptions about Raising Chickens for Meat. Ferrin Brook Farm. https://ferrinbrookfarm.wordpress.com/2015/03/11/5-common-misconceptions-about-raising-chickens-for-meat-2/

British Hen Welfare Trust. (2022, September 21). A Guide to Chicken Treats; Everything in Moderation. British Hen Welfare Trust. https://www.bhwt.org.uk/blog/health-welfare/chicken-treats-guide/

Bronze, K. (2019, November 8). More than Just a Turkey - Kelly Bronze. KellyBronze. https://www.kellybronze.co.uk/more-than-just-a-turkey/

Bupp, J. (2022, November 13). Defending Our Chickens Against Four-Legged Thieves. Lancasterfarming.com.

https://www.lancasterfarming.com/country-life/family/defending-our-chickens-against-four-legged-theives/article_82c4dd2a-6098-11ed-87af-8b31b24e30d2.html

Capps, A. (2014, November 21). These Amazing Conversations Between Turkeys & Humans may Change Your Mind about Eating Them. Free From Harm. https://freefromharm.org/videos/turkey-talk/

Carlson, R. E. (2023, October 11). Advantages and disadvantages of free range chickens: What you need to know. Homesteading Simple Self-Sufficiency Off-The-Grid | Homesteading.com. \

Chicken. (2016, April 25). Smithsonian's National Zoo; Smithsonian's National Zoo and Conservation Biology Institute. https://nationalzoo.si.edu/animals/domestic-chicken

Cole, T. (2019, February 22). Poultry houses: 197 designs, structures, plans & systems (PDF guide). The Big Book Project. https://thebigbookproject.org/agri/poultry-farming/houses-chicken/

Coogan, K. (2023, November 16). Four rare and threatened duck breeds. Backyard Poultry. https://backyardpoultry.iamcountryside.com/poultry-101/four-threatened-duck-breeds/

Country Smallholding. (2016, May 9). Chicken body language. Country Smallholding. https://thecountrysmallholder.com/country-smallholding/chicken-body-language-6260096/

Daniel. (2020, December 17). 7 Different Types of Poultry Birds. Agricfy.com. https://agricfy.com/types-of-poultry/

Daniels, T. (2012, May 8). The Beginner's Guide to Keeping Geese. Poultrykeeper.com; Tim Daniels. https://poultrykeeper.com/keeping-geese/beginners-guide-keeping-geese/

DeVore, S. (2019, April 5). Forage or Feed? Nutritional Benefits of Chickens that Forage. News From The Coop. https://newsfromthecoop.hoovershatchery.com/forage-or-feed-best-for-chickens-nutritional-benefits-of-chickens-that-forage/

Discover 11 Fascinating Pigeon Facts. (2022, March 9). Excel Pest Services. https://www.excelpestservices.com/11-fun-facts-about-pigeons/

Disease Control And Management. (n.d.). Tnau.Ac.In. http://www.agritech.tnau.ac.in/expert_system/poultry/

Diseases of poultry. (n.d.). Msstate.edu. https://extension.msstate.edu/agriculture/livestock/poultry/diseases-poultry

Duck. (2019, October 5). Animal Spot. https://www.animalspot.net/duck

Endangered. (2020, October 2). 10 Easy Things You Can Do to Save Endangered Species. Endangered Species Coalition. https://www.endangered.org/10-easy-things-you-can-do-to-save-endangered-species/

Farhat, G. (2023, April 6). An Evaluation of Different Chicken Housing Systems. MonoGutHealth. https://monoguthealth.eu/an-evaluation-of-different-chicken-housing-systems-2/

Farm, R. (2023, November 6). Jersey Buff Turkey: Characteristics & Best 7 facts. ROYS FARM. https://www.roysfarm.com/jersey-buff-turkey/

Farm. (2018, April 2). 9 Basic Considerations for Backyard Poultry. Farm and Dairy. https://www.farmanddairy.com/top-stories/9-basic-considerations-for-backyard-poultry/478093.html

Feed Additives for use in Poultry Diets | Animal & Food Sciences. https://afs.ca.uky.edu/poultry/feed-additives-use-poultry-diets

Feed additives. (n.d.). Food Safety. https://food.ec.europa.eu/safety/animal-feed/feed-additives_en

Feed Ingredients. (n.d.). Poultry Hub Australia. https://www.poultryhub.org/all-about-poultry/nutrition/feed-ingredients

Flank, L. (2017, September 8). Chicken Behavior: The Politics of the Pecking Order. Hobby Farms. https://www.hobbyfarms.com/pecking-order-chicken-behavior-history-science/

Foie Gras: Cruelty to Ducks and Geese. (2010, June 22). PETA. https://www.peta.org/issues/animals-used-for-food/factory-farming/ducks-geese/foie-gras/

Freedomrangerhatchery. (2022, July 7). Raising Turkeys 101 | Freedom Ranger Hatcheries. https://www.freedomrangerhatchery.com/blog/raising-turkeys-101-how-to-grow-happy-healthy-poults/

Fromm, I. (2018, October 23). 15 Fun Facts about Chickens. Carolinacoops.com. https://carolinacoops.com/resources/15-fun-facts-about-chickens/

Garrigus, W. P. (2023). Poultry Farming. In Encyclopedia Britannica.

Goldman, J. G. (n.d.). Nothing To Gobble At: Social Cognition in Turkeys. Scientific American Blog Network. https://blogs.scientificamerican.com/thoughtful-animal/nothing-to-gobble-at-social-cognition-in-turkeys/

Gomez, M. (2023, July 30). 10 Quail Facts about the Stout Small Pheasants. TRVST. https://www.trvst.world/biodiversity/quail-facts/

Haberfield, J. (2021, August 3). Pigeon & Dove Care – Learn How To Take Care of These Birds. The Unusual Pet Vets. https://www.unusualpetvets.com.au/pigeon-and-dove-care/

Hayes, B. (2022, February 4). 11 Benefits of Raising Chickens You Didn't Know. Homesteading Where You Are. https://www.homesteadingwhereyouare.com/2022/02/03/benefits-of-raising-chickens/

Health and welfare. (2020, July 20). Agriculture Victoria. https://agriculture.vic.gov.au/livestock-and-animals/poultry-and-eggs/health-and-welfare

Hotaling, A. (2021, June 30). Common Myths About the Backyard Chicken Flock. Hobby Farms. https://www.hobbyfarms.com/common-myths-about-the-backyard-chicken-flock/

How To Deal With an Aggressive Rooster. (n.d.). Raising Happy Chickens. https://www.raising-happy-chickens.com/aggressive-rooster.html

How to Read Turkeys' Body Language. (2020). Montanadecoy.com. https://montanadecoy.com/blog/how-to-read-a-turkeys-body-language/

Identifying 12 Backyard Chicken Predators. (2018, September 19). Predator Guard. https://predatorguard.com/blogs/news/identifying-12-backyard-chicken-predators

Ingram, B. (2019, November 6).Meet the Alpha Hen: Every Flock Has One. Hobby Farms. https://www.hobbyfarms.com/meet-the-alpha-hen-every-flock-has-one/

Ito, D., & Hendrix, H. (2021, April 7). Changing poultry housing systems, having the right breed for the right system - Laying Hens. https://layinghens.hendrix-genetics.com/en/news/changing-poultry-housing-systems-having-the-right-breed-for-the-right-housing-system/

Jagdish. (2020, November 28). Poultry Housing – Types, Equipment, and Construction. Agri Farming. https://www.agrifarming.in/poultry-housing-types-equipment-and-construction

Johnsgard, P. A. (1968). The Evolution of Duck Courtship . University of Nebraska-Lincoln. https://digitalcommons.unl.edu/cgi/viewcontent.cgi?article=1030&context=bioscio rnithology

Kubala, J., MS, & RD. (2022, April 8). How To Raise Chickens: A Complete Beginner's Guide. Healthline. https://www.healthline.com/nutrition/how-to-raise-chickens

Kunzmann, P. (2011, September 7). Ethics in the Poultry Industry – Answering Moral Questions of Society.Lohmann Breeders. https://lohmann-breeders.com/lohmanninfo/ethics-in-the-poultry-industry-answering-moral-questions-of-society/

Lesley, C. (2020, August 9). The 9 Rarest Chicken Breeds In The World. Chickens And More. https://www.chickensandmore.com/rare-chicken-breeds/

Lie-Nielsen, K. (2017, November 17). Questions Before you Get Geese. Hostilevalleyliving. https://www.hostilevalleyliving.com/single-post/2017/11/17/questions-before-you-get-geese

LineaPoultry Predator Identification: A Guide to Tracks and Sign. (2015, March 15). Ouroneacrefarm.com. https://ouroneacrefarm.com/2015/03/15/poultry-predator-identification-a-guide-to-tracks-and-sign/

Livestock and Poultry Predator ID Guide. (n.d.). Benton County, Oregon.

Macer, D. (2019). Ethical Poultry and the Bioethics of Poultry Production.The Journal of Poultry Science, 56(2), 79–83. https://doi.org/10.2141/jpsa.0180074

Malnourished conure. (2012, September 3). Parrot Forum Parrot Owners Community. https://www.parrotforums.com/threads/malnourished-conure.22576/

Matthews, S. (2016, September 16). An Organic Chicken Farm in Georgia Has Become an Endless Buffet for Bald Eagles. Audubon. https://www.audubon.org/magazine/fall-2016/an-organic-chicken-farm-georgia-has-become-endless

Mental Well-being. (n.d.). Org.Nz. https://kids.spcaeducation.org.nz/animal-care/chickens/mental-wellbeing/

Mitchell, A. (n.d).A Simple Guide to the Nutritional Requirements of Poultry. Thepoultrysite.com. https://www.thepoultrysite.com/articles/a-simple-guide-to-the-nutritional-requirements-of-poultry

Nicolaides, C. (1932). Fertility and Hatchability Studies in Poultry. University of Massachusetts Amherst. https://doi.org/10.7275/8V9B-8506

Oloyo, A., & Ojerinde, A. (2020). Poultry Housing and Management. In A. A. Kamboh (Ed.), Poultry - An Advanced Learning. IntechOpen.

O'Connell, N. (2022, May 12). Improved Housing Standards for Commercial Poultry. Queen's University Belfast. https://www.qub.ac.uk/Research/case-studies/improving-housing-standards-commercial-poultry.html

Pecking Order: Understanding Chickens' Social Dynamics. (2022, October 31). Strombergs. https://www.strombergschickens.com/blog/pecking-order-understanding-chickens-social-dynamics/

Pierce, R. (2022, November 18). 15 Ways to Deal with Aggressive Ducks. The Happy Chicken Coop. https://www.thehappychickencoop.com/15-ways-to-deal-with-aggressive-ducks/

Poisbleau, M., Fritz, H., Guillon, N., & Chastel, O. (2005). Linear Social Dominance Hierarchy and Corticosterone Responses in Male Mallards and Pintails. Hormones and Behavior, 47(4), 485–492. https://doi.org/10.1016/j.yhbeh.2005.01.001

Poultry - Diseases and Treatment. (n.d.). Khamarguru.com. https://khamarguru.com/poultry/en/diseases-treatment.html

Poultry Housing. (n.d.). State.Pa.Us. http://www.phmc.state.pa.us/portal/communities/agriculture/field-guide/poultry-housing.html

Praharee, T. P. (2023, November 19). Importance of Conservation of Indigenous Breeds of Livestock and Poultry. Pashudhan Prahree. https://www.pashudhanpraharee.com/importance-of-conservation-of-indigenous-breeds-of-livestock-and-poultry-2/

Predator Management for Small and Backyard Poultry Flocks. (n.d.). Extension.org. https://poultry.extension.org/articles/poultry-management/predator-management-for-small-and-backyard-poultry-flocks/

Predators of Poultry. (n.d.). Osu.edu. https://ohioline.osu.edu/factsheet/vme-22

Pros and Cons of Supplements. (2021, September 2). Food Darzee. https://fooddarzee.com/blog/pros-and-cons-of-supplements

Rafter W Ranch. (2023, April 2). The Top 4 Benefits of Pasture-raised Chicken. Rafter W Ranch | Colorado Grass Fed Beef, Lamb, Poultry, Produce. https://rafterwranch.net/top-4-benefits-pasture-raised-chicken/

Rhodes, J. (2022, September 11). Using Chickens for Garden Pest Control & Disease in Orchards. Abundant Permaculture. https://abundantpermaculture.com/using-chickens-for-garden-pest-control/

Roeder, M. (n.d.). 21-Day Guide to Hatching Eggs. Purinamills.com. https://www.purinamills.com/chicken-feed/education/detail/hatching-eggs-at-home-a-21-day-guide-for-baby-chicks

Selecting the Right Species of Poultry To Get for a Small or Backyard Poultry Flock. (n.d.). Extension.org. https://poultry.extension.org/articles/getting-started-with-small-and-backyard-poultry/selecting-birds-to-get-for-a-small-or-backyard-poultry-flock/

Should You Get a Chicken for Your Home? (n.d.). Green America. https://greenamerica.org/green-living/many-benefits-backyard-chickens

Small-scale Poultry Production. (n.d.). Fao.org. https://www.fao.org/3/y5169e/y5169e05.htm

Smith, T. W. (n.d.). Care and Incubation of Hatching Eggs. Thepoultrysite.com. https://www.thepoultrysite.com/articles/care-and-incubation-of-hatching-eggs

The Best Way to Hatch Chicken Eggs. (2020, September 6). Dine a Chook. https://www.dineachook.com.au/blog/incubating-chicken-eggs-pros-and-cons/

The Happy Chicken Coop. (2021, March 11). 9 Healthy Treats Your Chickens Will Love. The Happy Chicken Coop. https://www.thehappychickencoop.com/9-healthy-treats-your-chickens-will-love/

The Hidden Lives of Ducks and Geese. (2010, June 22). PETA. https://www.peta.org/issues/animals-used-for-food/factory-farming/ducks-geese/hidden-lives-ducks-geese/

THL. (2021, January 19). Actory-Farmed Chickens: The Cruelty of Chicken Farms. Thehumaneleague.org. https://thehumaneleague.org/article/factory-farmed-chickens

Turkey Welfare. (n.d.). Org.uk. https://www.ciwf.org.uk/farm-animals/turkeys/turkey-welfare/

Vanmetre, D. (2008). Infectious Diseases of the Gastrointestinal Tract. In Rebhun's Diseases of Dairy Cattle (pp. 200–294). Elsevier.

Virbac. (2019, April 25). How To Choose Good Feed for Your Poultry. Virbac.com. https://in.virbac.com/poultry/health-care/nutrition/how-to-choose-good-feed-for-your-poultry

What Are the Potential Risks Associated With Using Livestock Feed Supplements? (n.d.). SciSpace - Question. https://typeset.io/questions/what-are-the-potential-risks-associated-with-using-livestock-1m48uzjs2m

What is Small Animal Foraging? (1 C.E., January 1). Kaytee.com; Kaytee: Pet Supplies | Kaytee Products. https://www.kaytee.com/learn-care/small-animals/what-is-foraging

Why Nutrition Is So Important for Your Hens.(n.d.). ForFarmers UK.

Wild Turkey identification. (n.d.). Allaboutbirds.org. https://www.allaboutbirds.org/guide/Wild_Turkey/id

Willis, K., & Ludlow, R. T. (2016, March 26).11 Misconceptions About Chickens, Eggs, and So On. Dummies. https://www.dummies.com/article/home-auto-hobbies/hobby-farming/chickens/11-misconceptions-about-chickens-eggs-and-so-on-144654/

Worksheet Freelancer. (2019, March 8). Quail Facts, Worksheets, Habitat, Diet, Characteristics & Breeding for Kids.KidsKonnect. https://kidskonnect.com/animals/quail/

(2021). Unfccc.int. https://unfccc.int/sites/default/files/resource/SB2021_01.pdf

(N.d.). Homesteadingtoday.com. https://www.homesteadingtoday.com/threads/lgd-behavior-problems-how-to-resolve.386665/

(N.d.). Tamu.Edu. https://sanangelo.tamu.edu/files/2020/06/LGD-Puppy-2020-Final.pdf

(N.d.). Wur.Nl. https://edepot.wur.nl/283765

(N.d.-a). A-z-animals.com. https://a-z-animals.com/blog/10-incredible-donkey-facts/

(N.d.-b). Pethelpful.com. https://pethelpful.com/farm-pets/Twelve-Fascinating-Things-You-Never-Knew-about-Donkeys

Ali, Y. (2021, September 16). Livestock Guardian Breeds: Get to Know These Working Group Members. American Kennel Club. https://www.akc.org/expert-advice/dog-breeds/get-to-know-the-livestock-guardian-dog-breeds/

Animal predatory behavior. (n.d.). Psychology Wiki; Fandom, Inc. https://psychology.fandom.com/wiki/Animal_predatory_behavior

Barnes, A. (2021, March 23). Creating an enriching life for llamas. The Open Sanctuary Project; The Open Sanctuary Project, Inc. https://opensanctuary.org/creating-an-enriching-life-for-llamas/

Barnes, A., & Hess, T. (2018, April 12). Hello camelid companion! The new llama arrival guide. The Open Sanctuary Project; The Open Sanctuary Project, Inc. https://opensanctuary.org/the-new-llama-arrival-guide/

Barth, B. (2017, September 14). How to Choose a Livestock Guard Dog. Modern Farmer. https://modernfarmer.com/2017/09/choose-livestock-guard-dog/

Bennett, S. (2022, July 12). How to train A donkey: A simple guide. Farm & Animals. https://farmandanimals.com/how-to-train-a-donkey/

Boi, L. (n.d.). Three lessons from training llamas. Utah.edu. from https://accelerate.uofuhealth.utah.edu/improvement/three-lessons-from-training-llamas

Bryan, M. (2021, September 21). Donkey facts. Facts.net. https://facts.net/donkey-facts/

Bukowski, J. A., & Aiello, S. (2023, November 14). Routine Health Care of Dogs. Merck Veterinary Manual. https://www.merckvetmanual.com/dog-owners/routine-care-and-breeding-of-dogs/routine-health-care-of-dogs

Caring for Guardian Donkeys Farmers are increasingly turning to non-lethal techniques for predation management. Donkeys have become a popular protector of sheep that can perform very well under certain conditions. Following are some guidelines on management and caring for guardian donkeys to maximize the animal's capacity in regards to flock protection. (n.d.). Ontariosheep.org. https://www.ontariosheep.org/uploads/userfiles/files/-%20Caring%20for%20Guard%20Donkeys-.pdf

Department of Jobs, Precincts and Regions. (2023, November 3). Guard dogs. Agriculture Victoria. https://agriculture.vic.gov.au/livestock-and-animals/animal-welfare-victoria/dogs/guard-dogs

Differences between llamas & alpacas. (2022, March 23). Animal safari. https://animalsafari.com/whats-the-difference-between-a-llama-and-an-alpaca/

DipCbst, A. F. C. (2023, May 17). 11 Tips for Training Livestock Guardian Dogs. PetHelpful. https://pethelpful.com/dogs/Tips-for-Training-Livestock-Guardian-Dogs

Dohner, J. (2014, April 24). Selecting a guard llama. Mother Earth News – The Original Guide To Living Wisely; Mother Earth News. https://www.motherearthnews.com/homesteading-and-livestock/selecting-a-guard-llama-zbcz1404/

Dohner, J. (2014, February 25). More questions to ask yourself before selecting a livestock guard dog. Mother Earth News – The Original Guide To Living Wisely; Mother Earth News. https://www.motherearthnews.com/homesteading-and-livestock/selecting-a-livestock-guard-dog-zbcz1402/

Dohner, J. (2023, March 29). Should you get A guard donkey? Mother Earth News – The Original Guide To Living Wisely; Mother Earth News. https://www.motherearthnews.com/homesteading-and-livestock/guard-donkey-zbcz1310/

Dohner, J. (2023, March 30). Guardian llamas: Pros and cons. Mother Earth News – The Original Guide To Living Wisely; Mother Earth News. https://www.motherearthnews.com/homesteading-and-livestock/guardian-llamas-zbcz1309/

Dohner, J., & Giraud, C. (2018, December 2). Preserving the essential traits and behaviors of livestock guardians do. Jan-Dohner. https://www.jandohner.com/single-post/2018/12/02/preserving-the-essential-traits-and-behaviors-of-livestock-guardian-dogs

Donkey Listener. (2019, July 15). Training donkeys using gentle methods from the whole donkey approach. The Donkey Listener. https://donkeylistener.com/training-donkeys/

Donkey Listener. (2022, May 23). Training a rescue donkey {case study: Gucci}. The Donkey Listener. https://donkeylistener.com/training-a-rescue-donkey/

Exotic Animal Laws by State. (2023). Findlaw.com. https://www.findlaw.com/injury/torts-and-personal-injuries/exotic-animal-laws-by-state.html

Farm safety - handling animals. (n.d.). Gov.au. https://www.betterhealth.vic.gov.au/health/healthyliving/farm-safety-handling-animals

Farmbrite. (2023, January 10). How to Choose the Best Livestock Guardian Dog. Farmbrite. https://www.farmbrite.com/post/how-to-choose-the-best-livestock-guardian-dog

Flint, N. (2022, August 12). The 10 Best Livestock Guardian Dog Breeds, Large and Small. Pet Control HQ. https://petcontrolhq.com/blogs/news/best-livestock-guardian-dog-breeds

Franklin, W.L., N.K. Drufke, and K. J. Powell. 2012. Guard llamas: their use and effectiveness in North America for protecting sheep, goats, cattle, and poultry against canid predators. Pp. 21-36 in: Raggi S., L.A., Rojas S., I., Parraguez G., V.H. and Sepúlveda H., N. (eds.). Resúmenes VI Congreso Mundial Camélidos. Arica, Chile.

Griffler, M. (2019, July 4). How to be safely around A donkey. The Open Sanctuary Project; The Open Sanctuary Project, Inc.

https://opensanctuary.org/how-to-be-safely-around-a-donkey/

Griffler, M. (2019, June 14). How donkeys get along with other species. The Open Sanctuary Project; The Open Sanctuary Project, Inc. https://opensanctuary.org/how-donkeys-get-along-with-other-species/

Guard donkey. (2013, May 14). Jacobs Heritage Farm. https://jacobsheritagefarm.com/heritage-livestock/miniature-guard-donkey/

Guardian animals for livestock protection and wild dog exclusion. (n.d.). https://pestsmart.org.au/toolkit-resource/guardian-animals-for-livestock-protection-and-wild-dog-exclusion/

Guidelines for using donkeys as guard animals with sheep. (n.d.). Ontario.Ca. https://www.ontario.ca/page/guidelines-using-donkeys-guard-animals-sheep

Guidelines for using donkeys as guard animals with sheep. (n.d.-a). Ontario.Ca. https://www.ontario.ca/page/guidelines-using-donkeys-guard-animals-sheep

Guidelines for using donkeys as guard animals with sheep. (n.d.-b). Ontario.Ca. https://www.ontario.ca/page/guidelines-using-donkeys-guard-animals-sheep

Health and care. (n.d.). Psu.edu. https://extension.psu.edu/animals-and-livestock/llamas-and-alpacas/health-and-care

Heimbuch, J. (2016, June 14). 10 surprising facts about donkeys. Treehugger. https://www.treehugger.com/facts-will-change-way-you-think-about-donkeys-4869321

Introducing predator to prey. (2012, June 28). Horse Canada. https://horse-canada.com/magazine/behaviour/introducing-predator-to-prey/

Kansas Living Magazine. (2016, February 22). Guard donkeys. Kansaslivingmagazine.com. https://kansaslivingmagazine.com/articles/2016/02/22/guard-donkeys

Layers, A. (2013, June 20). Will donkeys keep predators away like foxes and dogs? BackYard Chickens - Learn How to Raise Chickens. https://www.backyardchickens.com/threads/will-donkeys-keep-predators-away-like-foxes-and-dogs.795604/page-2

LeBlanc, T. (2014, June 3). Modern farmer's guide to guard donkeys. Modern Farmer. https://modernfarmer.com/2014/06/modern-farmers-guide-guard-donkeys/

Lee, A. (2020, November 3). 13 reasons why your ranch needs a guard donkey. Helpful Horse Hints. https://www.helpfulhorsehints.com/reasons-to-get-a-guard-donkey/

Lee, A. (2020, October 29). Guard llama or guard donkey: Making the right decision for your farm. Farmhouse Guide; April Lee. https://farmhouseguide.com/guard-llama-vs-guard-donkey/

Lee, A. (2021, December 27). 9 ways donkeys show aggression (and how to stay safe around them). Helpful Horse Hints. https://www.helpfulhorsehints.com/ways-donkeys-show-aggression-and-how-to-stay-safe-around-them/

Liebenberg, L. (n.d.). Self-Rewarding Behaviours in LGD. Blogspot.com. https://predator-friendly-ranching.blogspot.com/2021/05/self-rewarding-behaviours-in-lgd.html

Livestock Guardian Animals. (2023, July 10). Landholders for Dingoes. https://landholdersfordingoes.org/livestock-guardian-animals/

Livestock guardian animals. (n.d.). Wild dog facts. Gov.au. https://www.daf.qld.gov.au/__data/assets/pdf_file/0005/76982/IPA-Wild-Dog-Fact-Sheet-Livestock-Guardian-Dogs.pdf

Livestock guardians. (n.d.). Alpaca Magic. https://www.alpacamagic.com.au/livestock-guardians/

Livestock ownership requirements for small landholders. (n.d.). Gov.au. https://www.agric.wa.gov.au/livestock-biosecurity/livestock-ownership-requirements-small-landholders

Llama. (n.d.). Cosley Zoo. https://cosleyzoo.org/llama/

Llamas and Alpacas. (2018). Govt.Nz. https://www.mpi.govt.nz/dmsdocument/46039-Code-of-Welfare-Layer-llamas-and-alpacas

Mies, C. (2018, April 20). Can dogs live with donkeys? Wagwalking.com; Wag! https://wagwalking.com/sense/can-dogs-live-with-donkey

Multispecies grazing. Country Folks; Lee Newspapers. https://countryfolks.com/multispecies-grazing/

Newspapers, L. (2018, December 11). Animals guarding animals: donkeys and dogs. Country Folks; Lee Newspapers. https://countryfolks.com/animals-guarding-animals-donkeys-and-dogs/

Newspapers, L. (2018, December 11). Animals guarding animals: donkeys and dogs. Country Folks; Lee Newspapers. https://countryfolks.com/animals-guarding-animals-donkeys-and-dogs/

Olson, E. (n.d.). Dogs in Ancient Egypt. DigitalCommons@USU. https://digitalcommons.usu.edu/fsrs2020/66/

Peterson, A. N., Soto, A. P., & McHenry, M. J. (2021). Pursuit and evasion strategies in the predator-prey interactions of fishes. Integrative and Comparative Biology, 61(2), 668–680. https://doi.org/10.1093/icb/icab116

Predation control of livestock. (2014, October 27). Center for Agriculture, Food, and the Environment. https://ag.umass.edu/crops-dairy-livestock-equine/fact-sheets/predation-control-of-livestock

Protection Dogs Worldwide. (2022, September 14). History of Guard Dogs | Protection Dogs Worldwide. https://www.protectiondogs.co.uk/history-of-guard-dogs/

Pugh, B. (n.d.). Chapter 13 Predator Control. Okstate.edu. https://extension.okstate.edu/programs/meat-goat-production/site-files/docs/chapter-13-predator-control.pdf

Purpose, benefits and considerations. (n.d.). Ontario.Ca https://www.ontario.ca/document/livestock-guardian-dogs/purpose-benefits-and-considerations

Quigg, M. (2022, April 5). Llama training tips. Franklinveterinaryclinic.net; Franklin Veterinary Clinic. https://franklinveterinaryclinic.net/llama-training-tips/

Raising llamas & kids. (n.d.). James Skeen. https://www.jamesskeen.com/raising-llamas-and-kids

Shena, T. (2022, January 24). Don't miss the cues with livestock guardian dog behavior. Farm and Dairy. https://www.farmanddairy.com/top-stories/how-to-troubleshoot-livestock-guardian-dog-behavior/700067.html

Sipes, R. (2022a, February 25). Introducing a new donkey to the herd! The Sassy Ass. https://thesassyass.com/blogs/news/introducing-a-new-donkey-to-the-herd

Sipes, R. (2022b, June 27). The basics of donkey training. The Sassy Ass. https://thesassyass.com/blogs/news/the-basics-of-donkey-training

subjecttopressure. (2018, January 27). Correction. Guard Dog Blog. https://guarddogblog.wordpress.com/2018/01/26/correction/

Trollinger, B. (2022, December 12). Beginner's Guide to Livestock Guardian Animals. EcoFarming Daily. https://www.ecofarmingdaily.com/raise-healthy-livestock/beginners-guide-to-livestock-guardian-animals/

Understanding donkey behaviour. (n.d.-a). The Donkey Sanctuary. https://www.thedonkeysanctuary.org.uk/all-about-donkeys/behaviour/understanding-donkey-behaviour

Understanding donkey behaviour. (n.d.-b). The Donkey Sanctuary. https://www.thedonkeysanctuary.org.uk/all-about-donkeys/behaviour/understanding-donkey-behaviour

Understanding the instincts of livestock guardian dogs. (2023, August 12). Off Leash Blog. https://blog.tryfi.com/livestock-guardian-dogs/

Usda Aphis. (n.d.). Usda.gov. https://www.aphis.usda.gov/aphis/ourfocus/wildlifedamage/operational-activities/sa_livestock/ct_protecting_livestock_predators

User, S. (2020, December 21). The livestock guardian dog: The best friend of livestock in extensive systems. Fawec.Org. https://www.fawec.org/en/what-do-we-do/inspiring-pilot-farms/363-le-chien-de-protection-de-troupeaux-le-meilleur-ami-de-l-elevage-pastoral

Using llamas as guardians: Benefits and considerations. (2023, May 15). The Thrifty Homesteader. https://thriftyhomesteader.com/llamas-as-guardians/

Verana, C. (2023, April 4). 15 donkey facts about the misunderstood equines. TRVST. https://www.trvst.world/biodiversity/donkey-facts/

Vistein, G. (2016, July 9). Donkeys as Guardians of your livestock. Farming with Carnivores Network. https://farmingwithcarnivoresnetwork.com/donkeys-guardians-livestock/

Weaver, S. (2016, March 31). Choosing a livestock guardian. Grit - Rural American Know-How. https://www.grit.com/animals/livestock/livestock-guardians-ze0z1603zcbru/

Weaver, S. (2019, April 26). Livestock guardian Donkeys. Grit - Rural American Know-How. https://www.grit.com/animals/livestock-guardian-donkeys-ze0z1904znad/

Wildlife Specialist. (n.d.). How LGD reduces predation. Tamu.edu. https://sanangelo.tamu.edu/files/2013/08/Livestock-Guardian-Dogs1.pdf

Wyzard, B. (2020a, September 9). Livestock Guardian Dogs and Food: What to Feed, When, and Problems to Avoid – For Love of Livestock. For Love of Livestock. https://www.forloveoflivestock.com/blog/livestock-guardian-dogs-and-food

Wyzard, B. (2020b, September 10). Training Livestock Guardian Dogs: The Ultimate Guide – For Love of Livestock. For Love of Livestock. https://www.forloveoflivestock.com/blog/training-livestock-guardian-dogs-the-ultimate-guide

Yokhna, D. (2009, February 18). Protect your flock with guard donkeys. Hobby Farms. https://www.hobbyfarms.com/protect-your-flock-with-guard-donkeys-2/

Image Sources

[1] https://www.pexels.com/photo/chicken-standing-on-the-cage-9821451/

[2] https://commons.wikimedia.org/wiki/File:Scheuerer_H%C3%BChnerhof.jpg

[3] https://www.pexels.com/photo/a-chick-and-eggs-on-a-nest-6897497/

[4] https://www.pexels.com/photo/girl-playing-with-chicken-on-pink-studio-background-5263998/

[5] https://www.pexels.com/photo/wooden-hen-house-with-straw-baskets-on-shelves-4577546/

[6] *Egan Snow, CC BY-SA 2.0 <https://creativecommons.org/licenses/by-sa/2.0>, via Wikimedia Commons: https://commons.wikimedia.org/wiki/File:Chicken_tractor_in_use.jpg*

[7] https://www.pexels.com/photo/four-assorted-color-roosters-1769279/

[8] https://unsplash.com/photos/brown-hen-on-brown-wooden-fence-ej5XXS8_2B8

[9] https://unsplash.com/photos/person-holding-brown-and-black-bird-6G0HWfLvP4Y

[10] https://unsplash.com/photos/white-and-pink-rabbit-plush-toy-on-yellow-plastic-basin-XOGg38VufZs

[11] *Michael Coghlan from Adelaide, Australia, CC BY-SA 2.0 <https://creativecommons.org/licenses/by-sa/2.0>, via Wikimedia Commons: https://commons.wikimedia.org/wiki/File:Pecking_Order_(5963393064).jpg*

[12] https://www.pexels.com/photo/white-chicken-on-brown-soil-4911723/

[13] https://www.pexels.com/photo/coyote-lying-on-grass-10226903/

[14] https://www.pexels.com/photo/brown-and-white-fox-on-green-grass-3739926/

[15] https://www.pexels.com/photo/closeup-photo-of-tan-rat-1010267/

[16] https://www.pexels.com/photo/close-up-photo-of-raccoons-14050298/

[17] https://www.pexels.com/photo/animal-animal-photography-big-big-cat-209032/

[18] https://pixabay.com/illustrations/arrows-direction-way-sketch-false-6268063/

[19] Phương Huy, CC BY-SA 4.0 <https://creativecommons.org/licenses/by-sa/4.0>, via Wikimedia Commons: https://commons.wikimedia.org/wiki/File:G%C3%A0_%C4%90%C3%B4ng_T%E1%BA%A3o_%E1%BB%9F_B%C3%ACnh_Long,_ng7th8n2022_(1).jpg

[20] https://commons.wikimedia.org/wiki/File:Tab41_H%C3%BChner_(Gefl%C3%BCgel-Album,_Jean_Bungartz,_1885).jpg

[21] Thomon, CC BY-SA 4.0 <https://creativecommons.org/licenses/by-sa/4.0>, via Wikimedia Commons: https://commons.wikimedia.org/wiki/File:Coq_la_fl%C3%A8che_noir.jpg

[22] Tim Daniels, CC BY-SA 4.0 <https://creativecommons.org/licenses/by-sa/4.0>, via Wikimedia Commons: https://commons.wikimedia.org/wiki/File:Old_English_Pheasant_Fowl.jpg

[23] https://commons.wikimedia.org/wiki/File:Tab19_H%C3%BChner_(Gefl%C3%BCgel-Album,_Jean_Bungartz,_1885).jpg

[24] Diandra Dills, CC BY-SA 3.0 <https://creativecommons.org/licenses/by-sa/3.0>, via Wikimedia Commons: https://commons.wikimedia.org/wiki/File:Gold_Onagadori.jpg

[25] https://commons.wikimedia.org/wiki/File:Dumpies_belonging_to_J._Fairlie,_Esq._Wingfield_1853.jpg

[26] Stephen James McWilliam, CC BY 4.0 <https://creativecommons.org/licenses/by/4.0>, via Wikimedia Commons: https://commons.wikimedia.org/wiki/File:Magpie_Duck,_drake_(cropped).jpg

[27] Kororaa, CC BY-SA 3.0 <https://creativecommons.org/licenses/by-sa/3.0>, via Wikimedia Commons: https://commons.wikimedia.org/wiki/File:Cotton_Patch_Goose.jpg

[28] Dorkinglad, CC BY-SA 4.0 <https://creativecommons.org/licenses/by-sa/4.0>, via Wikimedia Commons: https://commons.wikimedia.org/wiki/File:Saxony_ducks.jpg

[29] inkknife_2000 (7.5 million views +), CC BY-SA 2.0 <https://creativecommons.org/licenses/by-sa/2.0>, via Wikimedia Commons: https://commons.wikimedia.org/wiki/File:Tree_Farm,_Turkey_12-8-12_(8297236231).jpg

[30] Internet Archive Book Images, CC0 1.0, via Wikimedia Commons. https://commons.wikimedia.org/wiki/File:Image_from_page_82_of_%22Natural_history%22_(1897)_(20734677882).jpg

[31] mar_qs, CC0, via Wikimedia Commons: https://commons.wikimedia.org/wiki/File:Rottweiler_-52773841920.jpg

[32] Lauris Rubenis, CC BY 2.0 <https://creativecommons.org/licenses/by/2.0>, via Wikimedia Commons. https://commons.wikimedia.org/wiki/File:Fox_eating_mole.jpg

[33] Bernard Landgraf, CC BY-SA 3.0 <http://creativecommons.org/licenses/by-sa/3.0/>, via Wikimedia Commons: https://commons.wikimedia.org/wiki/File:Uncia_uncia.jpg

[34] https://unsplash.com/photos/herd-of-cattle-on-grass-field-during-daytime-0vVQWN_D26c

[35] https://unsplash.com/photos/black-and-white-car-dashboard-p79nyt2CUj4?utm_content=creditShareLink&utm_medium=referral&utm_source=unsplash

[36] https://unsplash.com/photos/adult-white-dog-sitting-beside-sheep-during-winter-XTNyfggdKTo

[37] *HeartSpoon, CC BY-SA 4.0 <https://creativecommons.org/licenses/by-sa/4.0>, via Wikimedia Commons: https://commons.wikimedia.org/wiki/File:Great_Pyrenees_Mountain_Dog_2.png*

[38] *Zeynel Cebeci, CC BY-SA 4.0 <https://creativecommons.org/licenses/by-sa/4.0>, via Wikimedia Commons: https://commons.wikimedia.org/wiki/File:Anatolian_Shepherd_Dog_01.jpg*

[39] *Nikki68, CC BY 2.5 <https://creativecommons.org/licenses/by/2.5>, via Wikimedia Commons: https://commons.wikimedia.org/wiki/File:Komondor_delvin.jpg*

[40] *Canarian, CC BY-SA 4.0 <https://creativecommons.org/licenses/by-sa/4.0>, via Wikimedia Commons: https://commons.wikimedia.org/wiki/File:CaucasianOwcha1.jpg*

[41] *Canarian, CC BY-SA 4.0 <https://creativecommons.org/licenses/by-sa/4.0>, via Wikimedia Commons: https://commons.wikimedia.org/wiki/File:Maremma_Sheepdog_male.jpg*

[42] *https://commons.wikimedia.org/wiki/File:Kuvasz_named_Kan.jpg*

[43] *Jerry Kirkhart from Los Osos, Calif., CC BY 2.0 <https://creativecommons.org/licenses/by/2.0>, via Wikimedia Commons: https://commons.wikimedia.org/wiki/File:Akbash_Dog_in_CA.jpg*

[44] *Pleple2000, CC BY-SA 3.0 <http://creativecommons.org/licenses/by-sa/3.0/>, via Wikimedia Commons: https://commons.wikimedia.org/wiki/File:Tosa_inu_786.jpg*

[45] *Alexandr Frolov, CC BY-SA 4.0 <https://creativecommons.org/licenses/by-sa/4.0>, via Wikimedia Commons: https://commons.wikimedia.org/wiki/File:Tibetan_Mastiff_%D0%A2%D0%B8%D0%B1%D0%B5%D1%82%D1%81%D0%BA%D0%B8%D0%B9_%D0%9C%D0%B0%D1%81%D1%82%D0%B8%D1%84_02.jpg*

[46] *https://commons.wikimedia.org/wiki/File:German_Shepherd_puppy_eating_out_of_a_human_hand.jpg*

[47] *https://unsplash.com/photos/woman-hugging-a-dog-FtuJIuBbUhI*

[48] *Ralf Roletschek, GFDL 1.2 <http://www.gnu.org/licenses/old-licenses/fdl-1.2.html>, via Wikimedia Commons. https://commons.wikimedia.org/wiki/File:18-08-25-%C3%85land_RRK6596a.jpg*

[49] *https://unsplash.com/photos/brown-and-white-llama-on-green-grass-field-during-daytime-sXDVbYSjcaY*

[50] *NasserHalaweh, CC BY-SA 4.0 <https://creativecommons.org/licenses/by-sa/4.0>, via Wikimedia Commons. https://commons.wikimedia.org/wiki/File:Equidae_Equus_africanus_asinus.jpg*

[51] *https://unsplash.com/photos/woman-in-black-and-white-striped-long-sleeve-shirt-kissing-brown-horse-during-daytime-wg8hYS_1alw*